BASEBALL'S
BAD HOPS
AND LUCKY
BOUNCES

Baseball's
BAD HOPS
AND LUCKY
BOUNCES

MIKE BLAKE

BETTERWAY BOOKS
CINCINNATI, OHIO

Baseball's Bad Hops and Lucky Bounces. Copyright © 1995 by Mike Blake. Printed and bound in the United States of America. All rights reserved. No part of this book may be reproduced in any form or by any electronic or mechanical means including information storage and retrieval systems without permission in writing from the publisher, except by a reviewer, who may quote brief passages in a review. Published by Betterway Books, an imprint of F&W Publications, Inc., 1507 Dana Avenue, Cincinnati, Ohio, 45207. First edition.

99 98 97 96 95   5 4 3 2 1

Library of Congress Cataloging in Publication Data

Blake, Mike.
   Baseball's bad hops and lucky bounces / by Mike Blake.
     p.   cm.
   Includes bibliographical references (p.) and index.
   ISBN 1-55870-368-3
   1. Baseball—United States—Anecdotes. 2. Baseball—United States—
   Humor. I. Title.
GV867.3.B53   1994
796.357′0973—dc20   94-32963
                                              CIP

Edited by Tom Clark
Designed by Angela Lennert

Betterway Books are available at special discounts for sales promotions, premiums and fund-raising use. Special editions or book excerpts can also be created to specification. For details contact: Special Sales Manager, Betterway Books, 1507 Dana Avenue, Cincinnati, Ohio 45207.

Dedication

To my lovely and loving wife, Jan . . . the luckiest bounce I ever caught, and the best teammate a guy ever had.

To Mom and Dad who put up with my bad hops.

To Cliff and Merle who welcomed me onto their team.

To Bill Brohaugh, Editorial Director of Betterway Books, who, with a marvelous sense of humor, goes the full nine, touches all the bases and comes through for me in the clutch.

And to the players . . . those who have played the game and thrilled, disappointed, amazed, awed and befuddled the countless masses who love baseball.

ACKNOWLEDGMENTS

It seems as though it is the same people who, time after time, come through for writers such as I, who need the information, documentation, fact-checking, contacts, entry into the files and entree to the ballplayers who make the dreams of books literary realities. These kind, generous people deserve the applause, the kudos and, above all, the thanks. Without their benevolence, there'd be a lot of empty space on the bookshelves.

Tim Mead, former Vice President Media Relations of the California Angels, who got what he deserved — to be named Assistant General Manager of the Halos — and whose picture must be listed twice in the dictionary . . . once under the phrase "nice guy" and again under the phrase "consummate professional."

Jeff Idelson, former New York Yankees Media Relations Director who went on to handle World Cup Soccer — a pro in any arena.

Rob Butcher, current New York Yankees Director of Media Relations, who handles the goldfish bowl of the Big Apple with talent, aplomb and generosity.

Dave Cunningham, Angels beat writer (Long Beach *Press-Telegram*) and friend, who is as quick with his help as he is with his wit.

Larry Babcock, Director of Baseball Information, California Angels, who really digs deep to help us all (writers) out with the facts whether they are important or nebulous.

John Sevano, Assistant Vice President and Director of Media Relations and Broadcasting for the California Angels, who generously provides contacts and friendship.

Ken Kondo, Media Relations Assistant for the California Angels, who digs quickly and efficiently for required facts and verification.

Carolyn LaPierre, Media Relations Assistant for the California Angels, who runs the show behind the scenes without complaint.

Joe McDonnell, sports talk show host (KMPC-710 AM/Los Angeles), whose sense of humor is pennant-winning and whose benevolence and acts of kindness all too often go unreported. And special thanks to him for sharing his classic outtakes tapes with me, which served as foundation for the chapters on role models and tantrums.

Ernie Harwell, the all-time voice of the Detroit Tigers who is as velvet-smooth as a human being as he is a broadcaster.

Richard Topp, the former president of the Society for American Baseball Research, who is always there with a laugh, a checked fact and his loyalty, and to his wife Barbara who, with Ozzielike grace and precison, catches what we dish out.

Paul Olden, golden-voiced sports announcer (New York Yankees), who asked Tommy Lasorda *the* question.

Alan Elconin, a childhood buddy who went on to broadcast for the California Angels and San Diego Padres and who remembers his roots and his friends.

Fred Roggin—a real hero—and Mike Cunningham, Sports Producer for KNBC-4 (Los Angeles), who provide humor and were nice enough to offer taped info; Frank Boal, WDAF (Kansas City), who tracked down that info further and Jim Bracciano, Sports Director for "The Lawrence Report," Sunflower Cablevision-6 (Lawrence, Kansas), who eagerly and kindly gave me the finished product of that info for use in this book.

Lee "Hacksaw" Hamilton, XTRA (San Diego), who thoughtfully shares his sense of humor as well as his contacts.

Mike Bass of the Cincinnati *Post*, a member of the brotherhood of journalists and who goes the distance to help out fellow writers in need.

Betsy Richards, whose shared contacts in high places were welcomed gratefully by this writer.

Ben "Doc" Kaufman, Van Nuys High Class of Summer '68 and a true buddy, who benevolently gave me live leads and living contacts even though many of the leads I have given him are dead . . . literally.

And to the following information providers and fact-checkers: Bob Rowe, KMPC-710 AM (Los Angeles); Steve Pascente, KPNX-12 (Phoenix); Bart Ripp, *The Morning News Tribune* (Tacoma, Washington); Del Boue, Chicago Cubs; Jerry Mezerow, Pacific Coast League Historical Society and member of SABR; C. Stanley Gilliam, SABR; Joe Wayman, Grandstand Baseball Annual and SABR, John Phillips, SABR; Michael L. Brint, SABR; Ron Selter, SABR; Joe Naiman, SABR; Paul Treese, SABR and David Vincent, SABR; Fred London, SABR and Bart Swain (Cleveland Indians).

And my thanks to the following, for reasons too numerous to mention:

Muppet Curtis Blake (OK, so she's my dog . . . she helps me, all right?!); Kimberlee Ann Dixon; Greg Dixon; Tony Kubek; John Robbins; Don and Peggy Powell; Roger and Giulii Kraemer; John Peter Zenger; R.F. Outcoult; Inigo Montoya; Eliseo Camacho and Yolanda Davalos (California State University, Fullerton) and all the guys on my Tustin, California, softball team — The Dream Team — who constantly supply me with stories (most of which I can't use) for publication: Richard Poe, pitcher; Mike Miller, outfield; Mike Jarrard, third base; Devo DeVincenzi, first base-catcher; Jerry Gardner, first base; John Dal Poggetto, second base; Bernie Merry, second base-outfield; Terry Flinn, outfield-pitcher; David Massey, outfielder-pitcher; Tom Bowers, outfield; Jim Bickley, outfield; Larry Butler, outfield; Ranie Martini, umpire (SCMAF) and Peggy Poe, our ever-faithful fan.

And thanks to Laila Nabulsi, Angela Kropko and Tom Liebig of Data Logic who saved my floppy drive, my data and my butt when I was on deadline.

And of course, enormous thanks must be given to all the boys of summer who laced up the cleats, buttoned the unis, pounded the gloves, swung the bats, iced up the bruises and sweated the good sweat on the ballfield. You are the pages of this book and the life of the game.

And a heartfelt thanks to Larry King, a man who does things he doesn't have to . . . just to be nice. He is one with the rightest of right stuff, who makes this business worthwhile. His kindness, graciousness and generosity is of championship caliber, and his efforts on my behalf have made my literary career a success, to me . . . regardless of copies sold.

And to Roy Firestone, for whom the term "nice guy" was created. His sense of humor is exceeded only by his altruism. His friendship is one of the richest benefits I have received in the book business.

ABOUT THE AUTHOR

Author of such diverse works as *The Minor Leagues: A Celebration of the Little Show*, *The Incomplete Book of Baseball Superstitions, Rituals and Oddities* and *Baseball Chronicles: An Oral History of Baseball Through the Decades* — baseball books — *Survivor: He Walked in the Shadow of Death* — a book on the holocaust — and *King of the Penny Stocks* — a book about a Denver industrialist, Mike Blake describes himself as a writer who takes the assignment at hand and writes to the audience at large.

Having completed three films for the United States Air Force and two as yet unproduced though once-optioned feature films for theatrical release — teenage adventure film, *The Prank*, co-written with his private eye buddy Logan Clarke, and a mystery-thriller, *The Last Vampire*, Blake is one who embraces the project, and researches it until he can sink his teeth into it and make it entertaining and informative.

That credo has allowed him to write and have published more than five hundred articles for a variety of newspapers and publications internationally on subjects ranging from investigative reporting to sports to business to political commentary to humor to religion to American history.

Blake again takes the humorous road to the world of baseball with *Baseball's Bad Hops and Lucky Bounces*, a subject he never stops researching. "The game is relentless," he says. "History is being rewritten every day, and the game is such a part of the American fabric that its audience seems to rebuild every season."

And as this book is a humorous side of the game, Blake says, "This project is perfect. Baseball humor is the consummate literary marriage for me. Baseball is the subject nearest and dearest to so many Americans, and humor is the art form I find that is most entertaining. What is better than making people laugh while sharing a few baseball yarns along the way?"

Blake is a sought-after public speaker on such topics as baseball, baseball humor, journalism, packaging, business and motivation, and is represented by the internationally known speakers bureau, The Speakers Connection, based in Sarasota, Florida. He has been a guest on more than one hundred television and radio shows across America, including *The Larry King Show*, *Up Close With Roy Firestone*, *A.M. Buffalo* and *The Tom Synder Show*.

And Blake is heard on *The Fan* — KFXX-1520 AM, Portland, Oregon — with his weekly spot, *The Odd and Obscure in the World and the World of Sports*, and on the Kevin Toon-"Poolside" Tony Ruzecka Show each Friday morning at 9:05 A.M., investigating the previous week's highlights and lowlights while taking a humorous, if jaundiced, view of life.

TABLE OF CONTENTS

PROLOGUE

Why another baseball anecdote book? Perhaps it is best summed up by Groucho Marx, who is credited with saying "Outside of a dog, a book is man's best friend. Inside of a dog it's too dark to read."

Why this author, who had already written three baseball anecdote books? Perhaps, to paraphrase George Bernard Shaw, "He who can, does. He who cannot, teaches. And he who can't teach, writes books."

But what is better than *another* book on baseball? Baseball is different from other sports. It is pastoral. Innocent. Historical. Baseball is Americana, and throughout its history, it has been proven that baseball fans, to the contrary of other sports fans, fanatically read about the game. Some even go as far as to declare "Where baseball fans love to read, basketball fans don't read, football fans won't read, and hockey fans can't read."

So to paraphrase—all right, butcher—Shakespeare (in *Henry V*), once more into the bleachers, dear friends, once more. Or close the wall at Fenway to dead-pull power hitters. In peace there is nothing so becomes a man as modest stillness and humility, and the author hopes this book will not simply lend the eye a terrible aspect of baseball, but stiffen the sinews and summon up the blood to enjoy the game further and humble the warriors of the diamond who provided us with thrills as well as a lot of laughs. And that's what we're here for—baseball and laughs.

What this book covers is the funny, odd, strange, superstitious, sleazy and silly goings-on between the white lines and in the clubhouse. And what may be slightly different from its myriad predecessors is that while this work covers much of baseball's past, from the 1880s on, there is a dugout full of material covering today's heroes and pretenders, proving today's boys of summer are just as idiosyncratic, superstitious, silly and fun as their counterparts of days gone by.

This is a book of luck, of scoreboard saints and stadium sinners, of aberrant behavior and ritualistic conduct, of mental preparation and comfort zones, of obnoxious nicknames, of slovenly dietary habits, of poor role models, of slaves to fashion, of foulmouthed tirades, of weird injuries, and of seldom-told tales that give baseball its lofty sobriquet of America's Pastime. And it's all for fun.

This book is not politically correct; the players in here aren't, so to be journalistically pure, neither are we.

Since this work is full of statistics, vignettes, player bios, the household names and the obscure, we hope to present an easy-to-read, comedic look at the sport through locker-room stories of the behavior behind the performances that make our daily news-papers and TV recaps.

Some chapters of this work deal with mannerisms, tics, jerks and choreographed characteristics. To the untrained eye, the many gyrations, motions and routines employed by baseball play-ers on the field are just nervous habits or loosening-up drills. But to those who understand the game and the players, these actions are not haphazard; they are deliberate. And they are merely the tip of the iceberg. They pale in comparison with the procedures employed by athletes off the field in an effort to gain success or override failures. Many of the deeds are perpetuated as supersti-tions or jinxes or as ways to hex opponents. Perhaps they are really idiosyncrasies, phobias, paranoias, neuroses or other psy-chological maladies affecting the players. But looking at it that way isn't funny. What is funny is that these guys are successful and they make our larger-than-life bubble gum card icons the heroes they are.

Other chapters cover the bizarre—those little hide-in-the closet, sweep-under-the-rug or raise-your-eyebrows-in-amaze-ment nuggets that permeate all families that have been around for 125 years. And the baseball family is no different. It is filled with its proud sons, prodigal sons, black sheep, mentors, students, rich uncles, kind grandfathers and ne'er-do-well cousins, and if they're funny and we had room for them, we included them here.

Warning: Several chapters include some really vulgar lan-guage, and even by BLEEPing the offensive words, most readers should be able to accurately break the code and uncover the de-scriptive vulgarisms. While this may mean that this work should carry a warning label, this is the actual language of ballplayers and managers—actual language (though BLEEPed)—not hear-say. We've got the tapes, transcribed for this book—and very few ballplayers are choirboys. They are rough-and-tumble boys of the locker room and this is real locker-room language—if you fill in the BLEEPs. No apologies though for the four-letter wordage or BLEEPage. This is real, and if you are of faint heart or of virgin ears, skip the chapter on tantrums (chapter three) and occasional stories in the role models chapter (chapter seven), because these are tirades from the gut, no holds barred and no implications omitted. Note: The words are theirs, not the author's. The author does not curse in this book, but, hell, you lie down with dogs, you get up with fleas.

And, to address the use of BLEEP in lieu of the actual, more colorful language, even though the author's newspaper buddies might disagree and say we're copping out and changing the truth, the real truths are (1) this book is not meant to be meanspirited — it's just for fun; and BLEEP is much kinder and gentler and in a funnier vein than the words we've thinly camouflaged; (2) we've got kids reading this book; (3) your newspaper editor wouldn't let you get away with these words in your columns, so get off our case; (4) this isn't cable — it's a book; (5) most readers should be able to read between the lines; and (6) BLEEP is funnier than most of the actual words anyway.

Some of what is covered here is beautiful baseball lore — true and factual, but lore nonetheless. And some of what is told between these covers isn't pretty. But life isn't all pretty and baseball is life — at least it is to those we've uncovered here. Baseball, with all its blemishes, warts, embarrassing figures, and misshapen and misguided warriors, is still the best-looking girl at the dance in America. We brought her here, so we're leaving with her.

What we tried for was a mix of information and controversy, with an emphasis on humor — not in all cases, but in most cases.

So go ahead. Read it, put it down, pick it up and enjoy it with no BLEEPing strings attached.

CHAPTER ONE

Lucky Bounces (Good Luck)

"Luck is the residue of design."
— BRANCH RICKEY

The lucky bounces in this book, under the umbrella of "good luck," come from many quadrants—some by design, some by accident, and some by just plain dumb luck. This chapter encompasses superstition, habits and rituals, charms, idols, voodoo, being in the right place at the right time and numbers.

Borrowing from William Shakespeare (in *The Merry Wives of Windsor*), ". . . good luck lies in odd numbers."

Some good luck maxims aren't completely provable, but bear repeating. It is said that the team with the fewest ex-Cubs wins the World Series (see chapter two), good pitching beats good hitting, you have to be a good pitcher to lose 20 games, a manager does his best job of managing with a losing team rather than with a pennant-winning club, and play for a win on the road and a tie at home.

What is a lucky bounce? Anything that fortuitously comes your way, whether you are expecting it or not, and becomes a key to success. You can be in the right place at the right time, make the right move that converts the lucky opportunity into victory, have something grand just fall in your lap without any effort on your part whatsoever, or go through complicated, well-choreographed rites to summon up rainbows and pots of baseball gold.

Many players claim they would rather be lucky than good. The following athletes sought, and in many cases received, good fortune through a variety of external factors from genetics to movie plots to precise ceremonies designed to exact success.

LUIS POLONIA, JOE VU AND MUGHAMBI

In a case of life imitating art and let's see if the media will bite, California Angels outfielder Luis Polonia came to the ballpark one day with an ugly, big-nosed, bulging-eyed doll named Joe Vu.

Polonia explained to members of the press, hungry for a story regardless of truth, that Joe Vu was a voodoo idol made expressly for him and given to him by his Dominican voodoo man.

The beat writers bit. So did ESPN. But it wasn't true. Polonia told the author he had seen the movie *Major League*, and liked the character Pedro Cerrano, a big, Latin ballplayer played by actor Dennis Haysbert, who derived his power from a rum-drinking idol named JoeBoo. Polonia decided, "If it worked for him, it can work for me," and he looked all over town — many towns — for an ugly, imposing fetish worthy of food, cigars, drink and idolatry. He finally found one after a game in Milwaukee.

Polonia discovered the perfect juju, a brown, hunch-backed gargoyle with a protruding reddish nose, open mouth, thrusting tongue and rotating head, attired in gray slacks and black boots. He named it Joe Vu and placed it in his locker at Anaheim Stadium and began the legend. Then the legend turned real in 1991.

Keeping the plastic idol at his side, Polonia began the season on a tear and was hitting .351 after a three-hit performance against Seattle April 24.

And Polonia wasn't stingy with his good-luck charm. Joe was working so well for him, he decided to spread the luck around. Teammate Jim Abbott was off to a horrible start in 1991, losing his first four decisions, going 0-4 with a 6.00 ERA. He was about to be sent down to the minors for the first time in his career and was given one last chance, versus Baltimore, May 5. Before the game, Polonia sneaked the statue into Abbott's locker, gave the idol a cigarette, some coffee and a good-luck rub and left it there for the pitcher. Abbott responded with his first win, 6-4 over the Orioles, and proceeded to win five in a row and 18 of his next 25 decisions to finish the season at 18-11 with a 2.89 ERA.

By June 4, Polonia was still hitting .337, but then Joe turned ugly, thanks to Chris Berman of ESPN. Until this time, Joe had been covered only by print media and hadn't been touched by anyone other than Polonia's teammates. But on June 4, Berman purloined Joe Vu and brought him out of the locker room for some national exposure on ESPN's pregame show prior to an Angels-Red Sox game that night. Apparently Joe Vu wasn't opposed to a little press, but national TV and the kidnapping got him nervous. Polonia went 1-for-5 that night in California's 3-0 loss to Boston, and he began to slide. Over the next month, Polonia's average fell nearly 50 points to .289.

Finally, Polonia took his friend aside and had a man-to-idol talk with him, and "got him a woman." Soon the ballplayer brought his average back up to .300, before finishing at .296.

With his good-luck charm restored, Polonia again loaned it out secretly to those in need of help.

Slumping Junior Felix had his only four-hit game of the season on September 2, with Joe Vu in his locker. Polonia, now the "Robin Hood of the Caribbean," put the plastic beast of fortune in pitcher Joe Grahe's locker to stop Grahe's six-game losing streak. The pitcher beat Milwaukee 2-1.

Polonia admitted that when things go well, he gives his doll food, drink, a girlfriend or two, smokes, caresses, a few lit candles, and a cup of good strong coffee. When things go bad, the talisman is punished. Polonia said, "I twist his head down or backward and tell him he'll stay that way until I get some hits. Then I turn his head back, talk to him, and give him a cigar if I go 3-for-4."

Polonia thought that good luck has its rewards and bad luck its consequences, so after his eight-game hitting streak was snapped against New York, May 8, 1992, he hanged the fetish by the neck from a light fixture above his locker. All it took was 0-for-4 and the lynching took place. The idol responded, and beginning the next day, Polonia was on another seven-game hitting streak.

In 1993, things got dark for Polonia and Joe Vu. The talisman went into a slump, and Polonia felt the good luck had been used up. On June 13, the Angels dropped a 12-7 decision to Seattle, their ninth loss in 12 games, and Polonia's average dipped to .270. That was too much to bear, so the little left fielder grabbed Joe, pulled him out of his locker, doused him with rubbing alcohol and set him ablaze, filling the clubhouse with smoke. Polonia said, "I wanted to make it disappear to take care of all the evil spirits. It started out as a good-luck charm, but it wasn't good luck anymore. Now it's gone."

Polonia remained doll-less for ten days and saw his average plummet. He searched for, and found, a replacement.

Having scrapped Joe Vu, Polonia brought in Mughambi, a much better looking idol who, Polonia claimed, possessed voodoo powers. Polonia, however, found this talisman, not in New Orleans or the Dominican Republic, but in Kansas City.

In the throes of an 0-for-20 slump, Polonia brought his newest charm into the clubhouse, gave it a doughnut and a cigar and promptly banged out three hits in an 8-7 win over the Royals.

Mughambi may not have delivered many wins on the field for the Angels or hits for Polonia, but it did reward his idolatry with a multimillion-dollar contract and a return to the New York Yankees in 1994.

Polonia said, "I don't believe in voodoo, but I believe in good-luck charms, and Joe and Mughambi are mine."

And speaking of good-luck dolls. . . .

MIKE HENNEMAN

Big Mike Henneman, the 6'4" relief pitcher for the Detroit Tigers, relied on imposing pitching to record an amazing 56 wins in relief against only 30 losses to go along with 128 saves during his first seven seasons in The Bigs. With a record like that, he wouldn't appear to need good-luck charms — especially when being backed up by the booming bats of Cecil Fielder, Mickey Tettleton, Rob Deer, Lou Whitaker and Travis Fryman. Yet Henneman does indeed count on the luck of the Irish and a tiny doll he has misnamed.

In 1990, Henneman found what he termed a "Leprechaun Doll" in a gift shop. He rubbed it before big games and responded with 22 saves and eight wins. He loaned the long-haired, smiling mite to Dan Petry and others, and they nearly always came through with big games. The doll, marketed as a "Troll Doll," had found a home and a new ethnicity — in Henneman's locker.

In April 1991, with Rob Deer and Pete Incaviglia struggling, Henneman bought each a replica of his "Leprechaun" doll while on a road trip in Kansas City. (What is it about Kansas City and good-luck dolls?)

Henneman put the players' bats in the middle of the clubhouse, rubbed them with the two dolls and removed the "strikeout spirits from the lumber." He walked over to the team's bat rack and waved the little charms above all the team's wood. Then he hung the two fetishes in the players' lockers, and that night Deer belted a grand slam to help the Tigers top the Royals 13-7. Deer then went on a 10-for-22 streak during which he hit four homers.

The Italian Incaviglia apparently didn't know of the luck of the Irish. He went 5-for-60.

But as Henneman — who hasn't worn a jock strap (bad luck, he says) since 1988 and wears spandex biking shorts instead (good luck, he says) and always buttons the left rear pocket of his baseball pants — reasons, "Whatever works . . . works."

JERRY REUSS

Another good-luck doll was the Chicago White Sox bobble-head doll of 1989.

Fun-loving Chicago lefty Jerry Reuss picked up a White Sox bobble-head doll at a concession stand and for a joke painted its hair white and put tiny glasses on it, creating a bobbling spitting image of team pitching coach Sammy Ellis.

With the team 24 games under .500, the White Sox needed a laugh, so Reuss brought his "Ellis doll" to the bench during a game at old Comiskey Park and set it on a shelf behind Ellis and manager Jeff Torborg. The Sox won the game.

Reuss, sensing something special with each bobble, brought the doll back out the next day and the next and the next. The ChiSox won eight straight, lost, then won three more in a row. Now Torborg was hooked and demanded that the doll make the team's next road trip.

In Boston Reuss knocked the doll off a shelf, and it shattered into uncountable pieces. He rushed into the trainer's room to glue it together.

Late in the game, with the White Sox down by two runs, Reuss heard Torborg scream, "Where's the doll?" Reuss hurriedly glued the doll's broken jaw and head together and carried it out to the bench. As the doll bobbled onto the ledge behind Torborg, White Sox outfielder Ivan Calderon connected with the game-winning three-run homer.

Although the doll remained with the club for the second half of the season, neither the glue nor the luck held, and the Sox fell to 69-92 — but one game over .500 with the Ellis doll.

On to more voodoo, but without the dolls. . . .

FREDDY KUHAULUA

Unsteady Freddy Kuhaulua, the Hawaiian hurler who spent brief cups of Kona coffee with the Angels in 1977 and Padres in 1981, reported to the Angels' spring training camp in 1977 unable to lift his arm. The Angels medical staff examined the 5'11" 175-pound lefty, but found nothing physically wrong.

Kuhaulua told the doctors his condition was something much more serious than a mere physical ailment. The pitcher told the club that one of his Hawaiian girlfriends was unhappy with the way he had treated her during the off-season and had her mother put a spell on him to prevent him from lifting his pitching arm.

Nonplused, the Angels' executives called Tom Sommers, their farm director, and asked him what to do. He informed the officials that they had no alternative but to call the girl's mother and convince her to remove the curse.

After several phone calls and much negotiation and pleading, the mother called Kuhaulua and removed the curse.

Unable to lift his arm to even comb his hair before the phone call, Kuhaulua was able to throw batting practice immediately after the spell removal.

Why was this good luck? Well, although the pitcher only lasted three games and went 0-0 with a 15.63 ERA, he did make The Big Show, and how many people can say that?

ASSORTED VOODOO

Cardinals and Astros infielder Julio Gotay sprayed "voodoo perfume" on all his bats in the 1960s. The spray was to kill evil "out" spirits and to promote good "hit" spirits. He must have run out of spray as Gotay hit .260 for his career.

Minnesota Twins outfielder of the 1960s and 1970s Cesar Tovar drove teammate Leo Cardenas, a voodoo devotee, nuts by altering the shortstops voodoo charms. Cardenas, who employed a series of rituals, had an entire collection of voodoo dolls, clothed in various uniforms, fed myriad potions, and performing a plethora of tasks. Tovar would change clothes, body parts and positions of the tokens and really mess with his buddy's mind.

Cardenas also had to have a baseball in his back pocket, or he absolutely couldn't take infield practice. He literally couldn't walk to the mound without the horsehide on his hip. And if he was in a slump, the shortstop would lock his bats in the trunk of

9

his car to punish them. No hits — no light and no air was his credo.

Cincinnati Reds pitcher Jose Rijo has a voodoo doll, voodoo spray and snake oil in his Riverfront Stadium locker and also keeps a picture of Pope John Paul II in his shaving kit. When he starts a game, he takes the Pope out and hangs him on a hook near the voodoo doll. Rijo reasons, "If the Pope falls off the hook, we lose. If he stays up, we win."

In early June 1991, Phoenix Firebirds (of the Class AAA Pacific Coast) manager Duane Espy appeared on a Phoenix radio show on KAMJ, hosted by Jeff Aaron. Aaron was discussing baseball superstitions with the author of a baseball book on the subject when the three talked about Tito Fuentes (San Francisco Giants shortstop from Havana), who used to spray what he called "voodoo juice" on his bats for good luck. While Fuentes didn't have great success at the plate, he did play for 13 years in The Show with a .268 average.

Espy, aware that his own team was slumping at the plate, took up Aaron's offer on the air to mix up some special voodoo juice and spray his team's bats. Whether Espy picked up the placebo concoction or not is unclear, but several players heard the broadcast and came to the park *thinking* their skipper had doctored the bats. The Firebirds' sticks came alive, and they swept four games from PCL rivals, the Calgary Cannons, 16-7, 15-2, 9-6 and 9-8 — 49 runs in four games.

Sometimes it's not what you do, but what your team *thinks* you've done.

TY COBB

When you're arguably the greatest hitter in baseball history — .367 average, 4,191 hits, 1,139 extra-base hits, 2,245 runs scored and 892 stolen bases in a 24-year career from 1905 to 1928 — how can you be superstitious? Well, for Cobb, it didn't hurt him any. He was one of the most superstitious ballplayers of his time, and he played it into good-luck rituals and 12 batting titles.

Cobb's list of rituals included eating the same breakfast of flapjacks, grits, six eggs, 12 slices of bacon, four slices of toast and a small melon every day during his 40-game hitting streak of 1911 — and he was a trim 6'1", 175 pounds. He also took the same route to the ballpark every game, circling from the park in Detroit from Michigan Avenue or what is now known as Cochrane Avenue. He hung his shower towel on the same hook in the locker room before and after every game, and he refused to wash his uniform, preferring the dirt and sweat of good luck.

Cobb also loved his black bat, which he called his "magic bat." No one but no one was allowed to touch his lumber. He even brought it with him to a wedding once and often brought it to lunch and dinner with him, insisting that the wood was never out of his sight.

Hey, for a .367 lifetime average, I'd take my bat to dinner and a movie, buy it flowers, and ask for its label in marriage.

BIG RED GENE POOL

Luck bounces a player's way in various forms — sometimes on the field and sometimes as an act of nature. It's good luck, apparently, to be part of the Big Red Machine gene pool. While the Cincinnati Reds were winning four National League pennants and two World Series in the 1970s, their warriors were begetting future baseball talent. Six second-generation Reds were playing organized ball in the early 1990s, with five drafted in the first round of the amateur draft having already made their marks on the game.

Outfielder Ken Griffey, Sr., begat Seattle outfielder Ken Griffey, Jr.; second baseman Julian Javier begat Oakland outfielder Stan Javier; outfielder/dh Hal McRae begat Kansas City outfielder Brian McRae; pitcher Ed Sprague, Sr. begat Toronto third baseman/catcher Ed Sprague, Jr.; first baseman Tony Perez begat California outfielder/first baseman Eduardo Perez; and second baseman/outfielder/first baseman Pete Rose, Sr. begat Cleveland third base prospect Pete Rose, Jr.

Note: At the time the other offspring were prospering, the son of the banished-from-baseball Rose, Pete Jr. was also banished — cut by the Indians prior to the 1994 season. Still, with those genes, it's a good bet Rose will smell sweet in another organization. But maybe it's only good luck to have chromosomes donated by those in good standing with the Commissioner's Office.

Still, I can see a test tube team of the future — the Cincinnati Clones.

ROGER MARIS

Roger Maris set the baseball world on its ear with a 61-home run performance in 1961 to break Babe Ruth's hallowed 60-home run mark set in 1927. Maris, respected by his teammates and opponents alike for his all-around ability as a hitter, base runner, fielder, thrower and strategist and for his knowledge of the game, remarked to the author in 1980 that there were times he wished he hadn't broken the record, but had hit only 55 or 56, because after setting the new standard, he was perceived by fans to be a one-dimensional player—a home run hitter and that's all.

Maris found good luck in his sweet, compact swing, in the short right field porch at Yankee Stadium, and in discovering ways to achieve peace and serenity. He found it on a September day in Detroit in 1961.

With teammate Tony Kubek at second base, Maris stepped in against Terry Fox. Suddenly, Maris stepped out of the batter's box and stared off into right field—his home run territory. All heads turned to see what Maris was watching, and they discovered he was following a skein of about 200 Canadian snow geese in flight. For a solid minute, Maris watched the geese as home plate umpire Nestor Chylak debated about letting Maris delay the game. The entire game was at a standstill, and when the geese disappeared from view, Maris stepped in and promptly belted Fox's first offering deep into the right-field stands—right below the spot where the geese first appeared. It was home run number 58 for Maris, who found that fowl was fair for him and very foul for Fox.

BRIAN HOLTON

Big strong reliever Brian Holton was a setup man for the Dodgers and Orioles from the mid-1980s to 1990.

But all those games spent sitting in the bullpen appeared to give him too much time on his hands and too much time to think about rituals and superstitions.

For Holton's entire career, he set the following schedule: His wife, Wendy, made him pancakes for breakfast and spaghetti for lunch. He drove to the ballpark, speeding up or slowing down to arrive precisely at 3:50.

Getting out of the car, he went to the clubhouse, put a dip of tobacco in his cheek, had a cup of coffee and read the paper.

After taking his swings in batting practice, he taped his right big toe and got dressed in this order: baseball sleeves; pants; spikes—right shoe first, all laced up, then left shoe. His baseball jersey still hung in the locker.

At this point, he went to the pitching coach — in Baltimore it was Al Jackson — and got two baseballs, which had to be placed in his glove, never his hand.

Then he put his game jersey on, grabbed a towel and wrapped it around his neck, took his jacket and hit the field exactly 30 minutes before game time.

Now it was off to the dugout and his own personal spot on the bench, exactly four places from home plate. And his teammates wouldn't even think of placing a bottom on Holton's spot.

Hitting the field again, he played long toss, throwing his last four as if he were a quarterback.

When Holton was chosen to enter the game, the routine got serious.

He screwed himself into the mound with a right-hand spin. Then one more turn around the mound. Then four kicks to the rubber with each foot. Then came nine warm-up pitches — four fastballs, three curves and two more smokers that he signified with a "hook 'em Horns" hand sign.

Between innings, Holton lassoed a teammate with a tiny rope he kept in his back pocket.

Despite all he did to bring himself good luck, Holton wound up with a 20-19 record and three saves in 185 appearances.

That's a lot of work for 20 wins.

NOLAN RYAN

Nolan Ryan is the greatest strikeout pitcher in baseball history with 5,714 K's over his amazing 27-year career that saw him fire a record seven no-hitters on his way to winning 324 games.

With a 100-mile-an-hour fastball and a Major League curve, he didn't need much luck. Still, he seemed to be at his best when an ill wind blew his way.

Good luck for Ryan, and bad luck for opposing hitters, seemed to be whenever Ryan, who pitched until he was 46, was feeling his age.

On May 1, 1991, Ryan tossed his seventh no-hitter in beating Toronto 3-0. He woke up that day with a stiff back. He took aspirin or Advil all day long. He undertook an extra pregame stretch, wore a heating pack on his back, and complained all day of his aching back, sore ankle and aching fingers. Pitching through the discomfort, Ryan fashioned a gem.

Eleven months earlier, on June 11, 1990, Nolan Ryan woke up with a sore back. His son, Reese, spent the day rubbing his dad's back, patting his legs and massaging his stiff neck. The elder Ryan, who had a stress fracture in his back, gutted it out and pitched his sixth no-hitter, a 5-0 triumph over Oakland.

And on September 26, 1981, a tired, younger Ryan, fought through a leg cramp and an aching elbow to throw his then-record fifth no-hitter, a 5-0 win over Los Angeles.

Three painful aches and three no-hitters.

Pain was good luck for "The Express," but it made him just that much tougher on the hitters.

"BROADWAY" BILL SCHUSTER

Known for his love of the nightlife — hence the nickname — journeyman reserve shortstop Bill Schuster (1937-1945) was also called "Monkey on a String" for his monkeyshines on and off the field. For luck, however, Schuster would yell at the top of his lungs — when he needed a hit, got a hit, made a good play — in a sound reminiscent of Sabu's calls to the elephants in jungle pictures of the same era. For that reason, Schuster was also called "Sabu."

The yells didn't help often, though, as Schuster hit only .234 for his career.

DON LARSEN

Speaking of loving the nightlife, Don Larsen, the 6′4″, 235-pound, no-windup pitcher, who propelled himself among the baseball immortals by tossing a 97-pitch perfect game against the Brooklyn Dodgers in the 1956 World Series, also made a legend of himself for his nocturnal habits. His manager, Casey Stengel, called Larsen "Night Rider" because Larsen never met a curfew he couldn't break.

Larsen's drinking and carousing became a good-luck charm for him, and the night before his perfect game, October 8, 1956, he was partying until dawn. When asked if he ever went to bed early, Larsen replied, "One time I did go to bed early, and I had the worst game of my career. That was the start just before the perfect game. And when Casey came out to take me out, I told him that's the last time I'll ever go to bed early."

Drinks all around. I'll bet Brooklyn wishes New York was a dry state in 1956.

Tagline: In a roller-coaster-like baseball oddity, the same day Larsen threw his perfecto, his wife filed for divorce.

PETE BROWNING

Known as "The Gladiator," Louis Rogers "Pete" Browning played from 1882 to 1894, mostly with Louisville. Finishing with a career batting average of .343, with 232 stolen bases, Browning was considered by many to be one of the greatest hitters of his time—nicknamed "The Louisville Slugger"—and one of the more brutal outfielders of his era—called "The Gladiator" for the way he fought every fly ball.

Browning did at least two things for luck.

Taking a page out of Don Larsen's book, Browning was an admitted heavy drinker. He once said, "I can't hit the ball until I hit the bottle." He would often take a bottle with him into the locker room and down an entire quart before game time. A quick hop to his locker during a game also often produced a shot of "courage" for him.

Equipment was more important to him than his health, and while playing in Louisville, he talked local lumberman John Hillerich into making a bat to his specifications. It was known as the Louisville Slugger. As Browning's average soared with his new custom-made lumber, other players demanded bats made for them as well, and Hillerich's company, Hillerich and Bradsby, began a baseball legacy that has endured for a century—Louisville Slugger bats.

It has been said that Browning went down to the mill and selected the wood for his bats to make sure they were perfect.

Ted Williams later took it one step further. Ted used to go out to the forest and choose the tree from which his bats would be made, then follow the wood through the entire process to make certain his bats were up to his stringent requirements. Williams, it has been reported, could tell if a bat was a half ounce too heavy or a sixteenth inch too fat or too thin. But it all started with Browning.

JACK "LUCKY" LOHRKE

Any chapter on lucky bounces or good luck must include one of the luckiest men ever to walk on a diamond—or anywhere else for that matter. Jack Lohrke played from 1947 to 1953, mostly with the New York Giants. A third baseman, Lohrke hit .242 in 354 games and hit 22 homers. Not much luck on the field, but man, did he have luck elsewhere.

As a member of the 35th Infantry Division for the Allied Forces during World War II, Lohrke fought at the Normandy invasion and in the Battle of the Bulge. On four occasions, GIs on both sides of him were killed, yet Lohrke came through the war unscathed.

In 1945, scheduled to fly from Fort Dix, New Jersey, to his home, Los Angeles, to be discharged, he was bumped from the flight. The plane crashed and all aboard were killed.

In 1946, he was on a bus trip with the Spokane Indians of the Western International League. When the bus stopped at Ellensburg, Washington, Lohrke got word to report immediately to the San Diego Padres of the Pacific Coast League. He stepped off the bus, and 15 minutes later, it crashed off a cliff in the Cascade Mountains, killing eight players.

From then on, regardless of what happened on a ball field, he was known as "Lucky" Lohrke.

JACK McDOWELL

Chicago White Sox ace pitcher Jack McDowell, the goateed 1993 Cy Young Award winner, says being happy equals wins, so he collects yellow happy faces. He collects them on anything he can lay his glove on—banks, buttons, T-shirts, coffee cups, and even a cookie jar, all emblazoned with yellow, smiling, happy faces. He has even painted the happy yellow fellas on his sneakers.

The right-hander from Van Nuys, California, went 22-10 in 1993 to run his six-year record to 81 happy faces and 49 losses.

Mac uses the little yellow guys to keep him in a laughing mood. "They make me laugh because yellow is supposed to be an angry color and it's supposed to make you feel angry," he says. "But when the funny face is yellow, the angry color makes me laugh. It's a dichotomy, and making me laugh makes me win." It made him win 22 times in 1993, anyway.

I would like to see what happens if a happy face McDowell

fastball meets a happy face Juan Gonzalez bat.

BATS

Whenever Yogi Berra would get into a slump—even back-to-back hitless games—he would change bats. The reasoning, from Yogi's own mouth, was "I never blame myself when I'm not hitting, I blame the bat. If it keeps up, I change bats. It's not my fault. How can I get mad at myself? I'm the same player I was yesterday when I wasn't mad and got two hits."

Philadelphia Phillies prospect first baseman Jeff Grotewold hit 15 home runs for Reading in the Class AA minors in 1990, the year before he was homerless for more than a month. Taking a page out of Phillies-legend Richie Ashburn's book—Ashburn, a career .308 hitter from 1948 to 1962 and two-time batting leader admitted to kissing his bats when he needed some hits—Grotewold's teammate Greg Legg grabbed his buddy's lumber one evening, gave it a big kiss and whispered those sweet words: "You're going deep." Grotewold responded by belting his first AAA homer in 1991. Another teammate Gary Alexander was also homerless when he watched Grotewold's first dinger. He asked Legg to perform oral luck on his stick, and Legg placed his lips against the wood and cooed, "You're going deep." Alexander pinch hit later in the contest and homered. Legg never homered during his brief two-year stay in the Majors (14 games in 1986-87). Grotewold made The Show in 1992, hitting only .200 with three round-trippers. Alexander was still looking for the big break. They should have stuck with Legg's lips.

Other bat kissers have included the Mets' and Dodgers' Darryl Strawberry, Chicago "Black" Sox hitter "Shoeless Joe" Jackson and Negro Leagues slugger Josh Gibson.

Perennial all-star slugger Joe Carter, the toast of Toronto, slept with his bat on an ESPN All-Star show. He's been hitting home runs at an increased clip ever since. I hope he kissed it afterward to show his appreciation.

Yankee clubhouse man Nick Priore revealed that Yankee outfielder Bobby Brown (1980-81) took his six best bats and soaked them in linseed oil for a month. They came out like concrete, and Brown swung the heavy lumber for a .260 average with 14 homers in 1980. The marinated ash preparation didn't work the following year as he managed only .226 with no four baggers and a one-way ticket to Seattle.

Hall of Fame slugger Reggie Jackson (563 homers) used to methodically shave all the black paint from the handles of his bats to improve his grip and bat speed. He rejected the idea of selling "Reggie Shavings" at memorabilia shows.

His Yankee teammate and fellow slugger Dave Winfield shaves his bat handles to thin them out. He also doesn't like the feel of paint or lacquer and prefers natural wood. The thinned bats have helped him collect more than 3,000 career hits, as did Hall of Famer "Stan The Man" Musial, who shaved his bats to obtain just the right feel during his storied career with the Cardinals from 1941 to 1963.

Detroit Tigers Hall of Fame outfielder Al Kaline used to put his bats in his locker 12 at a time for hits by the dozen—he got 3,007 of them in his career. He'd also bone his bats, an ancient baseball ritual that makes the grain deeper and has been practiced since the 1800s and is still seen today. Kaline also would not let pitchers use his bats either in a game or during batting practice. He apparently didn't want those nonhitters to get "out germs" on them.

Hall of Fame slugger Johnny Mize, who played first base for the Cardinals, Giants and Yankees from 1936 to 1953, had five dozen bats to start each season. "The Big Cat" used a different one for each pitcher and used longer bats against lefty pitchers. And while he was with the Giants, he banged out 91 homers in two years (1947-48) by swinging his bat in the clubhouse and puffing on a "hit cigar" before he stepped to the on-deck circle. Carrying the cigar theme further, he would swing his bat up in his hotel room before a game, look out the window, and find a flag or a tree and watch the wind blow. Then he'd take a big home run swing, puff on his stogie and growl, "I'll hit one or two today if the wind is blowing out." He finished with 359 homers, 341 of them in his first 12 seasons.

Other bat men include Hall of Fame second baseman Eddie Collins, who buried his bats in graves "to keep them lively"; Hall of Fame second baseman Frankie Frisch, who hung his bats in a barn "to cure them and make them harder to bang out more hits"; Cardinals and Giants first baseman Orlando Cepeda, who used a new bat after each hit saying each piece of wood only had one good hit in it (although, he got 2,351 hits, so he must not have changed bats *every* time . . . otherwise there'd be no Sluggers left in Louisville); and Yankee outfielder Bobby Murcer, who stored his bats in a sauna "to keep them warm and break-free."

Switch-hitting first baseman David Segui employs that time-honored boning technique, and he uses a real bone — a two-foot-long bone he picked up from the son of an all-time hitting great, who got it from a local butcher shop. Segui was given the bone by Pete Rose, Jr. when the two were roommates at Frederick in the Class AA minors. Rose boiled the bone, and Segui has been using it ever since. After hitting only .263 for his first four seasons, Segui may want to exchange Rose, Jr.'s gift for one given to him by the other five, more successful members of the Big Red Gene Pool.

And Leo Durocher, then a manager with the Houston Astros, threw a broken bat on the floor of the team's clubhouse in 1973 and instructed the team's batboy and everyone else to leave it where it was. The 'Stros won eight in a row.

ODDS AND EVENS

Some players excel every other year. Not every year, just every other year. If you're a rotisserie league player or a general manager deciding on whether to pay big bucks for an athlete, it may be wise to check out a player's biorhythms. Sometimes these big year-off year-on types have dramatic statistical ups and downs. Check out the following three ballplayers, who, when they were good, they were very, very good, but when they were bad . . . they could take a whole team with them.

Bret Saberhagen, the exceptional righty hurler for the Kansas City Royals and New York Mets, is an odd guy. Well, an odd-year guy, anyway. During the first 10 years of his fine career, Saberhagen won 120, lost 90, and fashioned an ERA of 3.24. In odd years he was great, at 81-37 with an ERA under 3.00. In five even years, he was 39-53 with an ERA over 3.50. The record:

Year	W-L	ERA	Year	W-L	ERA
1984	10-11	3.48	1985	20-6	2.87
1986	7-12	4.15	1987	18-10	3.36
1988	14-16	3.80	1989	23-6	2.16
1990	5-9	3.27	1991	13-8	3.07
1992	3-5	3.50	1993	7-7	3.29

Don't pick up this guy in an even year. Remember ... he's odd.

An even guy for most of his 22-year career with the Dodgers, Cubs and Red Sox was first baseman Bill Buckner. "Billy Bucks" was an outstanding hitter who fell on gimpy ankles—he pioneered the use of high-top baseball shoes—late in his career. Though it was during an even year, 1986, that a ground ball through his wickets cost the Boston Red Sox the World Series, he was on an even keel for most of his career.

Discounting his early seasons (1969 and 1970 when he played in only 29 games) and his final year (1990 when he called it a career after only 22 games), Buckner was a classic even-year hitter, odd-year flop. In evens, he hit better than .300 six straight times; he hit better than .300 only once in an odd year. Two of his three 100-RBI seasons were even years, and three of his top four stolen base years (31 in 1974, 28 in 1976, and 15 in 1982 and 1983) were evens.

Year	Avg.	HR	RBI	Year	Avg.	HR	RBI
1971	.277	5	41	1972	.319	5	37
1973	.275	8	46	1974	.314	7	58
1975	.243	6	31	1976	.301	7	60
1977	.284	11	60	1978	.323	5	74
1979	.284	14	66	1980	.324	10	68
1981	.311	10	75	1982	.306	15	105
1983	.280	16	66	1984	.272	11	69
1985	.299	16	110	1986	.267	18	102
1987	.286	5	74	1988	.249	3	43
1989	.216	1	16				

Keep this man out of your lineup in odd years.

Another even guy for most of his career was Los Angeles Dodgers' outfielder Willie Davis, the "3-Dog" ballplayer who was into chanting and Eastern religions to such an extreme that it even drove his Japanese teammates to distraction when he finished up his career in the Far East. In even years, Davis picked up his top five RBI years, six of his top eight batting years, and four of his top six homer years. Davis's numbers:

Year	Avg.	HR	RBI	Year	Avg.	HR	RBI
1960	.318	2	10 (22 games)	1961	.254	12	45
1962	.285	21	85	1963	.245	9	60
1964	.294	12	77	1965	.238	10	57
1966	.284	11	61	1967	.257	6	41
1968	.250	7	31	1969	.311	11	59
1970	.305	8	93	1971	.309	10	74
1972	.289	19	79	1973	.285	6	77
1974	.295	12	89	1975	.277	11	67
1976	.268	5	46	1977	.250	0	2

*rare good odd year

Other players were on and off to a certain extent.

Whitey Ford, the crafty Hall of Fame lefty pitcher for the Yankees, won 18, 18, 11, 16, 25, 24 and 16 in odd years from 1953 to 1966, totaling 128 wins against only 52 losses, an average of 18-7. In even years during that period, Ford won 16, 19, 14, 12, 17, 17 and 2 for 97 wins against 49 losses, an average of 14-7. Still not bad, but no 20-win seasons.

St. Louis Cardinals fireballer Bob Gibson won 130 games in seven even years from 1962 through 1975 (an average of 18½) versus 115 wins in eight odd years (an average of 14).

And while Tigers Hall of Fame outfielder Harry Heilmann (1914 to 1932) was consistent during his entire career—a .342 lifetime average, 12 consecutive .300 seasons—his four batting titles and his four best seasons were all in odd years: 1921—.394; 1923—.403; 1925—.393 and 1927—.398. That's an odd year average of .397, while the four even years along the way saw him average *only* .345.

Even Hall of Fame Yankee slugger Mickey Mantle had an on-off switch. He found it easier to bomb homers in even years than odd—though I'd take the odd totals as well. Despite belting 54 homers in 1961, his odd-year homers totaled *only* 246 in nine years, an average of 27 each (with one home run crown), while his even-year four-baggers totaled 290, an average of 32 (with three homer titles). Three of his four 100-plus RBI seasons were in even years, and the Mick hit better than .300 in six of nine even years and four of nine odd years.

Hey, I'd take these last four anytime, any year. But every other year they were really something.

Outfielder Candy Maldonado has a different odd-even streak going; he played in five consecutive odd-year play-off series — with the Dodgers in 1983 and 1985, the Giants in 1987 and 1989 and Toronto in 1991. He broke the string with the Blue Jays in 1992 and ended his odd-year run when he spent 1993 in Cleveland. Maybe it has something to do with the Cleveland curse (about which we'll talk more in the Bad Hops chapter).

One guy who seems to have broken his odd-even-itis with a change of scenery is shortstop Walt Weiss. Weiss, a steady defensive infielder from Tuxedo, New York, with a propensity for injuries . . . every other year . . . broke in with the Oakland A's and played 16 games in 1987. In helping lead the A's to four divisional flags, Weiss fared well in even years, playing 147 games in 1988, 138 in 1990 and 103 in 1992. In odd years, he got hurt, suffering a damaged left knee while turning a double play in 1989 that limited his play to 84 games and sustaining torn ligaments in his left ankle while running out a grounder to short, which cut his season to 40 in 1991.

Drafted by the expansion Florida Marlins, Weiss played an entire 1993 injury-free and appeared in 158 games. He declared himself healthy and free of odd-even-itis in 1994 when he signed with the sophomore Colorado Rockies, making him the first player to wear the uniforms of the game's two newest franchises.

Maybe his body didn't like the odd climate in Oakland.

MOUTH MUSIC

Gutteral sounds are good luck — at least that's what James "Grunting Jim" Shaw thought. Shaw pitched for the Senators from 1913 to 1921, before a hip injury ended his career. Although Shaw predated tennis stars Jimmy Connors and Monica Seles by six decades, just before every pitch he emitted a low-pitched, loud roar that seemed to reverberate from his feet to his mouth. These grunts could be heard in the stands, and some people even said they heard these roars on the street outside the ballpark.

They didn't help him win though, as he went 83-98 and twice led the league in walks.

A more pleasant sound can still be annoying, but Joaquin "Jackie" Gutierrez and Jon Warden felt whistling would make them better on the field.

Jackie Gutierrez was a shortstop for the Red Sox and Orioles in the 1980s. He should have whistled louder, since he hit only .237 and made 67 errors in 356 games. He did set a Major League record for the BoSox in 1984 for fewest assists and total chances by a starting shortstop in a full season—347 assists and 606 chances in 150 games. That whistling *did* get him into the record books.

Another whistler was Jon "Warbler" Warden, a pitcher who went 4-1 in 28 relief appearances for the Tigers in 1968, his only year in the Majors. Warden was seemingly always whistling, even while on the mound. He must have forgotten the tune the next season.

STUFF IN YOUR MOUTH

Keeping your mouth full seems to be a good-luck charm to many ballplayers.

Lots of guys chew tobacco, and ChiSox second baseman Nellie Fox (1947-1965) was among those who chewed licorice and found success. And you can hardly walk around a Major League ballpark these days without crunching your shoes on spit-out sunflower seeds. But these are other items diamond athletes like to spit out of their mouths—including toothpicks.

"Sad Sam" Jones, also called "Toothpick Sam" Jones, hit and pitched with a tiny piece of wood in his mouth from 1951 to 1964, covering 322 games. His best year was 1959 when he won 21 and lost 15 with the San Francisco Giants, sporting an ERA of 2.83 to lead the league. Jones would chewed on the stick during the game and flicked it in and out of his mouth with his tongue. He changed toothpicks whenever he needed to get his team some runs or some outs—or maybe just when the old one began to splinter.

Another toothpicker was "Toothpick John" Titus, an out-fielder from 1903 to 1913, mostly with the Phillies. He was a steady ballplayer who twice hit over .300., and his quiet, unassuming manner also earned him the nickname "Silent John." He played each game with a toothpick in his mouth, and he chewed the thing until the game was over, regardless of how splintered and soggy it got.

On the other hand, or tongue-in-cheek, sticking stuff out of your mouth can help prolong a career, too. Bobby Shantz, the diminutive hurler with a lot of heart and a great curve, pitched from 1949 to 1964, mostly with the Yankees and Philadelphia A's, for whom he won the Most Valuable Player Award in 1952, going 24-7 for a fifth-place team. Shantz, a Gold Glove fielder for eight seasons who fought injuries later in his career, had success both as a starter and reliever. Shantz's good-luck habit was sticking out his tongue and biting it with every pitch. It was his way of bearing down, and it worked for 16 years.

LUCKY SOD

In May 1993, the Los Angeles Dodgers had been playing well at home on natural grass, but were playing terrible ball on the road and on artifical grass. L.A. outfielder Cory Snyder solved the problem. He grabbed a flat of sod—the same Bermuda grass that is used at Dodger Stadium—and took it with him on the team's next road trip. The Dodgers placed the grass on their dugout floor, watered it, fertilized it and talked to it—even prayed to it— and went on an 11-game winning streak to move up from last place in the West to a contending third.

Snyder's two-and-a-half yards of sod cost $9.28 and sprouted its first win at Pittsburgh's Three Rivers Stadium May 28, after the Dogers had lost their first nine games on artificial turf that year and compiled a road record of 7-16.

Eventually, crabgrass set in, and the Dodgers cooled off and fell out of contention.

But, what if the players had all glued sod to the bottom of their shoes? Then they could be called "The Grasshouse Gang."

LUCKY MUSIC

Pitcher Bill Swift went through six seasons in Seattle with a 30-40 record. When he changed uniforms and addresses in 1992, moving on to throw for the San Francisco Giants, Swift thought a change of music would add to the change of scenery.

On days he was to pitch, he insisted that the clubhouse CD machine play only music from Frank Sinatra and only those Chairman of the Board songs written by Sammy Kahn or Jimmy Van Heusen. Swift went 10-4 in 1992 and 21-8 in 1993.

I did it myyyy way.

The 1992 Toronto Blue Jays became the first Canadian-based team to win the World Series. They did it with hitting, pitching and fielding, and they also did it with music. The Jays listened to the most loud and raucous rock and metal tunes as they took batting practice for the Series. When their Fall Classic opponents, the Atlanta Braves, took their practice swings, the Toronto Sky Dome loudspeaker played funereal chamber music. Toronto took two out of three at the Dome. When the Series returned to Atlanta for game six, Atlanta retaliated and played such downbeat music for the Blue Jay batters as "Be My Love," by Mario Lanza, and "The Itsy-Bitsy Spider." The Jays won the game anyway, 4-3, to wrap up the Series.

"TURK" WENDELL

Steven John "Turk" Wendell, the superstitious right-hander for the Chicago Cubs, *thinks* he knows what good luck is. Having spent six years in the minors — 32 days in the Majors — with a sub-.500 record, Wendell believes the following behavior will bring him good luck. Among other practices, he jumps over — we're talking high hurdles here, three feet in the air — the foul line on his way to the mound; waves to his center fielder and second baseman before pitching an inning; chews licorice (exactly three pieces at a time) exclusively on the mound; and brushes his teeth between innings.

Other Wendellisms (picking up from the four above):

5. He will not catch a ball before going to the mound to pitch, preferring instead to have someone, the umpire is best, roll the horsehide to him. Then he can pick the ball up from the ground — even after a foul ball is hit on the prior pitch.
6. If he has gotten the ball from the catcher, he walks behind the mound, crosses himself three times, turns, goes to his knees and draws three more crosses in the dirt behind the pitcher's rubber. Then he waves before going to the mound to pitch.
7. He circles the mound counterclockwise, walks to the rubber then squats. If the catcher is already squatting, he must stand up. Then when the catcher squats, Wendell stands.
8. Then Wendell licks his hand, the one he used to draw the crosses in the dirt.
9. To get ready for his pitching assignments, on the night before a scheduled start, he listens to the national anthem on his CD player.

10. After each inning he spits out the licorice, brushes his pearly whites, then pops in another three sticks.
11. He never wears socks, saying they're useless and without purpose. He certainly doesn't wear socks off the field, and on the diamond, he resorts only to stirrups and black tape.
12. He throws to first base for luck. Even during an inning, if no runner is at first, he'll still throw over.
13. He wears two watches, one with his home (Massachusetts) time on it and another reflecting the time zone he's in — or the twilight zone he's in.

Wow. If all this brings him *good* luck, imagine how lousy his stats would be if he just went to the ballpark and pitched.

WARREN CROMARTIE

Warren Cromartie was a slick outfielder for the Montreal Expos from 1974 to 1983 who chucked the American game at age 30 to play in Japan, where he became a legend. Signing with the Yomi-uri Giants of the Japan Central League, Cro smashed better than 30 homers a year in each of his first three seasons — 104 total — and maintained high averages — .321 for his career there as opposed to his .280 average in the United States — and good power for his seven-year tenure there before returning for a shot with the Kansas City Royals in 1991.

Cro became a hero in Japan and learned Japanese rituals that brought him good luck. He had several "good-luck elephants," all with their trunks symbolically in the "up" position, that he stationed above head level in and above his locker.

He says, "God forbid if I put my shirt on backward or inside out . . . it would ruin my whole day and game. And if I'm hot, I'll put my clothes on exactly the same way in the same order for the entire streak."

He says he's very superstitious and even has secret superstitions that he won't reveal. "If anyone finds out my personal ones, they won't work anymore, so I have to protect them from the public . . . and from writers."

NINTENDO NO-HITTER

Major league prospect Raphael Quirico was very lucky July 24, 1991, while pitching for the Yankees' Class A affiliate, Greensboro of the South Atlantic League. He finished the day with two no-hitters.

Just before he took the field to pitch against the Charleston Rainbows, he opened his travel bag, took out a Nintendo electronic baseball game, and "pitched" a no-hitter. Teammate Luis Gallardo, his catcher, told him he would now pitch one in the real game, which Quirico did, blanking the Rainbows 2-0.

The left-hander said that was his first no-no on either game and is looking for his second in both arenas.

"Next time I no-hit my Nintendo, I'll bet I can do it again on the field," he said.

THUNDERBIRD THUNDER

The Cleveland Indians found a way to put some bombs and thrust into their lineup—they just schedule the U.S. Air Force Thunderbirds aerial team to perform in the skies during a game.

On September 5, 1992, the Tribe, suffering though another long season (76-86 and a fourth-place finish), were involved in a tight game against the Seattle Mariners and ace pitcher Randy Johnson.

In the fourth inning, the Air Force jets performed an exciting, ear-splitting maneuver above Cleveland Municipal Stadium and visibly shook up Johnson, who at 6'10" and on top of the pitcher's mound was closer to the show than the rest of the players on the field. Johnson gave up four runs during a fifth-inning Indian rally.

And with the score tied in the ninth, the four jets flew in formation and screamed across the sky as Albert Belle singled in the winning run for the victory.

You'd think it would be easy to schedule the Air Force to fly overhead a measly 81 times a year, right above Cleveland's new ballpark, but apparently the flyboys have other things to do.

LOOK, UP IN THE SKY . . . AGAIN

They weren't airplanes, but they were airborne. On June 11, 1993, in Milwaukee, some 100 sea gulls swooped down on County Stadium during a Brewers-Yankees game. Several times during the game, just as Yankee players hit pop-ups, the horde of white birds filled the sky making it impossible to determine what was the white ball and what were the birds. As Yankee pops fell in for hits, the Brewers tried noise, horns, sirens, whistles and scoreboard lights to no avail. They even played the theme to Alfred Hitchcock's movie, *The Birds*, but the gulls owned the air.

With the birds flying in formation above, Yankee pinch hitter Kevin Maas hit a two-run homer in the ninth off Doug Henry to beat the Brew Crew 5-4.

Apparently the Yankees didn't shoo the gulls away and the Brewers did, creating good luck for the New Yorkers.

RELIGIOUS LUCK

Tom Lasorda, longtime skipper of the Dodgers, prays to "That Big Dodger in the sky." He may be on a first-name basis with the Big Guy.

In 1980, playing on a Sunday in Cincinnati, Lasorda met opposing manager John McNamara at a local church. They both made their peace with the Lord, prayed for a victory and walked out together.

On the church steps, Lasorda turned to his friend and said, "Wait for me, Mac, I forgot something." McNamara waited as Lasorda darted back inside the church.

He kneeled down, lit a new candle, prayed for a Dodger win, and blew out McNamara's candles.

The Dodgers won the game 13-2.

Someone up there likes him.

MORE RELIGIOUS LUCK

On the other side of the religious coin is the case of Leo Durocher, who in 1951 was the manager of the New York Giants.

During the 1951 National League pennant play-off between the Giants and Dodgers, Durocher fretted over whom he should send out to pitch game two. Durocher's wife, Laraine Day, suggested that the skipper should pray for guidance. Durocher knelt, prayed and heard the divine name, Sheldon Jones.

The field boss started Jones and was shellacked by the Dodgers 10-0.

After the game, Durocher glared at his wife and growled, "Does your Friend have any other bright suggestions for me?"

Maybe Lasorda is right and God *is* a Dodger fan.

LIP READING

Mitch Webster, the eccentric Dodger outfielder from Larned, Kansas, got some help from the lips of his opponent. On June 1, 1992, while in Pittsburgh to play the Pirates, opposing pitcher Denny Neagle had a conference on the mound, discussing with his catcher how to pitch to the switch-hitter. Webster watched Neagle's mouth and made out what he thought was the word "curveball."

The next pitch was indeed a curveball, which Webster belted into the left-field seats for a three-run homer.

Webster, who only hit six home runs all season, said he was lucky. "What if he was saying, 'I'll throw this guy anything *but* a curveball'?"

Another good-luck item for Webster is his "Mayberry ritual." In his mind, whenever he steps on the field, he is not at Dodger Stadium, or Three Rivers, or Wrigley, but in Mayberry, home of Andy, Opie, Barney and Goober.

Before every game, he sits in front of his TV and catches the reruns of *The Andy Griffith Show*. He mentally puts himself alongside Aunt Bee, Floyd and the gang as he drives to the park. And if he's on the road and can't find Andy anywhere, he'll rent a car and visit local gun shops or archery ranges and swap Mayberry-esque hunting tales with the locals — just to get in the mood.

He's at peace when he takes the field. And after more than a decade and 1,100 games in uniform, he considers himself lucky regardless of his .265 average.

HAIR OF THE DOG

When Lou Piniella was manager of the Cincinnati Reds (1990-1992), he would go along with owner Marge Schott's idiosyncrasies and demands. He allowed her dog Schottzie to romp and dump on the home field carpet before games, and when Schott sent the skipper strands of dog hair when the club was on the road, Piniella dutifully rubbed them on his chest for good luck.

Did it work? Well, he kept his job for three years and won a World Championship. Woof.

WET MOUND

No, Schottzie didn't wet this mound; Mother Nature did. On July 28 1991, Montreal Expos pitcher Dennis Martinez went to the hill to pitch the first inning against the Dodgers and complained to umpire Bruce Froemming that the mound was wet and he couldn't pitch from it. Froemming convinced him that it would dry out within three innings, but Martinez told him he didn't know if he'd be around that long.

Wet was something the Nicaraguan right-hander didn't want to hear. Just a day earlier, he had encountered something that reminded him of his wet past. As a recovering alcoholic, Martinez knew about excuses given for missing a routine and for taking that one more wet one before going home. On this day, Martinez contemplated skipping Sunday Mass because of inconvenience. His wife, Luz Marina, excused him from his religious duties, but Martinez risked missing his bus to the ballpark by going to church. Any excuse had an all too familiar ring to it.

So now on the mound, Martinez decided not to use a wet mound as an excuse for a bad outing. Whatever happened, he said to himself, was what God wanted to happen in conjunction with what he did himself, i.e., taking responsibility for his performance.

He needn't have worried. The wet mound became as dry as Dodger bats that day, and Martinez fashioned a gem, a perfect game, the 14th perfecto in Major League history.

There are a lot of pitchers out there today who can use a wet mound . . . or Divine intervention . . . or something. Anything. Just to retire the side now and then.

DON'T MESS WITH THESE GUYS

You may have heard that there are guys who are competitive to the point of meanness on the field, but are pussycats off the field. They certainly are.

There are ballplayers who fit that mold and who work themselves into frenzies before they cross the white lines.

Mel Hall, of Cleveland, New York and Japan, was one big, tough outfielder. A solid, strong, 6'0", 200-pounder, Hall was not a guy you wanted to tangle with. He looked tough. He was tough. And he thought tough. Hall's ritual was to get angry — to work himself into a hatred for one player. Most of the time it was an opponent, but teammate Steve Howe used to purposely get under Hall's skin to make him angry, so that by 7:35, game time, Hall's adrenaline would be flowing, spiked with anger — home run anger. He was home run angry 134 times, anyway.

"Bullet" Bob Gibson, the Cardinal right-hander with the mean fastball, also practiced hatred. The hitter was his enemy. All hitters. Even hitters on his team. And during All-Star games—he was in six of them—he made certain he didn't talk to his fellow All-Stars: he didn't want to make friends with them and then have to hate them the next day. He said, "It doesn't make sense to make friends with a guy I plan to knock down, then strike out."

The Hall of Famer used his hatred to win 251 games and strike out 3,117 in 17 years on his way to the Hall of Fame.

Even mild-mannered Yankee Captain Don Mattingly uses hate to succeed. He develops a personal hatred toward the opposing pitcher for those nine innings of a ball game. He said, "For those nine innings, it's a personal battle that I want to win. I hate that guy. Afterward, we can be the best friends in the world. Even before the game, we can be buddies. But during the game, I am Patriot missiles with the intent to bomb the pitcher's incoming scuds." Mattingly has hated his way to a batting title, an MVP Award, and an average over .300 for more than a decade.

THE TOMAHAWK CHOP

Before the Atlanta Braves became a power in the National League, their fans would go through various waves and cheers just like every other Big League club. Then, in 1991, Deion Sanders arrived on the scene.

Sanders was a two-sport athlete—baseball with the Yanks and Braves and football with the Atlanta Falcons—who was having trouble finding stardom in baseball. He was a sub-.200 hitter—he had hit only .178 in two years with the Yankees and just .191 in 1991 for Atlanta—and the Braves had been nonpennant winners since 1982, finishing dead last in the West for three straight years.

Then Sanders rediscovered a good-luck charm, the tomahawk chop.

In college, Sanders was a star gridiron player for the Florida State Seminoles. Seminole fans have been using a similar chop for years as a rallying ritual.

Upon Sanders' arrival in Atlanta, his fans greeted him with a Seminole chop for luck.

During the season, as the Braves began to challenge for the

pennant, Sanders and teammate Jeff Treadway et al. returned the fans' ceremonial chops with chops of their own. Soon, everyone on the team and in the stands seemed to adopt the chop, accompanying it with a "war chant" that is nonsensical if you ask any Native Americans.

Still, the ritual helped Sanders bring his average up to .304 in 1992, and he soon became one of the premier leadoff hitters in the game. While the chop and chant brought controversy — and a cry from many Native American groups to cease and desist, calling it a racial slur — the newly named "Tomahawk Chop" didn't do the Braves any harm, helping to inspire them to three consecutive National League West pennants.

Not bad for a bogus, racially insulting device used to honor a sub-.200 hitter.

WHATEVER IT TAKES

When hard-luck pitcher Kyle Abbott began the 1992 season for the Phillies with an 0-11 record, he thought long and hard about how to change his luck.

Using the mixed-bag approach, he grew a beard, saw his old college coach to talk about games he had won in the past, and caught a 50-cent piece that was tossed to him from the stands as he warmed up.

Abbott faced the Dodgers that night and earned his first win, 14-3.

HAIR TODAY, GONE TOMORROW

In 1992, Boston's perennial batting leader Wade Boggs went hitless in 18 at bats. He shaved off the moustache he had worn for the last three years and went 2-for-3. He finished the season at a career-low .259 and was gone the next year, having signed on with the New York Yankees. With a new moustache on his face, he hit .302 for New York in 1993.

Baltimore Oriole relief ace Gregg Olson, a superstitious pitcher who feared pitching in domes and during the day, grew a moustache and beard in order to look intimidating. Here's a guy who had saved 131 games in four years with a 2.36 ERA, and he wants to look initimidating. At 6'4", 210 pounds, he *was* intimidating. With facial hair in tow, he finished 1993 at 0-2 with 29 saves, but was gone from Camden Yards, having signed with Atlanta for the 1994 season, minus the brush.

Said Olson, on his hairy look, "The idea was to look nasty. Goose Gossage looked nasty. Of course, he could also throw it 98 miles an hour."

Good point. Give me a good fastball — and put some hair on it.

MOTHER'S DAY

Some players seem to perform their best for Mom. It must have something to do with all those home-cooked meals and hugs and words of endearment.

Tim Wallach, first with Montreal and then the Dodgers, absolutely loves Mother's Day. When the third baseman homered on Mother's Day 1993 (May 8), it ran his four-year Mom Day totals to 9-for-19 with three homers and 12 ribbies. He followed it up with another "I love Mom" performance in 1994, his fifth straight Big Show for his mother. With a 2-for-5, one homer, two-RBI day against the Giants in 1994, he increased his Mother's Day stats over a half decade to 11-for-24 (.458), four homers and fourteen RBIs.

And Yankee great Mickey Mantle, slumping in 1967, had begun the year with 496 homers and was stuck on 499. He called his wife, Merlyn, and she sighed and asked him, "Are you gonna hit that thing (number 500) or not?" Mantle replied, "I guess I'll give it to you for a Mother's Day present."

On Mother's Day of that year, Mantle belted career homer number 500 off Stu Miller.

Another star center fielder who loves Mom and Mother's Day is Pittsburgh Pirates team leader Andy Van Slyke. Van Slyke seems to wait for Mother's Day to get going. On the morning of Mother's Day 1994, Van Slyke was hitting an anemic .227 in 26 games. He finished the day batting .283. Van Slyke led the Pirates to a doubleheader sweep of the Cubs by going 4-for-5 with a homer, a double and four RBIs in the first game (won by Pittsburgh 9-2) and followed it up with a 4-for-4 nightcap to help the club win 9-3. The Pirates' star banged out eight consecutive hits and brought his Mother's Day totals since 1992, to 13-for-18, including two doubles, a triple, two homers and nine RBIs, for an average of .722.

Also on Mother's Day, 1994, California Angels lefty ace Chuck Finley had entered the game without a victory — 0-3 in six starts on May 9. Bearing down to win one for the team, as well as to honor his mom and his wife, Finley registered the Angels' first complete game of the year (in game 32) and shut out the Oakland A's 7-0 as teammate Bo Jackson ended his 0-21 slump with a run-scoring single.

But you may have to be a male ballplayer to find Mother's Day lucky. The Colorado Silver Bullets, an all-female barnstorming team, played its first game on Mother's Day 1994, and in front of 8,179 fans in Fort Mill, South Carolina, fell to an all-male squad made up of former Major Leaguers and AA and AAA players. The score was 19-0 in favor of the "Northern League All-Stars," as ex-Big Leaguer Leon "Bull" Durham homered twice. Maybe the women are luckier on Father's Day.

QUEEN ELIZABETH II

In 1991, the Oakland A's, who had won only two of 12 road games and were on a three-game losing streak, met England's ruling monarch before a game in Baltimore. Ballplayers shook her hand, won the game and went on to win four out of five. Of course, Harold Baines had something to do with it as he owned Baltimore early in the year, going 11-for-16 with four homers and 11 ribbies in five games. Still, the A's were losing until their audience with Her Majesty.

God save the queen.

BOGUS GOOD LUCK

John Tortes "Chief" Meyers, a catcher for the Giants and Dodgers from 1909 to 1917, was a good hitter and excellent catcher who appeared in four World Series. He was a star until the demands of catching eroded his skills.

The Cahilla Indian, who openly disapproved of his nickname, was educated at Dartmouth College and had an Ivy League demeanor and a great sense of humor.

In 1965, on a trip to New York to see the Dodgers play the Mets, he pulled a fast one on Mets president George Weiss, an old friend who had hired him to manage a Minor League team in New Haven for the Yankees 38 years earlier.

Meyers marched into Weiss's office and presented the executive with a small leather pouch filled with stones. Meyers explained that they were a gift from some Kwakiutl Indians he had known in Vancouver, Canada, and were imbued with the powers to bring good fortune and long life.

Weiss was humbled and accepted the stones with graciousness and heartfelt thanks.

Meyers related later that the stones were actually plucked from the bottom of his flowerpot at home, and he had no idea where they came from before that.

Weiss kept the stones and the bad-luck (and just plain bad) Mets, who finished dead last (tenth place) their first four years, and finished ninth, tenth and ninth the next three years before climbing to a pennant and World Championship in 1969. Although Weiss voluntarily resigned in 1966, he remarked that he was happy to see the Mets go so far so fast, and he often looked at Meyers' good-luck stones and mused that "they didn't hurt."

GOOD LUCK NUGGETS

It's good luck to be the brother of the godson of a Major League manager. That's what Dodger catcher Mike Piazza found out, as his father and Dodger skipper Tom Lasorda are best friends. Little Mike grew up with encouragement from Godpa-once-removed Tom. It also helps to have talent and power. Piazza was National League Rookie of the Year in 1993 with a .318-35 homer-112 RBI season. And not once did the Godfather make National League pitchers an offer they couldn't refuse. Piazza did it on his own.

It is also good luck to have a Hall of Famer as your godfather, particularly if your *father* was also a Big League star. That's how it worked out for Barry Bonds, son of Bobby Bonds and godson of Willie Mays. Once again, it seems that parentage and a baseball godfather—as well as God-given talent—have paid off handsomely.

Baltimore Orioles pitcher Mike Cuellar was a gamer if ever there was one. He was also afraid of evil spirits. For good luck, he would stuff paper in the keyholes and window and door crevices of his hotel rooms during the season. Given his career mark of 185-130 from 1959 to 1977, the team could have bought him some caulk.

Cuellar's Orioles teammate Chico Salmon, a utility player from Panama, knew that paper alone wouldn't do. He chewed special packs of gum and put the sticky chicle into the keyholes of his hotel rooms to keep evil spirits out. Think how much lower his

.249 career mark might have been if he had been inundated with evil spirits.

Another tough pitcher, White Sox righty Dick Donovan (122-99 from 1950 to 1965) made certain he placed his glove and warm-up jacket in the same spot at the end of the bench during each appearance. And for good measure, he'd talk to the bench—not the guys on the bench, just the pine itself—to help him win ball games. It worked 122 times, anyway.

An even tougher tough pitcher, "Bullet" Bob Gibson, St. Louis Cardinals Hall of Famer who won 251 games and lost 174 from 1959 to 1975, was intense. His good-luck charm was a mean fast-ball and silence. When he walked into his hotel room the night before a start, he demanded, and got, complete silence from his teammates, often until game time. And if you ever saw him stare down a hitter, you wouldn't want to mess with Gibson when he was demanding something.

And in Brooklyn, a nonpitcher hit someone other than an opponent for luck. In 1936, after scuffling in the Dodger clubhouse, Brooklyn manager Casey Stengel and right fielder Stanley "Frenchy" Bordagaray didn't much care for one another. It didn't take long for Bordagaray to make his feelings clear. The next day, just before a game against the Cincinnati Reds, while warming up on the sidelines, Bordagary fired a high hard one that hit Stengel in the ear and knocked him out. The skipper regained consciousness and the woeful Dodgers (who finished the year in seventh place, 25 games behind the Giants) beat Cincy. The following day, during a pregame team meeting, Bordagary suggested, "I hit you in the head yesterday and we won. That means hitting you is good luck. Let me hit you in the head again and we'll win today. In fact, I'll hit you every day and maybe we can win every game."

In 1991, Boston Red Sox reserve shortstop Tim Naehring was presented a door knocker by a 12-year-old fan. The door knocker was in the shape of a baseball player, and Naehring hung the thing in his locker with a string attached to it. Whenever a BoSox player wanted a "knock" (baseball slang for hit), the player would pull the string. It worked for Wade Boggs who hit .332, Phil Plantier (.331) and Mike Greenwell (.300), but it didn't do much for Naehring who hit .109 in 20 games. He fared much better a few years later as the club's starting shortstop when his knocker was discarded and his ability had improved, giving him all the knocks he needed.

In game three of the 1992 American League Championship Series between the Minnesota Twins and Toronto Blue Jays, Twins third baseman Mike Pagliarulo, who once wore a red ribbon around his baseball garter for good luck—it was given to him by his grandmother—grabbed some coffee to stay awake and then went deep into the clubhouse to hit some practice balls off a hitting tee. He did not start that day and began a regimen to put himself in game condition. After a few more swings and a quick trip on the stationary bike, he was summoned to pinch hit. He delivered the game-winning home run in the tenth inning off reliever Mike Timlin.

Seattle Mariners ace pitcher Randy Johnson spent the afternoon before a game at Yankee Stadium by flying around New York in a helicopter taking photographs of Manhattan. He shut out the Bronx Bombers on four hits, winning 1-0. Mariners officials contemplated buying him a helicopter for all his starts.

Psychotherapy has mixed results (see stories in several chapters) but it seems to have been a good-luck charm for Rangers pitcher Kevin Brown. Brown used sessions with psychologist Harvey Dorfman to help post a 15-12 record with a 3.59 ERA for Texas in 1993, but went on his own in 1994. Through four starts, Brown was a miserable 0-4 with a 10.86 ERA. He went back to the good doctor, held a few sessions, and pitched with renewed confidence and luck. He went 2-0 with a 1.06 ERA in two starts after he resumed therapy. Stick with the couch, Kevin.

Atlanta Braves ace pitcher John Smoltz uses visualization techniques to help him perform well on the field (see chapter on Twitches, Tremors and Theatrical Tic Douloureux). But his good luck comes when he promises something. In midseason 1991, a rotisserie league owner came up to Smoltz in Atlanta and told the pitcher he was ruining his rotisserie team's season with his 2-12 record and 5.16 ERA. Smoltz pleaded with the fan. "Don't dump me," he said. "I promise you a hot second half. Stick with me and I promise you'll be glad you did." The fan stuck with the 6'3" 210-pound right-hander and watched with glee as Smoltz kept his promise. He went 12-1 with a 2.16 ERA the rest of the way.

It's good luck to have an American legend present you with a gift. On May 6, 1948, Babe Ruth traveled to New Haven, Connecticut, to honor the Yale University Library with a donation of a signed manuscript of the book, *The Babe Ruth Story*. Ruth handed the document to Yalie first baseman and team captain George "Poppy" Bush. Bush accepted the book, and with the Bambino in the stands, went 2-for-4 and led Yale to a 14-2 drubbing of Princeton. Then Bush went on to become the youngest fighter pilot in America during World War II and, eventually, President of the United States from 1989-1993 — maybe all because he was given Babe's book.

California Angels assistant general manager Tim Mead was once one of the finest media relations directors in the Majors. He helped the team in various ways, including his game-winning device of not totaling the game stats until the game was over. He found that if the Angels were ahead and he totaled the home club's statistics, the visitors would come back to win. In similar circumstances on the road, the Angels would go quietly in the ninth, and the home team would emerge victorious. Judging by the Angels' failure to get into the World Series, however, perhaps another good-luck device should have been employed as well.

Perhaps the most expensive ritual for luck came during the 1930s and 1940s whenever Brooklyn restaurant owner Jack Pierce took his seat at Ebbets Field — he rarely missed a game. Holding the tickets for all ten seats behind the visitors' dugout, Pierce brought along with him two large boxes of balloons, a hydrogen tank, and a couple of bottles of Scotch. After consuming a few glasses of Scotch, Pierce would spread a large blue-and-gray banner on which was printed "Cookie," in reference to Dodger third baseman Cookie Lavagetto. Then he'd inflate each of the balloons and yell out "Cookie" as he popped it.

Did it work? Well, it made Pierce happy, but Lavagetto only had one big season with Brooklyn — .300 in 153 games with ten homers in 1939 — and the Dodgers didn't win a World Championship until 1955. Still, Pierce *thought* he was bringing the club luck.

Ending this chapter, what can be better than a call from home?

BRIAN ANDERSON

Brian Anderson was first-round draft pick for the California Angels in the June 1993 amateur draft. The 6'1", 190-pound lefty pitcher was scheduled to pitch a minor league game for the Angels' AAA affiliate, the Vancouver Canadians of the Pacific

Coast League, when California starter Mark Langston was put on the disabled list.

A hurried call was placed, and Anderson was told to get to Milwaukee immediately; he was to pitch against the Brewers the next day—April 10, 1994 .

The pitcher left Nat Bailey Stadium in Vancouver, picked up some clothes from his Vancouver apartment, and made it to the airport with just moments to spare. His flight from British Columbia to Seattle went fine, but his connection from Seattle to Denver was delayed by a snowstorm and arrived ten minutes after his Denver-to-Milwaukee leg had departed. Stranded in Denver.

The next flight to Milwaukee wasn't until the next morning and wouldn't arrive in Milwaukee until 2 P.M., one hour after game time.

Anderson called the Angels who were sympathetic. Traveling secretary Frank Sims told the 21-year-old, "Be here. You're pitching."

His options included private charter and driving some thousand miles to the ballpark.

Anderson talked his way onto a flight that arrived in Minneapolis, one leg closer to success, at 1 A.M. He checked into a hotel and was asleep by 2:30 A.M. At 5:50 A.M. he received a wake-up call from his mother, Janice Anderson, in Geneva, Ohio, who told her son, "Honey, it's time to get up. It's time to get ready to pitch."

With barely three hours of sleep, Anderson doggedly returned to the airport and caught another flight, this one to Milwaukee. He eventually arrived in the Angels' clubhouse at 9:15 A.M., 90 minutes before the team arrived. He sat alone, waiting for the team bus.

Buoyed by his mother's phone call, Anderson, on three hours of sleep and following a 21-hour journey, won his first Major League game by shutting down the Brewers on five hits, allowing only one run in 8⅓ innings, for a 4-1 victory. It was only his ninth professional appearance.

He said it was the call from Mom that did it.

The next day, in Anaheim, teammate Bo Jackson called Anderson's mother. He called to tell her what a great game her son had pitched the previous day. She didn't believe it was really

Jackson—she thought it was a prank—until her son got on the line and convinced her the caller was, indeed, Bo. But Jackson was not a lucky son. In the Angels' ball game that afternoon, he struck out as a pinch hitter to end a ninth-inning rally as the potential tying run at the plate in a 9-6 loss to Cleveland.

Had Anderson been sent up to pinch hit, it might have been another story. After all, he had talked to his mom earlier that day. And what's luckier than dear old Mom?

CHAPTER TWO

Bad Hops (Bad Luck)

"Ill luck, you know, seldom comes alone."
— MIGUEL DE CERVANTES (DON QUIXOTE DE LA MANCHA)

These are the book's bad hops, though it seems that sometimes the victims were accidents just waiting to happen, like waiting for the ball to come to you instead of charging it hard to get the out.

What is bad luck? It comes in many forms. Sometimes it is what a player doesn't do that causes the bad luck. Sometimes, superstitiously so, it is what a player does consciously that creates the ill omen. And quite often, it is a swing that follows something over which the victim has no control.

Bad luck is appearing on the cover of *Sports Illustrated*. Time and time again, the heroes honored for great performance go downhill just as the issue hits the newsstands. It is worse yet for a manager who gets a vote of confidence from the team's owner or general manager. More often than not, the public show of support comes just days before the skipper gets dumped.

What is a bad hop? Anything that ricochets into you, over you, past you or through you and derails you despite all your good intentions. For example, your career has taken a bad hop if you make a superstar look bad in front of the Boss. Just ask George Zeber.

GEORGE ZEBER
June 14, 1978

It's definitely bad luck to show the ineptitude of a million-dollar marquee name, at home and in front of the boss — especially when that name is Reggie Jackson, that home is Yankee Stadium, and that boss is George Steinbrenner. It was a career killer for George

Zeber in one of the coldest moves in recent memory.

Zeber, a second baseman for the Yankees playing behind Willie Randolph, was coming off a superb .323 season in 25 games as a reserve in the Yanks' 1977 World Championship season. Though seldom used—and ferried up and down to the Yankees' AAA Tacoma team reportedly because of a salary conflict with Yank GM Cedric Tallis—Zeber was a good backup and was penciled into the starting lineup in a summer game at Yankee Stadium aginst Seattle.

With the Bronx Bombers up 1-0 after one inning, Mariners left fielder Bruce Bochte led off the second with a single to center. That brought up designated hitter Lee Stanton. Stanton pops one into short right field, and in the twilight sky at Yankee Stadium, Zeber couldn't find it. Zeber hollered, "I don't see it." Yankee center fielder Paul Blair couldn't find it, but Yankee right fielder Reggie Jackson called for it. Zeber backed off as Reggie came in and pounded his glove to indicate he had it all the way. Suddenly, Reggie, the Yanks' 1977 World Series hero, stopped. He'd lost it. In a desperate attempt to make the play, Zeber lunged, and the ball fell between him and Jackson, who was only five feet behind him. The official scorer gave Zeber an error, though he claims he never touched the ball. The misplay led to a five-run rally by Seattle.

Up in the Yankee stands, owner George Steinbrenner witnessed the play and yelled to his staff that Zeber made "his man," presumably Reggie, look bad and that the second baseman was gone. Before the end of the game, Zeber had been banished to the minors, but no one told him.

The Yankees, down at one point in the game 6-1, came back to win 11-9 in 10 innings. The next day Zeber headed to the ballpark, feeling good about the win and the two fine plays he'd made in the third and fifth innings.

Then Zeber walked into the Yankee clubhouse and stood in front of his locker. There, standing in his locker, wearing his uniform—number 25—was Brian Doyle, the second baseman the Yanks had called up to replace Zeber. Zeber looked down and saw that his bags were packed with all his gear in them.

Cold.

ANAHEIM STADIUM . . . THE CURSE OF THE ANGELS
1700s to 1994

It's bad luck to play ball on a home field erected on an ancient Indian burial ground.

A rumor that has dogged the Angels, football's Los Angeles Rams, and pro soccer's ill-fated California Surf is that the ballpark, known as "The Big A," just a few miles from the Enchanted Kingdom of Disneyland, is cursed. The author, along with *Long Beach Press-Telegram* sportswriter Dave Cunningham, investigated the hearsay and came up with the following history.

During the 1700s, the Gabrieleno Indians settled in a village called Hutuk on the north bank of the Santa Ana River, about seven miles north of The Big A's home plate. Only one known branch of the Gabrielenos, some 85 miles away on Santa Catalina Island, buried their dead, though a self-proclaimed modern-day chief of the tribe claims to have visited Gabrieleno burial grounds within 15 miles of the ballpark. Other Gabrieleno tribes burned their dead in funeral pyres above ground. This is where the story gets hot. They would have staged the fiery funerals down river, some seven miles from the center of camp, or right about where home plate is located.

Curse scorecard: Now we're not even going to get into bad trades—got Von Hayes in 1992 for Ruben Amaro and Kyle Abbott; poor moves—let Nolan Ryan leave the fold in 1979; injured acquisitions—Kelly Gruber in 1993; injured amateur selections—Pete Janicki in 1993; or rookie flashes who fizzled spectacularly—J.T. Snow in 1993. Heck, every team runs into those, and many are far worse than those suffered by the Halos.

But the big bad bounces, the ones that seem metaphysically linked, have occurred with startling frequency since the Angels announced they were moving to Anaheim, which became their home in 1966. Among the ills suffered by the Angels while residing on the site in question are

1. The Angels' first bonus baby, Rick Reichardt, a $200,000 signee in 1964 when the team was still safe and in Los Angeles, who Joe Garagiola likened to the picture on the front of a Wheaties box, was just hitting stardom when an illness befell him after ground for the new ballpark had already been defiled. The illness

43

necessitated the removal of one of Reichardt's kidneys.

2. Pitching ace Ken McBride, winner of 10 straight games, was involved in an automobile accident that injured his neck and back. He won only four more games the rest of his career.

3. With the new ballpark under construction, pitching prospect Dick Wantz, a 6'5", 175-pounder with promise, got into only one game before suddenly falling ill with a brain tumor and dying in midseason.

4. In 1968, Don Mincher, power-hitting first baseman who belted 25 roundtrippers the previous year, got skulled by Cleveland's Sam McDowell. He slumped for the Angels upon his return. His career in Anaheim over, he went to Seattle where he hit 25 homers in 1969, then to Oakland where he hit 27 more in 1970.

5. Also in 1968, third baseman Paul Schaal got beaned by the Red Sox's Jose Santiago. The pitch broke Schaal's jaw and soon his Angel days were over. He caught on with Kansas City in 1969 and rebounded with a good season in 1971.

6. In a catastrophe that went full circle with Angel-curse overtones, Angel pitcher Jack Hamilton, a wild fastball hurler, fired a high, hard one that smashed into the face of Boston star hitter Tony Conigliaro. The resulting injury left Tony C. with impaired vision and little hope for a resumed career. He fought back and re-achieved stardom with 36 homers in 1970. Then the Angels acquired him in 1971. His vision failed, he retired that season, and he died in 1990 at the age of 45.

7. Righty relief ace Minnie Rojas—27 saves in 1967—had a sore arm that destroyed his 1969 season and was then paralyzed in an automobile accident in 1970.

8. In 1972, utility infielder Chico Ruiz was killed in an automobile collision. Ruiz had only appeared in 31 games for California in 1971, but the curse got him anyway.

9. On May 17, 1973, shortstop-outfielder Bobby Valentine caught his spikes in the outfield fence at Anaheim Stadium while attempting to snare a home run off the bat of Oakland's Dick Green. A multitalented player with the "can't miss" and "superstar" tags all over him, Valentine never walked straight again and was only a fill-in player.

10. In 1974, left-handed pitching prospect Bruce Heinbechner, a product of Cal State Northridge, was killed during a spring

training automobile accident. He was expected to be the team's top lefty in the bullpen.

11. In 1977, shortstop Mike Miley was killed in an off-season auto accident. He was expected to be the team's shortstop for the 1980s.

12. In 1977, the Angels signed free agents Don Baylor, Joe Rudi and Bobby Grich and looked like pennant contenders. Baylor slumped that year (though he performed well during his tenure with the club), Rudi broke his hand and was a shadow of his former Oakland self, and Grich suffered a herniated disk while lifting an air conditioner at home, helping to kill off a season that began with promise.

13. Lyman Bostock, a superstar hitter who played his college ball at Cal State Northridge, signed as a free agent. He was just rounding into form as a member of the Halos, when in 1978, he was shot to death in the backseat of a car driven by his uncle.

14. It appeared the Angels had escaped the jinx when the club won its first AL West pennant in 1979. In a celebration party, however, pitcher Jim Barr, the team's million-dollar free agent du jour, who had gone 10-12 during the season, broke his right (pitching) hand and fell to 1-4 the next season before drifting north to San Francisco for his final two years.

15. On Oct. 12, 1986, the Angels were one strike away from their first World Series appearance when, in the ninth inning of the fifth game of the ALCS, Donnie Moore surrendered a home run to Dave Henderson in a four-run inning that spelled doom for the club. Moore would take his own life three years later.

16. Matt Keough, upon returning from a stint in the Japan Leagues, came to Anaheim to win a spot on the Angels' pitching staff. On March 16, 1992, while sitting in the dugout at Scottsdale Stadium during a spring training game in Arizona, he was struck in the head by a line drive off the bat of San Francisco Giants prospect John Patterson. The concussion almost killed Keough, who recovered but never pitched in the Majors again. In a bizarre continuation of the story, after his recovery, Keough went back out to Scottsdale Stadium in a scouting role, and with Patterson up at the plate again, a wicked line drive again went foul and this time struck Albuquerque Dukes pitcher Chris Nichting, who was in the same dugout and in nearly the same place as was Keough during the initial beaning.

17. Batting coach Deron Johnson died of lung cancer in 1992.

18. On May 21, 1992, the team was involved in a bus accident on their way to Baltimore, leaving six players injured and putting manager Buck Rodgers out of action for three months.

19. On January 17, 1994, an earthquake measuring 6.7 on the Richter scale struck Southern California, its epicenter some 75 miles away near Northridge. The deadly temblor killed more than 50 people and devastated the San Fernando Valley portion of Los Angeles as well as pockets within the center of the city. Neighboring Orange County, home of the Angels, escaped largely unscathed. While there was minor damage in areas surrounding The Big A's neighborhood, only one piece of major destruction hit that city (Anaheim): The 35,000-pound Jumbotron scoreboard, the signature attraction at The Big A, tumbled and fell, taking out some 800 seats and causing an estimated $4 million in damage. . . .

And the calamities continue.

20. Tragedy befell a new Angel when pitcher Mark Leiter, signed near the end of spring training in 1994, suffered the loss of his nine-month-old son, Ryan, on opening day to a form of spinal muscular atrophy. The death was expected, but it did not come until after Leiter had signed on with the Angels.

21. Just a week and a half later, California catcher Chris Turner was notified that his 11-year-old nephew, Chad Turner, had died of a self-inflicted gunshot wound in Bowling Green, Kentucky.

22. A week after that, while running out an infield grounder, Jim Edmonds was struck in the throat by an errant throw (see the complete story in this chapter, as there is another bad luck aspect to this tale) and knocked unconscious and out of the lineup for a week.

And one mishap that hit the Angels right on the mound in 1994. . . .

23. During an otherwise quiet Sunday afternoon in Anaheim, May 1, 1994, California pitcher Joe Grahe was minding his own business between hitters when he felt a sharp pain in the neck. He lost his breath, tumbled down and thought he'd either been shot or suffered a stroke. It was neither. It was a Little League baseball, autographed by 15 young players and thrown from the upper deck by a 15-year-old "fan," who was goaded into it by five of his teammates from Oceanside, California. Great arm, poor

social habits. The teen was reprimanded and forced to write a letter of apology. Grahe recovered quickly, but was gone from that game and into the trainer's room before he could face another batter.

And then there's the biggest hurt of them all:

24. In nearly 30 years at The Big A, the Angels never got to the World Series.

That's a lot of continuing bad luck in 30 years. Coincidence? Or ticked-off Indian souls? You be the judge.

Speaking of ticked-off Indians, the Cleveland tribe has a curse of its own. . . .

LEAVING TUSCON

The Cleveland Indians hadn't won much of anything in years — except for the imaginary pennant in the movie *Major League*. With no AL pennant since 1954 and never a winner of an American League East crown, the Wahoos felt they had nothing to lose by abandoning their longtime spring training site — 46 consecutive years in Arizona — in favor of a new Grapefruit League location in Homestead, Florida. It is a move that many already regret.

The curse began eight months after the club signed a two-year pact — December 12, 1991 — to begin spring training play in Homestead.

Curse scorecard:

1. Six months before they were scheduled to move into their new spring headquarters, Hurricane Andrew ripped through South Florida — August 24, 1991 — and destroyed the team's complex.

2. In September 1993, a news conference was called to announce that the Indians were giving up on Homestead for 1993 and replacing it with Winter Haven, Florida. But remember, the Arizona spirits were still offended.

3. On March 24, 1993, tragedy hit the team during its first Florida spring. Pitchers Tim Crews and Steve Olin were killed and Bob Ojeda was seriously injured in a boating accident in Clermont, Florida.

4. As if to further embed themselves in bad luck, the team signed a ten-year contract to play their spring games in Winter Haven — October 9, 1993.

5. It took only ten days for the next piece of bad luck. Pitcher Bob Ojeda, limited to only nine games (2-1 with a 4.40 ERA in 43 innings) following his recovery from the boating accident, filed for free agency — October 29, 1993 — and, fully recovered, hooked on with the Yankees, making their starting rotation. True, he was through after only two starts in 1994, but he still left the Tribe without allowing them to get anything — or anyone — in return.

6. Pitcher Cliff Young was killed in an auto accident in Willis, Texas — November 4, 1993.

7. The team abandoned venerable old Cleveland Stadium, their home since 1932 (exclusively since 1947 and where their American League pennant was buried in 1949), for the new Indians park, Jacobs Field. A park of good luck or bad? Time will tell. And will leaving another old-time Indians' stomping grounds bring forth a new curse or cancel the old ones?

The answer may be yes . . . and no.

In 1994, the team's fortunes changed and had one of the best records in the American League all season. But the curse won't die, and a superb season was tarnished by labor-management woes.

THE EX-CUB FACTOR

Bad luck is having former members of the Chicago Cubs on your team. Or at least having a lot of them.

Since 1945, any team with more than three ex-Cubs on the roster loses the World Series. Actually, this isn't foolproof, but in the first 14 times this has occurred, 13 teams have lost. Only the 1960 Pirates triumphed, beating the Yankees in seven games despite being outscored 55-27, outhit .338-.256 (91 hits to 60 hits) and outhomered 10-4. A bad hop that caught Tony Kubek in the throat helped pave the way to an unlikely win.

And it seems that during the season, the teams with the most ex-Cubs on their squads have the most difficult time getting to postseason play. In the win column, less is more — less Cubs, that is. And that goes for current Cubs as well, as the Cubbies themselves have not been to a World Series since 1945, and they lost that one to Detroit. The Cubs haven't won a Series since 1908.

And speaking of the Cubs, they've endured a curse for nearly a half century, and now they've taken steps to reverse it.

THE CUBS AND THE BILLY GOAT CURSE
1945-1994

In the 1930s and 1940s, the Chicago Cubs were a decent club that had some good years and some bad years. They had won National League pennants in 1929, 1932, 1935, 1938 and 1945, and even though they hadn't won a World Series since 1908 and were on the losing end of the Boston Red Sox's last World Championship (in 1918, before Boston suffered the "Curse of the Bambino," by trading Babe Ruth to the Yankees), there was no reason to expect that over the next half century the Cubbies wouldn't tack on a dozen more pennants and many world titles.

No reason, that is, until the team drew the ire of a tavern owner with a temper, an attitude and a pet goat.

William Sianis, a Greek immigrant, owned a tavern in Chicago in the 1940s. Strolling down the street one day, he discovered a live goat that had fallen from a livestock truck. Sianis, who had herded goats as a child, thought of this as a good omen. He took the animal home, built it a pen behind the bar, and allowed it to wander freely in the establishment where it begged customers for peanuts and beer.

Sianis named the goat Sonovia, and the two went everywhere together, earning Sianis the name "Billy Goat" Sianis.

During game four of the 1945 World Series between his beloved Chicago Cubs and the Detroit Tigers, Sianis brought his genus capra pal to Wrigley Field to see if the hometown club could improve on its two games-to-one lead.

Sianis walked up to the gate, presented his ticket, and was stopped by attendants who told him to get his goat and go. Sianis was angry enough to decree, "If this goat can't go into the game, the Cubs will never win another pennant. No more World Series."

The Cubs lost the game 4-1 and lost the Series in seven games. The hex was in full swing, and it was only just beginning. The Cubs have been absent from the World Series ever since, and Sianis went 14 years without bringing a goat to a game.

He relented in 1959 when he brought a young goat — Sonovia had passed away but the hex was still in progress — to a Chicago White Sox game at Comiskey Park. The ChiSox won the pennant that year for the first time since 1919.

Just before his death in 1970, Sianis offered to end the hex on the Cubs, but did not bring his goat to the ballpark.

Four years later, Billy Goat's nephew, Sammy "Goat" Sianis—these guys are humans, so follow me here—went to Wrigley Field with his pet goat, Socrates, to take in a game.

History repeated itself when Wrigley attendants shooed the pair away, whereupon Sammy "Goat" Sianis restored the hex.

In 1984, saying enough was enough, Cubs management invited Sammy "Goat" Sianis to bring a new billy goat to a game at Wrigley to end the curse. The tavern owner and his animal attended, and the Cubs won their first pennant—albeit a divisional crown—since 1945. They lost the National League Championship Series to the San Diego Padres and haven't been close since.

The curse continued, and in 1994, the Cubs started the season poorly, losing their first 12 home games, a club record. With an 0-12 mark at Wrigley and 7-18 record overall, 9½ games out, and dead last in the National League Central Division, the team brought all-time Cub hero Ernie Banks to a pregame celebration and had him parade a goat, supplied by Sammy Sianis, around the field before the game on May 4, 1994. The goat, dressed in a blue Cubs jersey, bleated with approval as the Wrigley fans cheered.

The Cubs won the game over the first-place Cincinnati Reds, 5-2, to end the slide and, they hope, put an end to the curse that has kept them out of the Fall Classic for four-and-a-half decades. Still, you can't expect miracles. We *are* talking about the Cubs here.

Note: Not willing to break his newfound luck, Cubs manager Tom Trebelhorn packed a plastic goat in his travel gear and took it on the road with him for the Cubs' next game. The Plasticine capra helped, and the Cubs won in Pittsburgh, 10-1, on May 6. The win also was a first for hard-luck pitcher Anthony Young. Young, who set a Major League record in 1993 by enduring his 27th consecutive loss on the mound, had not won a game as a starter (he did pick up one in relief to stop the skein) since April 9, 1992. Young was the winner this time, as, according to Trebelhorn, "We paid homage to the goat and then went out and played a good game."

Prediction: It will be a long time before Cubs brass keep livestock from attending games at the friendly confines of Wrigley.

JOE "DUCKY" MEDWICK

It's bad luck, or at least bad form, to take out an opposing player with an unnecessary slide, especially when you're playing in the other guy's yard and the place is packed with boisterous fans in a game played for all the marbles. Hall of Fame outfielder Joe Medwick was a fan favorite for the St. Louis Cards of the 1930s and 1940s, but opposing fans turned against him with vigor and anger for his hard play in the World Series. In game seven of the 1934 World Series between the Cards and the Tigers in Detroit, Medwick took out third baseman Marv Owen, an .069 Series hitter, with an intentionally hard slide on a triple, even though no throw was made on him. With the score 9-0 in favor of the Cards, the Detroit faithful pelted the left fielder with food, garbage and bottles as a near riot began.

For his own safety, and for the safety of the game, Commissioner Kenesaw Mountain Landis, who was sitting in the Commissioner's box, ordered Medwick removed from the game. Chick Fullis replaced him in left. It didn't matter, as the Cards won the game (11-0) and the Series.

CASEY STENGEL

Casey Stengel, "The Old Professor," was one of the cagiest baseball mentors of all time, guiding the New York Yankees to ten pennants and seven World Championships in 12 years of running the Pinstripers. But Ol' Case found out it was bad luck to be an aging manager who made public how easy it was to run the club.

Yankee catcher Johnny Blanchard tells the story of an August 1960 ball game in which Casey arrived at Yankee Stadium late, just two minutes before game time. Yank coach Jim Turner made out the lineup and was at home plate, giving the lineup card to the umpire as Casey stepped into the dugout. Case walked to the end of the bench and fell asleep as the game went on.

Through eight innings, with Stengel catching a few Zs, the Yanks battled to a 1-1 tie. Yankee pitcher Bob Turley was due up in the eighth and Turner, who was still calling the shots while Casey slept, decided to pinch hit for the hurler, with Hector Lopez. Turner yelled at the snoring skipper, "You want to pinch hit for Turley?" Casey stirred. Turner said, "I'll put up Lopez, OK? Wave or something."

Casey groggily awoke. Turner said, "Look at the scoreboard.

Lopez, OK?" Casey growled, "Lopez, grab a bat."

Lopez hit a pinch-hit home run and the Yankees won 2-1.

As the game ended and the team walked down the ramp to the clubhouse, a fully awake Stengel stopped shortstop Tony Kubek and said, "Anybody in New York can run this BLEEP-BLEEP team."

Yankee bosses took Casey to heart, and despite winning 97 games during the regular season and barely losing the World Series four games to three, Casey was fired and replaced with Ralph Houk for the 1961 season. Houk's Yankees are now considered by many to be one of the greatest teams in baseball history.

Speaking of old managers. . . .

GEORGE STALLINGS

George Stallings was manager of the Boston Braves, Phillies, Tigers and Yankees on-and-off from 1897 to 1920. His "Miracle Braves" were in last place, 11½ games behind, on the fourth of July 1914 and came back to win the pennant and World Series, earning Stallings the nickname "The Miracle Man."

He thought everything was bad luck.

Scraps of paper, if left untended, would bring about losses, so if he saw one, he'd bellow at a player to pick it up and put it neatly in this pocket. Same thing with peanut shells—the worst bad-luck omen of them all, according to the otherwise mild-mannered Southerner—and other trash.

If a Braves player got a hit, Stallings knew he would jinx the rally if he moved, so he'd stay frozen in that spot until the inning was over.

Crossed bats were a sure sign of outs, so he would uncross any lumber he found when his team was at bat. Sometimes he reasoned that the bats were sleeping, so he shook them and patted them to wake them up.

Sometimes, watching his players was bad luck, so when a certain player was up at the plate, on the mound or in the field in a crucial situation, he'd turn his back to the field and ask his players what happened, too frightened to view the action.

And it was Stallings who figured that facial hair was bad luck and began a crusade to keep players clean-shaven—a tradition that lasted from the 1920s until the Oakland A's changed it in the 1970s. Stallings once threatened to release catcher John Henry if he didn't shave off his bad-luck moustache. Henry cut his ill-fated brush, and the Braves, losers of nine in a row and victims of seven consecutive moustachioed rainouts, won their next game.

It's bad luck to change your name yourself. . . .

TIM "ROCK" RAINES

For more than a decade, Tim Raines had been everything the Montreal Expos could ask for, winning a batting title, earning four stolen base crowns, and acting as a team leader as well. He lacked power numbers, but he made the offense go-go-go with a career average above .300, a pace of better than 60 steals per season, and about 80 walks per year.

Opting for free agency in 1991, he signed with the Chicago White Sox and announced he would no longer be known as "Tim." From now on, he was assuming the macho, powerful nickname "Rock."

Bad move.

As "Rock," Raines couldn't buy a hit or a steal. He hit "Rock" bottom. Through April, the leadoff man was hitting an anemic, make that microscopic, .106.

He announced to all his "Rock" fans that he wanted to be Tim again, and within a month, he was over .250, raising his average at one point during the season to .289 before tailing off at the end and finishing at .268, still far better than the rocky start he got off to during his stone age.

"BOBBY" KELLY

Roberto Kelly was a good-hitting, speedy outfielder for the Yankees during his first six seasons, averaging .280. From 1989 to 1992, he averaged better than 30 steals and double figures in homers. He was coming off a solid, healthy year during which he played in 152 games. But the Yankees, seeking more power and a lefty bat, traded him to the Cincinnati Reds prior to the 1993 season for Paul O'Neill.

Kelly got off to a slow start in Cincinnati, hitting only .227 in 10 games, with one homer and five RBIs.

On April 17, 1993, Kelly decided he wanted to fit in better in the Midwest and forsook his Panamanian name, Roberto, for something more American sounding. Kelly announced to all that he was changing his name to "Bobby."

The name change had an immediate effect. Kelly went on a 14-game hitting streak and by July 4 had brought his average up to .320, with nine homers and 35 RBIs.

Then the name jinx nailed him. He injured his shoulder diving for a ball and missed half the season, appearing in a career-low (since he became a full-timer in 1989) 78 games.

Prior to the 1994 season, Kelly changed his name back to Roberto, saying, "That Bobby guy was always hurt, so it's Roberto this year."

Apparently he'll take Roberto's durability over Bobby's batting average.

J.T. SNOW – ROGER CLEMENS

It's bad luck to be a rookie hitting over .400 while facing "Rocket" Roger Clemens for the first time.

California Angels rookie first baseman J.T. Snow was tearing up the American League. He had just been named AL Player of the Week by going 10-for-22, a .455 average, with four homers, eight RBIs, one triple and a 1.091 slugging percentage. This brought his average to .407, and he was on the cover of more magazines than Madonna. Then came a cool night at Anaheim Stadium against the Red Sox.

In a nationally televised game, Clemens decided to teach the kid a lesson in respect. Clemens rocked the rook with a 94-mile-an-hour rocket behind the kid's ear. Snow hit the dirt, brushed himself off, didn't dig in quite as deep as before, struck out and eventually, went hitless that night. Snow's avalanche had begun. His average tumbled — he hit only .124 in May — to .223, and he was exiled to the Minors in July. He came back in September, but he wasn't the terror who faced the Rocket Man the night his season went down in flames.

It might be good strategy to drop that tear under .400 if you're scheduled to face a feisty veteran with a good fastball. Either that, or it's a good time to come down with a tight hamstring and sit out a game.

ROGER CLEMENS'S NEW "DO"

As bad luck giveth and bad luck taketh away, fireballer Roger Clemens is bad luck for more players than with J.T. Snow. But Clemens, too, is subject to the whims of Lady Luck, and she apparently likes her men with long hair.

A little more than a month into the 1993 season, Clemens was sailing along with a 5-2 record, a sparkling 1.73 ERA and good control, issuing only 2.4 walks every nine innings.

Then he hit the barbershop for a new, shorter, more stylish hairdo. The do didn't.

Just as Samson lost his power when Delilah cut his locks, Clemens lost his power pitch. In his next two outings, he went 0-2 with a 10.97 ERA and an average of 6.75 walks every nine innings.

His hair grew out a bit and he won his next start, but he finished the season in un-Clemenslike fashion, compiling an 11-14 mark, an ERA of 4.46, and an average of 3.2 walks per nine innings.

Hair today, gone tomorrow.

MORGANNA ROBERTS

How can a kiss from a lusty, buxom blonde bring bad luck? Just ask some of the more than 25 players bussed by busty Morganna Roberts, "The Kissing Bandit."

Roberts, an exotic dancer with a 60-inch bust, made a career out of gate-crashing baseball games, jumping—or falling, as she once said in court to win a trespassing case—onto the field, and planting a big wet one on her intended target, the player du jour on her menu.

Pete Rose was Morganna's first score, in 1970, and though he had a fine year, he later ran into difficulties with baseball commissioners, the Internal Revenue Service and the Hall of Fame Committee.

Among those her lips have graced on Major League ball fields are George Brett, Nolan Ryan, Mike Schmidt, Steve Yeager, Fred Lynn, John Candelaria, Dickie Thon—and the list keeps growing.

Bad luck? She seems to provoke short-term slumps whenever she shares her lipstick. Following the smooches, Lynn went 0-for-10, Brett went 0-for-6 and Rose 1-for-11.

Only Brett got her back, interrupting one of her dances at a nightclub and planting one on her.

And a Morganna wanna-be, another exotic dancer similarly endowed, named Kathy Stathopoulous, aka "Topsy Curvy," pecked pitchers Roger Clemens one night and Scott Kamieniecki the next, resulting in losses by both hurlers.

So next time you see a big-busted woman make a beeline for you with lips smacking and body bouncing, just be safe and say, "Keep those things to yourself."

LARRY WALKER

Sometimes it's bad luck to be a nice guy.

Nice guy Larry Walker, the Gold Glove right fielder for the Montreal Expos, was given an error for a math error and an error in judgment—and his team lost, too.

On April 24, 1994, in a game between the Dodgers and Expos in Los Angeles, L.A. catcher Mike Piazza hit a one-out, one-on fly ball to right. Walker raced into foul territory to make a nice grab for out number two. As Walker crossed into foul territory, he thought it was the third out and he casually jogged to the right-field stands and handed the ball to a nine-year-old fan, Sebastian Napier, who had brought his glove to the game hoping to land a ball.

The 38,817 in attendance looked at the scoreboard and saw a big "2" under "outs." So did Dodger shortstop Jose Offerman, who tagged up at first. As he sprinted around the bases, Walker realized his mistake and calmly returned to Napier and asked the young fan if he could have the ball back. The boy acquiesced, and Walker fired toward the plate in hopes of keeping Offerman from scoring.

Umpires ruled the ball out of play after the Walker-to-Napier handoff, and Offerman was told to go back to third.

Walker promised the boy he'd give him another ball, and the next hitter, third baseman Tim Wallach, blasted a homer to left on the first pitch to put Los Angeles on top 4-0. A couple of innings later, Walker grabbed another ball and gave that one to young Napier to keep. In the seventh, following Walker's second act of kindness, Wallach came through with his second act of power, another home run to left to wrap up the game for the Dodgers 7-1.

Maybe you have to be cruel to be kind . . . to your own team.

And speaking of cruel, it's bad luck to be injured against the Yankees in a game in New York. . . .

JIM EDMONDS

California Angels rookie outfielder Jim Edmonds became part of the Angels' jinx as well as a victim to life in New York as he made his first trip to Yankee Stadium on April 25, 1994. In the second game of a two-game series, Edmonds tapped a grounder to short. Yankee shortstop Mike Gallego charged and threw off-balance, the ball going up the first base line. Edmonds, sprinting to the bag, was struck in the neck by the wild throw, knocking him down and into semiconsciousness.

Trainers put a neck brace on Edmonds, and he was carried off the field on a stretcher and whisked away to the hospital in an ambulance. Here's where the bad luck comes in.

As the emergency vehicle sped to the hospital, it came to a toll bridge, and the toll booth operator refused to let it pass until the $3 toll had been paid. The ambulance driver explained that he didn't have any cash and that this was an emergency. That didn't cut any ice with the toll booth operator who demanded $3.

Angels Assistant General Manager Tim Mead, who was in the back of the vehicle accompanying and reassuring Edmonds, grabbed a $10 bill from his wallet and threw it at the toll booth guy. After the operator examined the "Hamilton" to make sure it wasn't bogus, he allowed the vehicle to proceed.

Hey, maybe he was listening to the game on the radio and had heard the Angels were winning. Maybe this guy isn't cold and heartless, he's just a Yankee fan.

VOODOO AND AN ANGRY WIFE

A real bad-luck mixture to avoid is an angry spouse who uses voodoo. At least that's what Los Angeles Dodgers pitcher Bob Ojeda claimed after getting bombed by his ex-team, the Mets, in July 1991.

Following a 9-4 shellacking, Ojeda met with the press and explained his poor performance. He explained that his ex-wife, in dispute over alimony payments, had acquired a voodoo doll with Ojeda's face on it.

She apparently used pins and Mets bats to tag her ex-hubby with the loss.

Ojeda's claim went unconfirmed, but he did say he would rectify the situation. He must have, as Ojeda finished the season with a credible 12-9 mark and a 3.18 ERA.

GAYLORD PERRY

It was bad luck to face spitball pitcher and baseball mechanic Gaylord Perry, but not just because he won 314 games over his 22-year career. Perry was also a master of the head game. He admitted that many of his mound gyrations were designed to look as though he were doctoring the ball, just to mess with batters' minds.

True, he threw the spitball, resin ball, Vaseline ball, dirt ball, mudball, powder ball, greaseball and sliced cowhide ball, but just as often, there was nothing foreign on the sphere. But as long as the batter thought there was something on the ball, the pitch was just as effective as if saliva were dripping off the seams.

One mind game Perry played on his opponents was "the Vaseline trick." Perry would rub Vaseline or K-Y Jelly on his hands before a game and walk over to the hottest hitter on the opposing team. He said, "I'd shake hands with Bobby Murcer, George Brett, Johnny Bench or the like and get them thinking, 'That S.O.B. is gonna throw me greaseballs all game.' I got them psyched out and won more than 300 games that way."

Bad luck facing Perry. Worse luck seeing him before the game.

MIKE PAGLIARULO

In 1991, it was bad luck to be around Mike Pagliarulo, but it all ended well for the Minnesota Twins.

Pags, the slick-fielding third baseman who had spent his early years with the Yankees, was known for his superstitions. He wore a pink ribbon from his baseball garter, he chose number 13 to adorn the back of his uniform, he rubbed his Italian good-luck horn, the "maluckya," before every game, and he had certain pre-game rituals devoted to putting him in a game mood.

But when he came to the Twins in 1991 to replace Gary Gaetti, who had flown west to join the Angels, Pags brought misery to those around him.

After a couple of tough fielding games, a Minnesota sportswriter wrote that Pagliarulo was just a hole in the infield and that the Twins would be better off just throwing Gaetti's empty uniform out there. Mild-mannered Pags just laughed it off, but the next day, while taking practice swings by the batting cage, the writer in question stuck his nose in the area and *SMACK*; the third baseman swung and connected, breaking the writer's nose in two places.

Later that day, in a game against the A's, Pagliarulo fouled off a line drive into the Oakland dugout. It struck relief pitcher Gene Nelson on the pinky of his left hand, breaking the little finger. Pagliarulo quipped, "Nelson is a righty. He should have been wearing his glove on that left hand." Nelson replied that he was trying to protect his face, but it was just bad luck.

The Twins won their Western Division title, defeated Toronto in the ALCS, and took the World Series in seven games over Atlanta. Pags had three hits and a homer and played errorless ball for the champs.

It turns out the Pags *was* bad luck that year, but only for sportswriters and opponents.

FIGHTING MIKE GREENWELL

Mike Greenwell, the classy outfielder for the Boston Red Sox, is a steady player who shows a good work ethic with numbers to back that up. As a throwback to the old Boston way of doing things, it makes sense that challenging him is challenging Red Sox tradition. So it's no surprise that fighting with Greenwell has an adverse effect on the team in general.

In 1991, the Red Sox, under Joe Morgan, were poised to battle Toronto for the American League East flag. In June, the club was 37-35 and in second place, only three games behind, when left fielder Greenwell and shortstop Luis Rivera brawled in the dugout over who should have caught a fly ball. The Red Sox simmered down, and while Greenwell's average rose from .317 to .320 over the next month and Rivera's climbed from .271 to .284, the BoSox felt the ill effects of the bout and lost 22 of their next 35 games to drop to 50-57, 11½ games out.

Just when the Bostonians began to right themselves with a 12-win, and three-loss run to move over .500 at 62-60, 4½ games out, a second Greenwell fight put the club off its winning ways just enough to derail their pennant run.

Before a game at Anaheim Stadium on August 24, first baseman Mo Vaughn challenged Greenwell and insulted him. A fight in the batting cage was eventually broken up by teammate Jack Clark and coach Dick Berardino, but not until several punches had been landed. Greenwell suffered a cut near his blackened eye, and the BoSox suffered in the weeks to come.

Boston dropped their next two games, and though they recovered later in the season, it wasn't enough to offset the two Greenwell fight doldrums. They settled for second place.

STEAL BASES, NOT CASH

It's not bad luck to steal bases against an opponent, but it may be bad luck to have your hosts suffer a cash loss on game day.

On August 15, 1990, a few hours before the game between the hometown Philadelphia Phillies and the visiting San Francisco Giants was to begin, a thief, dressed in a Brooks Armored Car Service uniform, robbed the Phillies ticket office of $25,000.

Giants players heard about the robbery and began to joke about it. The joke was on them.

Phillies pitcher Terry Mulholland robbed them of their bats that night, tossing a no-hitter to beat them 6-0.

UMPIRES AND BAD CALLS

It's bad luck to be an umpire, or at least it was in the 1920s when a close call went against the local team in a Minor League game. Bill "Lord" Byron, "The Singing Umpire," who became famous for singing some of his calls, sung a man out on a close call at the plate to end the game in a loss for hometown Sacramento. Byron was chased from the ballpark by rock-wielding fans who tried to stone some sense into the man.

Following the game, as Byron relaxed at the Clunie Hotel, a ruckus began outside. A crowd had gathered and a rope was being dangled in preparation of a lynching—Byron's. Byron didn't flinch, walked out into the crowd, and sang to the rope-holder, "My boy, 'twas ever thus and so 'twill ever be. The man was out 'twas what I did see."

The crowd dispersed and the poetic umpire lived to call another game.

THE CONDO FROM HELL

Rob Murphy was a successful relief pitcher for the Boston Red Sox until he moved into the bad-luck condominium of all time.

Murphy was an emerging star, going 5-7 with a 2.74 ERA for the BoSox in 1989. The following season, he moved into a Watertown, Massachusett, condo, and his record dropped to a dismal 0-6 with a 6.32 ERA. He hasn't been the same since.

Murphy was traded to Seattle, and slugger Jack Clark moved into Murph's condo. Clark had been a steady power hitter for 16 years before coming to Boston. He began the season with terrible numbers, hitting an anemic .196 with four homers through June 9. He slowly picked up his season as he began staying in the condo less frequently.

But the curse took hold and Clark had a poor 1992. By 1993 Clark was out of baseball, had filed for bankruptcy, and was being investigated by the IRS.

Must be the condo.

BAD LIKENESS

On July 12, 1991, the Yankees visited Anaheim Stadium, and New York outfielder Mel Hall found an ad extolling the virtues of the Los Angeles Zoo. He put two full-color photos of surly looking gorillas over teammate Hensley "Bam-Bam" Meulens' locker.

Hall laughed and said, "They're a good likeness (of Meulens), don't you think?"

Meulens responded by going 0-for-4 that night and tore the photos from his locker.

"No more gorillas," he said. "They're bad luck."

BAD LUCK NUGGETS

It was bad luck to face Don Drysdale under the following circumstances:

1. If your pitcher had just hit one of Drysdale's teammates and you were the leadoff hitter the next inning, you *were* going to be hit. Drysdale's oft-recited credo: "If you hit one of ours, I'll hit two of yours."

2. If "Big D" caught you digging in against him, he didn't like it, and the next pitch would be under your chin.

3. If you had just hit a home run off him, you'd be on your wallet next time up.

4. If the batter before you hit a home run, the first pitch to you would be a blazing sidewinder behind your head.

5. If Don just felt like throwing one at you, he might do so.

Before one 1963 World Series game against the Yankees, Drysdale leaned against the batting cage and watched Mickey Mantle blast ball after ball into the seats 400 feet away. Mantle looked over at Big D and smiled. Big D gave Mick a steely-eyed stare and said, "Where do ya want to get hit today, Big Boy?"

Don was a fastball pitcher with an attitude, and that attitude got him into the Hall of Fame. But his trail there was littered with diving, battered and bruised batsmen. And if you think it wasn't done on purpose, consider this: Drysdale beaned a National League-record 154 batters during his career, yet his control was outstanding, walking only 855 hitters in 3,432 innings pitched, while striking out 2,486. He threw four pitches: fastball, curve, change-up and knockdown.

It's bad luck to be a pitching coach for the New York Yankees during the George Steinbrenner era. Billy Connors was the 29th Yankee pitching coach in the first 21 years of George's reign — and Steinbrenner stayed uninvolved his first year with the club (1973) and was suspended from the game in 1992-93. This coaching position has all the baseball longevity of a wild, sore-armed lefty with a 50-foot curve and a 70-mile-an-hour fastball. Of course, it's not great luck to be a Yankee manager under "The Boss's" guiding hand either, as 20 managers have been at the helm in 21 years — but then five of those managers were Billy Martin.

"Sunset Jimmy" Burke, a third baseman for the Cardinals and four other teams from 1898 to 1905, felt it was deathlike bad luck to eat dinner before sundown. Under no circumstances would he have his big meal until nightfall.

Hall of Famer Rogers Hornsby felt that watching movies was bad luck. He didn't watch them when he was a player, and he forbid his players from watching them when he was a manager. Hornsby felt that watching the flickering movie screens in the darkness of a theater would cause the ball to bounce when you saw it in the daylight. Hey, the guy hit .358 over a 23-year career. He might have been right.

Sometimes it's bad luck to watch yourself play. In 1988, Ivan Calderon, an outfielder for the Chicago White Sox, was in the clubhouse watching himself hit on videotape while a game against the Kansas City Royals moved on into the late innings. Calderon was still watching when ChiSox manager Jim Fregosi called his name as a pinch hitter. Fregosi looked around and there was no sign of the outfielder, so another man was put up in his place. After the pop out by the pinch-pinch hitter, Calderon emerged from the clubhouse knowing how to swing again. He walked up to Fregosi who promptly fined him $100 for being AWOL.

And finally, Chicago White Sox catcher Carlton Fisk, once he reached the age of 40, concluded that it was bad luck to play in any game in which the temperature was lower than his age, so he took those games off.

CHAPTER THREE

Tantrums

"To succeed in the world, it is not enough to be stupid, you must also be well mannered."
—VOLTAIRE (FRANCOIS MARIE AROUET)

"A good man does not argue; He who argues is not a good man."
—LAO-TZU

"Well done is better than well said."
— BENJAMIN FRANKLIN

Warning: This chapter contains harsh language. Harsh? Hell, it's downright vulgar and may be objectionable to children, adults or any others who haven't spent time with angry athletes in postgame locker rooms. To keep this chapter from being rated "X" for language and violence, we've resorted to the television technique of BLEEPing out the offensive jargon. Thinly veiled, maybe, but funnier, perhaps.

An old Latin saying goes *"Quos deus vult perdere prius demenant,"* or "Those whom God wishes to destroy, he first makes mad." Well, the following gentlemen may not have been destroyed, but they certainly went mad, or got mad, mostly at members of the press—the author's buddies.

So despite Benjamin Franklin's warning—he must have been a master of the tantrum, or at least of describing founding fathers' faux pas—that "It is ill manners to silence a fool and cruelty to let him go on . . . ," we will risk ill manners and let the following go on . . . and on . . . and on.

These are blow-by-blow, play-by-play transcriptions of some of the most creative, energetic, vulgar, English grammar-bedamned invectives in baseball history. These diatribes have a few things in common. They were all performed by short-fused ball-players or managers and were directed at the media, usually in postgame interviews held in locker rooms or the manager's office. In most cases the press bore the brunt of the blitzkrieg, but occa-sionally, the salvos were fired in the direction of umpires or op-posing players. They are true and accurate transcriptions of furi-ous fulminations of those diamondeers who lost their cool. These harangues are taken word for word from tapes made by media members who had the foresight to leave their recording devices on while those around them were losing their heads. Lucky for us — unlucky for the participants — these shock-jock acts were per-formed in front of open mikes — we've got the tapes — and whir-ring cameras and are a matter of public record.

Why print this here? Well, they haven't been printed anywhere else and this is as good a place as any to keep these jeremiads and obloquies for posterity.

Now, before you start your own rantings and ravings about book burning (this one) remember that this is history, nonfiction, and its printing here is all in fun. And to satisfy redeeming social value requirements, in many cases the delivered verbal abuse, usually aimed at members of the press, achieved for the speaker a desired result — most good, in some cases bad. And in many scenarios, the team prospered from the venom.

Of course, baseball is an action sport and in many cases action speaks louder than words, so also included in this chapter are some of the more well-choreographed pantomimes that are deli-ciously demonstrative examples of silent baseball verité.

To fully appreciate the drama and theatrical displays in this chapter, try to picture the bursting veins, red faces, bulging eyes, raised voices, kicked dirt, stamping, stomping, spitting and con-vulsive gestures. Your wildest images will probably be right on the mark.

Now, to keep this book from becoming an underground publi-cation, we've inserted BLEEPs where the really offensive detours in demeanor take place. But you can figure it out if you really try. The rationale and censorship belong solely to the writer and editors of this book, and we've left in some colorful and objection-able (to some, it is supposed) words for haranguing continuity.

BLEEPing LEGEND

BLEEP — Any part of speech (noun, verb, adjective, adverb, etc.) — ballplayers are extremely creative in the use of these words — usually either a body part, action word, act, bodily function, or nickname for an individual. Encompasses several euphemisms for the same act.

BLEEPS — Plural of BLEEP, usually anatomical parts or action people.

BLEEPin — Usually an adjective, as in "Those BLEEPin BLEEPS." Note: Most ballplayers and managers use "BLEEPin," rather than the more grammatically correct "BLEEPing."

BLEEPed — Action description, usually bodily function or physical act, oriented in the present tense. Can also be past tense of BLEEP.

BLEEPER-BLEEPERS — A real action word that would make Oedipus cringe in plural. Singular would, of course, be BLEEPER-BLEEPER.

BLEEPER-BLEEPin — Same action as BLEEPER-BLEEPERS, but used as an action description of individuals or events.

BLEEP-BLEEPERS — A different action word in plural that is anatomy specific. Can also be BLEEP-BLEEPin if used as adjective.

We have left in allusions to questionable heritage, as those are personal, social and perhaps sociological references. We also left in metaphysical locations and acts of condemnation when not combined with a deity.

HAL McRAE
Manager, Kansas City Royals ◆ April 26, 1993 ◆ 41 BLEEPS

Sometimes, when things aren't going well, a team needs a shot in the arm, or in some other anatomical area, to straighten itself out. When it does, it is often up to the manager to mix metaphors and provide that spark. This was the case when Royals skipper Hal McRae, in his third year at the K.C. helm, saw his team sinking around him with a 7-12 record. He reacted rather predictably, if seemingly unprovoked, to one question too many by the press following a tough loss at home to the Tigers. The result was a littered locker room, a clubhouse emptied of the dreaded media, and a dramatic turnaround to a nearly lost season.

It started out innocently enough: Mac was asked why he didn't send up his man to bunt in the ninth.

Picking up the action:

McRae: "If I bunt him, we got second and third ... they got some options, Wally's [Joyner] the next hitter. We'd like him to swing the bat. We got two rights comin' up, and Hennemen is a good closer; he's tough on right-handed hitters. So I didn't want to get myself into a situation where all I had to go after him was all right, and our lefts was swinging the bats well, so I wanted my left-handed hitters to hit."

So far, so mild. Now is where it starts to heat up, for no apparent reason.

Question: "Did you consider [George] Brett for [Keith] Miller with the bases loaded in the seventh?"

McRae: "No, no don't ask me all these stupid-BLEEP BLEEPin questions. No ... and, and, and uh ... BLEEP."

MacRae begins to throw anything he can find:

"Stop all these BLEEPin stupid-BLEEP questions every BLEEPin night. Why the BLEEP would I hit Brett for BLEEPin Miller? Miller started the BLEEPin game. He's batted against left-handed BLEEPin pitchers; Brett hasn't batted against left-handed pitchers. Why the BLEEP would I bat for Miller? You think I'm a BLEEP-BLEEP fool?"

Mac throws more towels, clears a table with a few vicious arm flails, throws other items at hand, slams door and tosses anything he can reach.

"Tired of all these stupid-BLEEP questions every night. And stay out of here asking these dumb-BLEEP questions. BLEEP you, too. BLEEP it. Ask me that stupid-BLEEP BLEEP every BLEEPER-BLEEPin night. Stupid-BLEEP BLEEP. BLEEP this BLEEP. I'm not takin' no BLEEP off you guys; I'm not takin' no BLEEP off the BLEEPin players. I'm sick and tired. I'm fed up with every BLEEPin thing. No BLEEP from you guys, no BLEEP from you BLEEPin players. And they can do any BLEEPER-BLEEPin thing they want to do. I'm sick and tired of all this bullBLEEP.

"Now, put that in your BLEEPin pipe and smoke it."

Now anything not tied down has been thrown, including towels, water bottles and tape.

"Try to be BLEEPin nice and courteous and you BLEEP-BLEEPERS take advantage of the situBLEEPination. That's what I get for tryin' to be a BLEEPin nice guy. You try to make a BLEEPin BLEEP out of me every BLEEP-BLEEP night. Well this is the last BLEEPin night."

Result: The club went on a tear and challenged for first place by winning 25 and losing only 13 over the next month-and-a-half. The team finished in third place at 84-78, or 11 games over .500 after the tantrum. One more tirade during a cold streak in June might have brought the Royals a pennant.

TOM LASORDA
Manager, Los Angeles Dodgers ◆ May 14, 1978 ◆ 18 BLEEPS

Tom Lasorda, the stalwart, true, rah-rah Dodger Blue and blue-languaged skipper for nearly two decades, takes good days by opponents personally. And when Dave Kingman, a Dodger nemesis who twice in his career blasted three monstrous homers in one game against the Dodgers, beat Los Angeles with a prodigious performance to win the game 10-7 in 15 innings for the Cubs, Lasorda answered reporter Paul Olden's rather innocent question with Ruthian umbrage, yet he really didn't seem agitated—just filled with matter-of-fact annoyance. Here's an excerpt:

Question: "What's your opinion of Kingman's performance?"
Lasorda: "What's my opinion of Kingman's performance? What the BLEEP you think is my opinion of it? I think it was BLEEPin horseBLEEP. Put that in. I don't BLEEPin . . . opinion of his performance? BLEEP, he beat us with three BLEEPin home runs. What the BLEEP can you mean, what is my opinion of his performance? How can you ask me a question like that? What is my opinion of his performance?

BLEEP, he hit three home runs. BLEEP. I'm BLEEPin BLEEPed off to lose a BLEEPin game, and you ask me my opinion of his performance. BLEEP. I mean that's a tough question to ask me, isn't it . . . what is my opinion of his performance?"

Olden: "Yes, it is. I asked it and you gave me an answer."

Lasorda: "Well. I didn't give you a good answer because I'm mad, but I mean that's a tough question to ask me right now . . . what is my opinion of his performance? I mean you want me to tell you what my opinion of his performance is. BLEEP. Guy hits three home runs against us. BLEEP I mean I don't wanna get BLEEPed off or anything like that, but, you know, you asked me my opinion. I mean he put on a hell of a show. He hit three home runs. He drove in what? Seven runs?"

Olden: "Eight."

Lasorda: "Eight runs. And what the hell more can you say about it? I didn't mean to get mad or anything like that but BLEEP-BLEEP. You ask me my opinion of his performance. BLEEP."

Yeah, but Tommy, how do you really feel about Kingman's performance?

Result: The outburst had its desired effect. The Dodgers went on to capture the National League West flag by three games over Cincinnati and the NL pennant in a play-off against the Phillies. Los Angeles then lost to the Yankees in six games. Bucky Dent and Brian Doyle were the hitting stars in the final game. In the pivotal game three, with the Dodgers up two games to none, Yankee third baseman Graig Nettles put on a spectacular fielding display, making four incredible plays to save five runs. The Yanks won that one 5-1 and swept the rest of the Series. I wonder what Lasorda thought of Nettles's performance.

LEE ELIA

Manager, Chicago Cubs ◆ April 29, 1983 ◆ 56 BLEEPS

Lee Elia was in his second year at the helm of the Cubbies. A year earlier, he guided the club to a fifth-place finish at 73-89. But in 1983, with such stars under contract as Bill Buckner (1b), Ryne Sandberg (2b), Larry Bowa (ss), Ron Cey (3b); an outfield

of Keith Moreland, Mel Hall and Leon Durham; Jody Davis behind the plate; and a pitching staff that included starters Steve
Trout, Fergie Jenkins and Dick Ruthven, with Lee Smith out of
the bullpen, fans and sportswriters from The Windy City expected much more out of the Wrigley crew. So, after a slow,
5-14 start, the boobirds took roost in the friendly confines and
the local press took the club to task. After losing another game,
this one to the Dodgers, Elia went wild at a postgame press conference following a seemingly innocuous question asking the skipper what he thought about all the boos that crescendoed throughout the home ballpark.

Elia responded with a memorable monologue, excerpted here.
We bow to the BLEEP master. Demeanor: Angry. Decibel level:
high.

Elia: "We are mired now in a little difficulty. We got all these
so-called BLEEPin fans who come out here and say they're
Cub fans that are supposed to be behind ya, rippin' every
BLEEPin thing ya do. I'll tell ya one BLEEPin thing, I hope
we get BLEEPin hotter than BLEEP just to stuff it up them
3,000 BLEEPin people that show up every BLEEPin day.
Because if they're the real Chicago BLEEPin fans, they can
kiss my BLEEPin BLEEP right downtown and print it.
They're really really behind ya around here. My BLEEPin
BLEEP. What the BLEEP am I supposed to do? Go out
there and let my BLEEPin players get destroyed every day
and be quiet about it? For the BLEEPin nickel-dime people
that show up? The BLEEPER-BLEEPERS don't even
work. That's why they're out at the BLEEPin game. They
ought to go out and get a BLEEPin job and find out what
it's like to go out and earn a BLEEPin livin. Eighty-five
percent of the BLEEPin world's working, the other 15 come
out here. A BLEEPin playground for the BLEEP-BLEEP-
ERS."

Result: Tough year all around in Chi-town. Elia lasted until August 22 and was fired with a 54-69 mark (49-55 after the BLEEP
speech) following another Cub loss and one punched-out camera-
man and was replaced by Charlie Fox, for whom the Cubbies
went 17-22. Attendance for the year was 1,479,717, so I guess
unemployment was down that year. The following year, the Cubs

won the pennant for manager Jim Frey, and attendance reached 2,107,655. More unemployed fans?

BILLY MARTIN
Manager, New York Yankees ◆ June 10, 1978 ◆ 16 BLEEPS

Billy Martin, the enigmatic and fiery manager of the New York Yankees and Oakland A's, among others, was arguably one of the finest managers of his era when it came to getting the most out of his players and his team (.553 winning percentage and five pennants) — at least over a few years at a time, as he usually wore out his welcome with ownership and players after two years. His "Billy Ball" style of play included knowing every nuance of the rule book, instilling fundamentals in his players, stealing runs with daring baserunning, using a timely hit-run-and-bunt strategy, and milking his pitching staff for all it was worth. Hired and fired by the Yankees five times, Martin was two different people. When he was not drinking or under the stress of managing a team in a pennant race, Martin was a kind, generous, soft-spoken man who was also one of the finest, low-key baseball analysts on the tube. When he was drinking or under the pressure of a tight race, however, Martin had the shortest of fuses, exploding often, as he did in the following tale, thanks to an ill-timed question by this author in a postgame locker room (causing Martin to storm off and close the clubhouse before many beat writers had been able to get the quotes they needed — sorry, guys).

The scene: Anaheim Stadium, June 10, 1978. The Yankees were 32-22, four games behind Boston, and coming off a 3-1 win the night before in which Rich "Goose" Gossage pitched a perfect ninth inning for the save. Gossage had pitched a lot recently, and before the game, the author, noted below as "Blake," asked Gossage if he had been getting too much work. Gossage replied, "I can really use a rest. I've pitched in five of our last six or seven (games), and my arm is tired. A few days off would serve me well."

During the game, Martin deftly used Don Gullett, Rawley Eastwick and Sparky Lyle to get to the ninth tied 3-3. With one out and two on in the ninth, Martin brought in Gossage to relieve Lyle, and Big Goose got Joe Rudi and Don Baylor to end the threat. Martin sent Gossage out again in the tenth and Goose retired the side in order. And in the 11th, Goose again got the side in order.

Sending his closer into his fourth inning of relief, Martin had no one up in the bullpen as Gossage tired and gave up a walk to Lyman Bostock and a two-out, game-winning single to Reggie Jackson, who had been 0-for-5. The Angels won 4-3, dropping the Yanks five games behind Boston.

After the game, Martin calmly and softly answered questions. A mere four questions into the postgame recap, Blake asked the one that blew the lid off.

Blake: "Since Gossage was complaining of a tired arm and had pitched in five of your last seven, did you give any thought to getting someone else up after Goose had already pitched three innings tonight? Or was it sink or swim with Goose no matter how long the game went?"

Martin (leaving his low-decibel answers of the previous questions behind in favor of a loud, squeaky scream): "Tired arm? Tired arm? Who the BLEEP told you he had a tired BLEEPing arm?"

Blake: "Goose did."

Martin: "Well, he never the BLEEP told me. Tired arm? He's my best reliever. He got the first eight men he faced, and there was no BLEEPing reason to believe he wouldn't go on like that for another two innings. Tired arm? He blew 100-mile-a-BLEEPing-hour fastballs past Jackson [in the 10th] and Mulliniks [11th]. Tired BLEEPing arm. Are you BLEEPing second-guessing me? You can all kiss my Dago BLEEP. You BLEEPing writers will write what you want to write anyway. You're out to get me, and it doesn't matter what I say, you'll just BLEEPing write whatever the BLEEP you BLEEPing want to BLEEPing write. So get the BLEEP out of here. The clubhouse is BLEEPing closed. BLEEPs."

A simple "No" would have sufficed. And it is interesting to note that Martin preferred the more grammatically correct "BLEEP-ing," ending in "g," than the more popular but sloppy bastardization, "BLEEPin," ending with "n" and no "g."

Outcome: On July 24, Billy resigned — or was fired — with the Yanks 52-42, in third place, 10 games out. Under his replacement, Bob Lemon, New York went 48-20 to win the flag in a play-off with Boston. Martin came back to the Big Apple in 1983 after a stint and a pennant in Oakland, and in 1987, as a broadcaster-analyst for the Yankees' cable-TV games, Martin, under no pressure, remembered the incident, apologized, and went on to talk softly about many things, including his baseball games in Japan—he introduced the double play break up and takeout of the second baseman to the Far East—and the science of baseball.

Nice guy—off the field.

RICH "GOOSE" GOSSAGE
Pitcher, New York Yankees ◆ 1982 ◆ 26 BLEEPS

For 22 years, Rich Gossage has been wheeling and dealing and firing his 90 to 100 mph fastballs to, through and by Major League hitters. From behind his menacing Fu Manchu moustache, Gossage was perhaps the most feared and most effective relief pitcher in baseball for a decade from the mid-1970s through the mid-1980s. He is one of the few pitchers to hit the magic 300-save mark.

Goose was always in charge. Once, when catcher Rick Cerone walked to the mound to talk with his pitcher, Goose barked, "Stay off my BLEEPER-BLEEPin mound. It's my BLEEPin mound, so stay the BLEEP off." Cerone returned to home plate and let his pitcher throw to the next hitter without any words of strategy.

Seldom one to lose control, Gossage lost it one day. A tough loss on an error during a poor team year, reverberating raspberries from disgruntled Yankee Stadium fans and some rapid-fire interviewing by a horde of New York journalists sent the Goose flying south, in about as loud a yell as a feathered friend can manage. Here's an excerpt:

Question: "You look angry. Who's making you angry?"
Gossage: "Everybody. The way they boo BLEEPin [Ken] Griffey and everybody else.

"And you BLEEPER-BLEEPERS [writers]. All you BLEEPER-BLEEPERS with a BLEEPin pen and a BLEEPin tape recorder, you can BLEEPin turn it on and take it upstairs to "The Fat Man" [George Steinbrenner].

I wonder if Gossage renewed his subscription to his New York newspapers.

Result: Goose left "The Fat Man" and his New York writer-buddies behind at the end of the year, signing a lucrative deal to play on the west coast with the San Diego Padres.

LOU PINIELLA

Minor League Player, Portland Beavers ◆ 1967 ◆ Uncounted BLEEPS

Lou Piniella, who, back in the 1970s as a member of the New York Yankees, told the author that the quote he lives by is "Patience is the key to contentment," has been a winner wherever he's gone; and while he may be content, he certainly has seldom exhibited patience in his on-field/locker-room behavior.

Former Major League hitter-extraordinaire Richie Scheinblum, a Minor League teammate of Piniella's, offers his favorite "Sweet" Lou tale.

The Beavers of the Pacific Coast League were playing a home game in Portland when the team owner visited the clubhouse and told the players to be on their best behavior; sitting right behind the dugout that night was a group of nuns — special guests of the owner. Looking at Lou, the owner exacted a promise that all players would be courteous and considerate.

A first-inning strikeout left Lou angered, but in control. He smiled at the nuns and laid his bat down.

A fourth-inning pop out raised his ire, but again he placed his bat gently in the bat rack.

A seventh-inning whiff enraged Piniella. He slammed his bat down, looked at the nuns, regained his composure, and slammed himself down on the bench.

Vesuvius was showing signs of eruption.

In the ninth, with a chance to win the game, Piniella went down swinging. He gingerly walked to the bat rack and carefully placed his lumber in the proper slot. He walked over to the nuns, smiled, pressed his face against the screen as close to theirs as possible, and let loose in volcanic vulgarity at the top of his lungs. (Too bad there were no tape recorders going to save this one for posterity. Scheinblum says it was a classic display of anatomical and action-erotic vocabulary.) A half minute of creative epithets later, the nuns were catatonic, and Piniella was a relieved, peaceful man, ready to bang out four hits the next day, without the women in habits in attendance.

Philippic Piniella isn't through with just this escapade. This is merely minor league stuff. He refined his performance for The Big Show.

LOU PINIELLA 2

Manager, Cincinnati Reds ◆ August 21, 1990

Since verbalization may not be Sweet Lou's long suit — his physical performance got him to the Bigs — the following pantomime is worth exploring in this chapter. It makes ESPN's highlight reel quite often.

While his temper seemed under control as manager of George Steinbrenner's Yankees — and if ever a situation screamed for a tantrum, that was it — Piniella let it all fly several times as skipper of the Cincinnati Reds for Marge Schott — another owner who seems to get the beast (not best) conduct from her charges (and not without reason).

Training for the baseball Olympics, Lou practiced his base throw and received perfect 10s from the fans in a one-man display that achieved its desired effect.

The first-place Reds had gotten off to a 33-12 start and were trying to go wire-to-wire to win the NL West. At this point, they held a 5½ game lead over the Dodgers, but had lost five in a row and were in danger of letting a fine season get away. The club needed a fire built under it, and Piniella used himself as the fuse.

In a game in which the Reds won, beating the Cubs 8-1, Piniella put on a great show.

Leading 6-1 with the bases loaded and one out in the sixth inning, Barry Larkin topped a grounder to Domingo Ramos, the Cubs shortstop, who fed Ryne Sandberg for the out at second. Then Rhyno pivoted and fired to first to nip Larkin for the double play in a photofinish. Here's how Piniella protested the "out" call at first base:

1. Ran full speed out to the field and ranted, raved, yelled, stomped, gestured and looked near convulsion as he screamed his disapproval.

2. Flung his cap at first-base umpire Dutch Rennert as the veins bulged from the skipper's neck and his eyes bulged nearly out of their sockets.

3. Yanked first base out of its foundation and heaved it toward second base with two hands.

4. Followed the bag and fielded it.

5. Picked up the tossed sack, whirled like a discus thrower, and flung it into right field one-handed, as the 22,759 fans in atten-

dance roared their approval.

6. Stomped, kicked dirt, yelled, screamed and hopped around as he made his way back to the dugout and exited stage right.

Piniella's postgame analysis: "Well, I was gone as soon as I threw my cap . . . and first base was just sitting there . . ."

Result: The Reds maintained their intensity for the rest of the season and won the NL West flag by five games over Los Angeles. They went on to capture the NL play-off in six games against Pittsburgh and the World Championship in a four-game sweep over Oakland. And in Lou's honor, the city of Cincinnati held a base-throwing contest at Fountain Square that drew more fans than were in attendance to watch the original performance.

Before we go back to "talkies," one more silent film bears reporting—a legendary production that was great theater to those in attendance.

BUDDY HUNTER
Manager, Winston Salem Red Sox ◆ May 13, 1980

Harold James "Buddy" Hunter was a seldom-used infielder for the Red Sox in the early 1970s, but he really hit his stride and baseball immortality for his stint as field general for the Carolina League Red Sox the following decade.

The night before this memorable moment in Minor League history, his slumping ball club had lost its 13th of its last 17 games, following a controversial call by umpire Bob Serino in which an apparent home run was taken away. On the road against the Durham Bulls at Durham Athletic Park, Hunter may have had reason to gripe. The right field fence at Athletic Park was metal, and if a ball hit metal, you could hear it "ping." Above the metal barrier was a wooden addition. A ball hitting the wood "thudded." The ball in question "thudded," it didn't "ping," so by sound as well as sight, it was a home run. Yet Serino called the ball "in play," the run didn't score and Hunter's team lost.

Move on to the next night, May 13. The Sox were losing to the home team Bulls 5-3 when, in the top of the eighth, the home plate umpire, Serino, called an inside pitch a strike on hitter Juan Pautt. Hunter went into action.

Knowing that protesting a strike call would get him thumbed out, he decided to show up Serino, and show him up he did.

Hunter ran toward the man in blue, turned his cap rapper style and, nose-to-nose, yelled and screamed, questioned his heritage, and called him everything he could think of. Then he ran to his dugout, grabbed a baseball, ran full speed to right field and threw the ball against the fence, right to the spot the blown-home-run-call ball had struck the night before.

Hunter pantomimed a coin flip and signaled "home run." He danced around and waved his arms and jumped up and down in celebration. Then he flipped the imaginary coin again and signaled "out."

After the "out" call, Hunter ran to the infield and slid into first base. He stood up and signaled himself safe, then out. He sat on the bag and took off his baseball shoes. He took a bite out of the toe of one, and, pretending it was a grenade, tossed it in Serino's direction and pantomimed a blown-up umpire. Hunter then ran toward second-base umpire Bob Duncan and "blew him up" with another "shoe grenade."

Not waiting to be escorted off the field, Hunter turned to the crowd and bowed. The standing ovation—from the opposing team's fans—was thunderous. The 2,011 in attendance rocked the stadium, and they yelled "HUN-ter . . . HUN-ter . . . HUN-ter" in obvious approval. They had just seen a very special baseball moment.

Result: Hunter lit a fire under his team, and the Sox won 27 of their next 41.

SPARKY ANDERSON
Manager, Detroit Tigers ◆ 1980s ◆ 30 BLEEPS

The white-haired mentor of the Cincinnati Reds' Big Red Machine and the Detroit Tigers' return to prominence, George "Sparky" Anderson has been a steady influence on his players while running the show from the bench for nearly a quarter century, winning more than 2,000 games.

Though the Baseball Writers Association of America might disagree, it can be argued that more than one beat writer has, shall we say, antagonized a manager or two while reporting on the hometown club. Asked his reaction to a headlined story that maligned the Tigers and Sparky's managing, as well as the Detroit skipper personally, Anderson replied coolly, never raising his voice. Here's an excerpt.

Anderson: "I don't give a BLEEP. To me, I don't care what the BLEEPin headline says. Whoever's writing the BLEEPin story ought to control the headline then because that's a lot of bullBLEEP. I don't need to come in this town and be made to look like a BLEEPin fool, and I'm not gonna buy that bullBLEEP. So they can stick it in their BLEEPin BLEEP. I don't really give a BLEEP about nothin'. . . ."

But I got people here too ya know. And then the BLEEPin brother-in-law calls you up and says what the BLEEP are you doing? It's a BLEEPin joke that you have to come home and have bullBLEEP like that. That's all I gotta say."

That's quite enough, actually.

TOM LASORDA 2
Manager, Los Angeles Dodgers ◆ 1978 ◆ 14 BLEEPS

Never one to pass up a question, no matter how tough the circumstances, Dodger field general Tom Lasorda offered his opinion of a 1978 World Series call that cost him a game.

With his mouth full of his postgame meal, an angry, shouting skipper protested the call to a reporter.

Question: "It took him a while to call that play."
Lasorda: "BLEEP-BLEEP right it took him a while to call it. And I tell you it was a horseBLEEP BLEEPin call. And you can BLEEPin put that in the BLEEPER-BLEEPin paper. I'll tell ya that right BLEEPin now. It was a horseBLEEP BLEEPin call. Keep the BLEEP out [to another writer who barged into the fray]. BLEEP-BLEEP shame to lose a BLEEPin BLEEPER-BLEEPin game like that, I'll tell you that. Get that BLEEPin microphone out of my BLEEPER-BLEEPin face."

EARL WEAVER – BILL HALLER
Earl: Manager, Baltimore Orioles, 15 BLEEPS; Bill: AL Umpire ◆ 1979

Did you ever wonder what managers and umpires really say to each other during those rare occasions when alternate views are discussed? Occasionally in baseball we see differences of opinion regarding plays on the field. These mild-mannered discussions often occur between managers and umpires, and they are usually good-natured, polite dialogues filled with smiles and warm-hearted discourse all around.

Right. And Marge Schott was a poster child for the B'nai Brith.

Anyway, what follows is one of those friendly exchanges of ideas between two guys who genuinely liked each other — if this conversation is proof enough for you — Earl Weaver, fiery skipper of the Baltimore Orioles, and Bill Haller, American League umpire. The scene was a big ball game in which an Oriole pitcher was called for a balk, a decision with which Weaver took slight exception. This touching intercourse then took place as the crowd roared with delight over the stomping and shouting on the field below. For decibel fans, Weaver said everything about as loud as a human being can say things, while Haller replied in a rather soft-spoken manner. Here are a couple of excerpts:

Weaver: "That is not a balk."
Haller: "Behind the rubber."
Weaver: "That is not a balk."
Haller: "Behind the rubber."
Weaver: "Bull. He did not go behind the rubber."
Haller: "For me, he did."
Weaver: "I had a good view of the hill. He did not go . . ."
Haller: "Aw, I ain't listenin' to that."
Weaver: "That's bull."
Haller: "Behind the rubber."
Weaver: "Oh bullBLEEP."
Haller: "BullBLEEP, yourself."
Weaver: "You just BLEEPed this call and shut the BLEEP up."
Haller: "You're out."
Weaver: "Who?"
Haller: "You."
Weaver: "That's right. And you BLEEP."
Haller: "Ahh, you BLEEP."
Weaver: "And you don't got the right to throw me out."
Haller: "Oh, Earl, you run yourself, Earl. You run yourself."
Weaver: "Get your finger off me."
Haller: "You hit me."
Weaver: "Yeah, 'cause you put your finger on me."
Haller: "Good. I'm glad you did. I'm glad you hit me."
Later that same tirade:
Weaver: "You ain't no good."

Haller: "No, you aren't either. Yeah, you aren't either."

Weaver: "You ain't no good."

Haller: "You're no BLEEPin good either."

Weaver: "You stink. Your BLEEP will never have our games again."

Haller: "I hope not. What do I care?"

Weaver: "What are ya doin' here now?"

Haller: "Well, why don't you call the league office and ask them."

Weaver: "Yeah, I will."

Haller: "Good."

Weaver: "Don't think I won't."

Haller: "Good."

Weaver: "The quicker you get out the better."

Haller: "And the quicker you get out it'll be better too."

Weaver: "Yeah."

Haller: "That's right."

Weaver: "You ain't goin' nowhere."

Haller: "You aren't either."

Weaver: "You ask who five damn BLEEPin years from now, who's in the Hall of Fame?"

Haller: "Oh you're gonna be in the Hall of Fame?"

Weaver: "You know it."

Haller: "Why?"

Weaver: "You know it."

Haller: "For BLEEPin up a World Series?"

Weaver: "You know it."

Haller: "You're gonna be in the Hall of Fame for BLEEPin up a World Series?"

Weaver: "You know it. I've won more than I've lost, kid."

Haller: "Oh no ya haven't, Earl."

Weaver: "You stupid . . . you don't even know what the BLEEP you're talking about."

Haller: "You better get going, Earl."

Weaver: "I'd better get going your BLEEP."

Haller: "You'd better get going."

Now throw in some stomping and dirt kicking and add a roaring crowd.

Weaver: "Tell the truth that you had your hands on me."

Haller: "Naw, that's wrong, Earl. Wrong."

And these guys are adults — well, chronologically speaking if not from a maturity perspective. Wouldn't you love a televised presidential debate to take this course?

TOM LASORDA — DOUG RAU
Tom: Manager, Los Angeles Dodgers, 32 BLEEPS; Doug: Pitcher, Los Angeles Dodgers, 7 BLEEPS ♦ 1977

And for those of you who want to know what a manager tells his pitcher during a mound conference when the skipper takes out his hurler, consider the following:

It's game four of the 1977 World Series. In front of more than 55,000 fans and millions more watching on television, with an organist playing some annoying tune in the background, this second-inning conversation transpired on the mound between beleaguered pitcher Doug Rau and his mentor, the colorful linguist, Dodger manager, Tom Lasorda.

Rau: "Let me stay in."

Lasorda: "BLEEP no. You can't get them BLEEPin left-handers out for BLEEP alBLEEPinmighty."

Rau: "BLEEPin Jackson, I got him jammed all the BLEEPin game (Remember, this is the second inning). I feel good, Tommy."

Lasorda: "I don't give a BLEEP you feel good. There's four BLEEPER-BLEEPin hits up there."

Rau: "They're all BLEEPin hits the opposite way."

Lasorda: "I don't give a BLEEP."

Rau: "Tommy, they got a left-handed hitter. I can strike this BLEEPER-BLEEPER out."

Lasorda: "I don't give a BLEEP, Dougie."

Rau: "I think you're wrong."

Lasorda: "Well, I may be wrong, but that's my BLEEP-BLEEP job."

Result: The Dodgers lost the game 4-2, but came back to win the next contest 10-4 before falling to Reggie Jackson's three-home run display in game six. Rau pitched in that game as well. He didn't gripe when yanked in that one.

RON LUCIANO
AL Umpire ◆ 1975

Tommy Harper was at the plate in this game in Baltimore for the California Angels against the Orioles. Harper drilled one right down the left-field line, and Luciano, the third-base umpire, called it fair. Orioles skipper Earl Weaver argued, and for one of the few times in baseball history, an ump changed his mind. Luciano ruled it foul.

Luciano explains:

"Two men on, Harper hits one down the left-field line. I look up and all I see is the sun; I don't see the ball. I know it went home run distance, but I don't see it. All I see is the sun. So I got a 50-50 chance, fair or foul.

"I jumped in the air, twirled around, made all kinds of motions and called it fair. The entire stadium wanted to kill me and out runs 'The Little General,' Earl Weaver. His veins are thumping out of his neck and I beat him to the punch, and I said, 'Earl, maybe I missed it.' So I run over to first-base umpire Bill Haller and asked him, 'Fair or foul?' Bill said, 'Ronnie, the worst call I've ever seen in baseball — foul by 40 feet.'

"I told him I'd change the call, and he said, 'Baseball tradition 100 years old says you can't change it.' I said, 'Foul?' He said, 'By 50 feet.'

"I knew if I changed the call, Angels manager Dick Williams would explode and I'd have to throw him out — over my mistake.

"I walked over and Dick was beautiful. I said, 'Dick, the ball was foul.' He said, 'Probably by 50 feet.' I said I'd have to change the call, and he said, 'Ohh, no. There's no way you can change the call. If you change the call, you're gonna have to throw me out of the game.'

"I said OK and was set to toss him, and he said, 'Ohh, no. Before I go, there's got to be two things: I want you to make an idiot out of yourself and jump up in the air and do all those stupid things you do when you throw me out of the game, and second of all, I want to talk about your heritage and you've got to take it.'

"Well, he started in and the obscenities flew, and after

four minutes of nonstop abuse, he said he was ready to be tossed, so I jumped up in the air three times, whirled and yelled, 'You're outta here.' The crowd was roaring, and as Dick was walking away toward the dugout, he stopped, walked up to me face to face and said this show was worth the home run."

It's amazing how long it takes to get a manager agitated and what it takes to get thrown out of a game.

DAVEY JOHNSON

Manager, Cincinnati Reds ◆ April 3, 1994 ◆ 8 BLEEPS

In the opening game of the 1994 season, a first-of-its-kind opening night in Cincinnati, it only took seven innings of the year to have Reds skipper Davey Johnson blow his stack, and it only took eight BLEEPs for Terry Tata to thumb the Cincy field boss.

While his club was absorbing a 6-2 loss to the St. Louis Cardinals, a Bob Tewksbury pitch seemed to strike Cincy batter Lenny Harris on the back foot. Home plate umpire Terry Tata did not award the hitter first base, ruling that the batsman did not make an attempt to avoid the pitch, and according to baseball rules, was not entitled to a free pass to first.

Johnson, in midseason form, became enraged and charged Tata, first just discussing the situation and then becoming more heated.

There were no tapes made of the conversation, but lip readers were easily able to distinguish the offending language and clearly saw — on the nationally televised game — Johnson utter the epithet bullBLEEP seven times as he got a negative response from Tata. Following the seven bullBLEEPs, Johnson changed his tack and shouted horseBLEEP and was immediately tossed.

For Johnson, it was seven innings and a change from the bovine to the equine. For Tata, it was listening unemotionally as he played matador to Johnson's bulls before roping Johnson's offending wild stallion.

Relax, Davey, there are 161 more to go.

TODD STOTTLEMYRE

Pitcher, Toronto Blue Jays ◆ October 23, 1993 ◆ 1 BLEEP

Todd Stottlemyre is a hard-working hurler who always gives his best. And while his best isn't always good enough to win, he gives an honest effort. He was coming off an 11-12 season with a 4.84 ERA in 28 starts for the AL champion Blue Jays when he was called upon to start game four of the Fall Classic against the Phillies in Philadelphia. With the Series standing at 2-1 in favor of the Jays, the mayor of the City of Brotherly Love, Ed Rendell, publicly lambasted Stottlemyre and Toronto. He verbally attacked Stot, impugning his ability, courage and heritage, and said he'd be happy to send a limousine to pick Stottlemyre up and bring him to the ballpark, just to make sure the Phils could hit against him.

Well, the good mayor was right about the Phillies having a field day on Stot's pitching. The hurler lasted only 2 innings, gave up 3 hits, 6 runs and 4 walks, for an ERA of 27.00. But then, it was a tough day for pitchers all around, as the Blue Jays outslugged the Phils 15-14 in a four-hour-and-fourteen-minute classic slugfest.

In a mini-BLEEP of a tantrum that should really be labeled "just desserts," Stottlemyre gave the good mayor what was coming to him in a public comment following Toronto's six-game conquest of the Phillies. On the air, Stottlemyre told the mayor how he felt.

Question: "Todd, what do you have to say about Mayor Rendell now?"
Stottlemyre: "Mayor, you can kiss my BLEEP."

Result: The Blue Jays shuttled Stottlemyre between the bullpen — he was Toronto's early-season closer — and the starting rotation the following season with good consequences.

JOHN ROSEBORO – JUAN MARICHAL
John: Catcher, Los Angeles Dodgers; Juan: Pitcher, San Francisco Giants
◆ August 22, 1965

On August 22, 1965, the Los Angeles Dodgers met the San Francisco Giants in a game at Candlestick Park. The rivalry was intense, the pennant race tight, and the pitching matchup a dream — Juan Marichal versus Sandy Koufax.

After Marichal had purposely dusted Dodgers Maury Wills and Ron Fairly, L.A. catcher John Roseboro called on ace pitcher Koufax to retaliate and hit Marichal, who was now at the plate. Koufax didn't play the game that way and preferred to simply strike Marichal out. This enraged Roseboro, whose return throws to the mound tipped Marichal's ear.

The Giants pitcher and Dodger catcher shouted obscenities at each other, and Roseboro threw his mask off to face Marichal. Marichal took a one-handed swing and blasted Roseboro over the head.

What ensued was a 14-minute brawl.

A semiconscious Roseboro was led away by opponent peace-maker Willie Mays. Dodger Bob Miller raced to the plate and tackled Marichal. Miller was punched by Marichal's best friend, Giant teammate Matty Alou. And Giant Tito Fuentes swung his bat at all Dodger comers.

TANTRUM NUGGETS

Jack Clark, the much-traveled slugger, was playing for San Diego when he was called out on strikes in the first inning of a late-season game against the Giants in 1990. Umpire Bill Hohn raised his right hand on a curve and endured a growl and a low-toned, obscenity-laced rap from Clark, who walked to the dugout, got his glove, and assumed his first-base position.

Clark then accelerated the tirade. He threw gum at Hohn, kicked dirt on the plate, and went back to first base and ripped it from its moorings. He threw it some 30 feet, toward the Giants' dugout, and before it hit the ground, he was thumbed out of the game — his fourth ejection of the season.

In 1993, third baseman Dave Magadan became the first Florida Marlin to be ejected and fined after arguing a third strike and throwing down his helmet and bat. He's in the record books for his $100 fine. His mother must be proud.

Chris Sabo, the blue-collar third baseman for the Cincinnati Reds, had a tough summer of 1991. He made an obscene gesture following a strikeout in July, destroyed the team's bat rack in August following a first-inning strikeout against Paul McClellan of the Giants, and yelled at teammate Jose Rijo that Rijo was throwing too many pitches in the game. After Rijo countered that McClellan wasn't exactly Cy Young, an enraged Sabo attacked his pitcher. Sabo took on as many as a half dozen Reds in a Cincy free-for-all that summed up a terrible year for the defending World Champs, who slid to fifth place.

Closing this chapter, it may be appropriate to end with a tantrum conceived and acted out strictly in the name of love.

TOM PRINCE – HECTOR VILLANUEVA
Tom: Catcher, Buffalo Bisons, 1 BLEEP; Hector: First Baseman, Iowa Cubs, 3 BLEEPS ♦ July 1992

Baseball Weekly editor Paul White was witness to this well-planned tantrum one Sunday afternoon in Buffalo, spearheaded by Pittsburgh organization catcher Tom Prince and Cubbie prospect Hector Villanueva.

The temperature soared on this lazy day that followed a late night game that left the players sapped. Buffalo had a huge lead, and Villanueva was nursing a heavy head from the prior night's partying as he stepped to the plate. He looked at Prince, who nodded, understanding the opponent's plight as only fellow players do.

Angel (pronounced An-HELL) Hernandez was the umpire behind the plate, and he called a close pitch on the corner a strike. Villanueva wagged his finger and said, "Nah, nah. Bad call." Prince, who got the benefit of the call, agreed and said, "Hector, you're right. Terrible call."

The next pitch shaved the same corner for strike two.

Villanueva looked down at Prince and asked, "Tommy?" Prince replied, "Yeah. That call was worse than the first."

Hernandez barked, "Cut it out. What the hell are you doing?"

Prince glared at the umpire and said, "You're making bad calls. When you make bad calls, I'll tell you. And by the way, BLEEP you."

Hernandez wheeled and thumbed Prince out of the game, and before you could blink an eye, he was off the field, in the dugout, into the clubhouse, into the shower, dressed, and out of the ballpark.

Manager Mark Baumgardner went out to talk to the umpire and told Hernandez that Prince's wife was about to give birth and Prince wanted to be with her. He knew that the team had an off day tomorrow and the last plane home was about to leave and he had to catch it.

Villanueva heard this and the lightbulb went on over his head.

He says softly to the umpire, "Hey, Angel? Why you throw that man out? He knows you can't see BLEEP, and I know you can't see BLEEP. See all the people in the stands? They know you can't see BLEEP."

Hernandez, sweating and in no mood for humor or critique, thumbed Villanueva out, and in a twinkling, Villanueva was off the field, showered, changed, and at the airport to catch a plane to Chicago to see his wife, Gizelle.

Ahh, love.

CHAPTER FOUR

Twitches, Tremors and Theatrical Tic Douloureux

"She slithers, she shakes, she crawls on her belly like a reptile."
—ANONYMOUS ANNOUNCER WHO INTRODUCED
BELLY DANCER LITTLE EGYPT

"Post hoc ergo propter hoc (After this, therefore because of this)."
—ANONYMOUS—LATIN DEFINITION OF FALLACY IN LOGIC

You've seen it before: The game is on the line, you've been sitting in your seat for three-and-a-half hours and want the game to end soon, and the pitcher tugs at his cap, adjusts his sleeve, goes to the rosin bag, and taps his glove three times before hitching up his pants twice and touching the bill of his cap. Meanwhile, the hitter is a human rain delay of his own as he steps out of the batter's box, adjusts both of his batting gloves, taps the dirt off his cleats with exactly four knocks on each shoe, adjusts his batting gloves again, takes off and puts on his batting helmet, swipes his hand across the lettering on his uniform, steps back into the box and digs in with precisely four back-foot digs and two front-foot jabs as he takes three practice cuts and on the last one, points directly to the pitcher with his lumber. Then the pitcher steps off the rubber and begins his ritual again, and before he moves back to the mound, the batter steps out and starts his routine again.

To the untrained eye, or to those who don't give a damn, this is meaningless, time-wasting theatrical calisthenics. The twitches, tic douloureux and tremors employed by baseball players are merely nervousness or gamesmanship or some physical ailment that needs to be looked at.

But to those who don't have lives save for baseball, there is a method to this madness. These movements and gyrations are practiced, precisely choreographed and designed to give the performer an edge, a comfort zone, a concentration point, a physical means of re-creating recent success by mimicking everything done before that last accomplishment was achieved or, perhaps, lucked into.

Many players believe that routine is the cornerstone to glory. If they do the same thing every time, they will be successful. Of course they only remember the good times. Convenient memory has allowed the average twitching player to forget that the last 20 times he tightened his belt, scratched his groin, and touched his bat to the tip of his nose, he struck out. He only remembers that 21 times ago, he hit a grand slam, and that good feeling is what he is trying to re-create. Used to practicing a swing, a batting stance, a pitching delivery or a fielding technique day in, day out for hours at a time until the movements are unconscious and second nature, a player brings that routine to what is hoped to be a luck-producing and success-yielding procedure by re-creating the exact circumstances surrounding his most vivid recent brilliance. If that selected memory is of gum-popping and neck-scratching routines in the on-deck circle or knee rubbing and tongue touching on the mound, then it is those movements that will be indelibly etched in the player's mind and will be re-created in every game hence ad nauseum.

Haphazard twitches, quavers and quivers? No way. Neruoses and idiosyncrasies? Maybe. Perpetuated paranoias? Perhaps. Strange and funny rituals? We think so.

Among those seemingly innocent or apparently silly mannerisms carried on with regularity by the game's greats, near greats and never-were-greats are the following:

AL SIMMONS

Philadelphia A's manager Connie Mack once said, "If only I could have nine players named Simmons." The Hall of Fame slugger played for the A's and several other clubs from 1924 to 1944, won two batting crowns, and hit .334 for his career with 307 home runs. He was a complete player, winning games with his hitting, baserunning, fielding and competitiveness, but he earned a nickname based on a flawed physical movement that didn't affect his play, but caused him no end of grief.

"Bucketfoot Al" Simmons, a name the outfielder despised,

came about because he would stand right-handed at the plate, plant his right foot (back foot) as the ball left the pitcher's hand and came toward him, and then as he made his step into the pitch, his left foot (front foot) would stride toward the third base dugout. He stepped, in baseball parlance, in the bucket. Many coaches and managers tried to get Simmons to change his technique and they all failed, just as Simmons succeeded to use the mechanics, teamed with a long bat, to belt out hit after hit.

Connie Mack finally told all to leave Simmons and his flawed technique alone, that he was better "wrong" than all his other players were "right."

DICK PORTER

Dick Porter was called "Twitchy" because he seemed to twitch all over whenever he played. He never stopped moving, whether in the outfield or at bat. The Indians outfielder from 1929 to 1934 moved and twitched often enough to bat .308 for his career. At the plate, he'd move, gyrate, wiggle and wag his bat, arms, leg and head, uncoiling just before each pitch.

GEORGE CUPPY

George "Nig" Cuppy went 162-98 pitching for the Cleveland Spiders and three other teams from 1892 to 1901. The 5'7", 160-pounder was one of the first pitchers to wear a glove. He also brought delay of the game and hesitation on the mound to an art form.

He would delight in taking as much time as possible between pitches and during his extra slow windup and delivery. He often exhorted hometown and visiting fans alike to count time out loud as he dragged on, much to the chagrin of wearying hitters.

It's not that he would stop in middelivery; he would just take so much time doing everything in slow motion during what was, in those days, a quick-moving ball game.

CHAN HO PARK

Now for real hesitation, look to the East. Chan Ho Park, known in his native South Korea as Park Chan Ho, is a young fireballer with the Dodgers. Taking a page from Satchel Paige's delivery book, as well as emulating many great Far East pitchers, Park incorporated a hesitation in his windup, sometimes coming to a complete stop for as much as 10 seconds in middelivery, to throw the batter off. Then he would complete the motion and throw — with startling speed and control.

Opposing American managers and hitters complained and the National League brass got together with umpires and said unofficially that the pitch would be a balk with men on base and an automatic ball with or without men on base.

Park parked his pitch, but don't be surprised to see it test the rules again.

"HERKY JERKY" HORTON
Also on the mound, Elmer Horton, who threw the pill from 1896 to 1898 for Pittsburgh and Brooklyn, seemed to put his body in opposite directions as he released the ball. This motion got him the nickname "Herky Jerky." He'd bend low and wiggle up, and his arms and legs would appear to go off to different compass points as he fired home. Horton didn't jerk enough, though, as he only went 0-3 with a 9.75 ERA.

KENT HRBEK
Big Kent Hrbek, the 6'4", 230-pound first baseman for the Twins, has an entire routine to enact before every game. He gets to the ballpark five hours before game time; most players are there two to two-and-a-half hours before game time.

He goes through various rituals and relaxation until he begins batting practice. He never stretches. Never. He said, "Other guys stretch 15 to 45 minutes a day. I stretch one or two times a season, if it's very cold."

Once up at bat, Herbie looks at the batter's box, smooths it out with his spikes then taps the plate. He said, "I read that those who tap the plate have better averages than those who don't tap. I'm a tapper."

He has also tapped the ball — 283 homers in his first 13 seasons.

TONY PHILLIPS
Oakland A's-Detroit Tigers switch-hitting infielder Tony Phillips, a steady performer for more than a decade, is a leadoff man, so he gets to the plate with a pristine batter's box awaiting him.

He carefully erases the back line of the box before looking in for that first pitch. He seems to do a particularly fine erasure job when he hits right-handed. He also generally hits higher righty than lefty.

His pre-at-bat gyrations include hip-wiggling and making certain he has dug in at the plate at least one full shoe width behind the now-erased legal back line. This overlooked cheating enables him to see the ball just that much longer and react later to the oncoming pitch. Sneaky but effective.

VISUALIZATION

What looks like transfixed stares to the outfield, statuelike catalepsy at the plate, indifference to the game at hand, or allegiance to an Eastern holy spot are often meditation or visualization techniques employed by ballplayers to get that all-important psychological edge. Why is this category in this chapter? Well, the chapter title is "Twitches, Tremors and Theatrical Tic Douloureux," and it looks pretty theatrical to me.

When Don Mattingly, the classy Yankee first baseman and team captain, isn't doing well, he visualizes all the kids in the stands watching him swing, and he concentrates on the swing to look good for the young fans. Generally, according to Mattingly, this attention translates into hits.

Mattingly also stops by the orange Yankee water cooler after each out he makes, stands nearby and takes off his cap and batting gloves, and follows the pitcher who has just gotten him. He says he's focusing on the pitcher and is trying to learn something he can use in his next at bat.

Former California Angels third baseman Jack Howell, who moved to the Japan Leagues when his days in the Majors were numbered, visualized and listened to music in a routine devised by Angels pysch-guy Ken Ravizza. Howell's act began when he got into the on-deck circle. He imagined hearing a familiar Christian rock tune, got into his stance, and faced the pitcher to time his swing. He imagined himself getting a hit. Then, still imagining hits and music, stepped into the batter's box. He cleaned out the batter's box with his spikes, erasing all other holes and marks. He took cleansing breaths, got rid of all negative thoughts, and put himself in control of the situation. After all this, Howell lasted only seven years in America with a .236 average . . . his worst two years (1990-1991) were his visualization years, in which he hit .228 and .207. That's a lot of effort for .207 and airfare to Japan.

Also largely unsuccessful is Chicago White Sox pitcher Kirk McCaskill's visualization technique. He stands on the mound, stares out to center field and picks out a spot on which to concentrate, like the 410-foot sign in dead center, the monuments at Yankee Stadium, the American flag, or a burned out light in the scoreboard. He says it helps him relieve stress and aids his concentration. The only thing is, all these spots are in home run territory, and McCaskill has seen his early career success (68 wins and 55 losses from 1985 to 1990) turn to 26-40 from 1991 to 1993 when he was at his visualizing peak. Here's a suggestion, Kirk, concentrate on the catcher's glove, or at least on a spot in foul territory.

A more successful visualization technique belongs to Atlanta Braves pitcher John Smoltz. In 1991, Smoltz was a dismal 2-11 in July when he sought out sports psychologist Jack Llewelyn. Llewelyn got the pitcher to concentrate on the psychologist's red shirt, which he wears to every Smoltz start. Smoltz sees the the shirt and he peers into home plate — Llewelyn has seats behind the plate — and finds it easier to concentrate on the task at hand, getting out opposing hitters. The pitcher went 12-2 the rest of that season and 2-0 in the National League Championship Series versus Pittsburgh and followed it up with a 15-12 1992 and 3-0 in postseason play. In his third red-letter and red-shirted year, Smoltz was able to find Waldo to the tune of 15-11. See, Smoltz concentrates behind the plate, not in front of it. McCaskill should look for red in foul territory. He'd be more successful.

CAUTIOUS CATCHERS

Gruff Yankees captain Thurman Munson confidently strode to the plate wearing his special helmet, the dirty one with the "NY" logo slightly off-center, then settled into the batter's box. Then before each pitch, he'd step out, open, tighten and close the wrist closure on his left batting glove, then his right. Munson hit .292 with 113 homers before his life was tragically cut short during his eleventh season.

Equally gruff Red Sox-White Sox backstop Carlton Fisk was a human rain delay at the bat. His routine before every pitch included stepping up to the plate wearing his always-smudge-brimmed helmet; tapping the stained headgear with his batting glove, gripping, loosening his grip and regripping the bat several times; pulling his shirtsleeves in every conceivable direction; getting each of his feet ready with proper kicks, stretches and minute movements; stepping out and then back in again; and taking three practice swings. Fisk played 24 years and bombed 376 homers.

Kirt Manwaring, the San Francisco Giants receiver stepped to the dish in a shiny helmet, tapped the plate once, swung his bat in a 360-degree arc, and then took two swings before each pitch. He never hit higher than .275 with 5 homers.

Sometimes it works . . . sometimes it doesn't. Maybe it's the dirty, off-kilter helmet that does it.

PERIPATETIC PITCHERS

Pascual Perez and his brother Melido Perez, both of whom pitched for the Yankees and others, ran off the mound at the end of each inning, contrary to the usual approach of walking leisurely off the mound. Melido said, "It shows respect to the hitters." Pascual said, "I don't want to be out there any longer than I have to be. The sooner I get into the dugout, the better."

Relief pitcher Doug Jones, who spent most of his career in Cleveland, will not look at the hitter until he goes into his delivery, and only when he is about to release the ball.

This is reminiscent of Dodger screwball pitcher Fernando Valenzuela's no-look technique in which he would stare skyward as he was about to deliver the pitch, focusing on the hitter only as he began his release of the ball.

Brian Holton was a Dodger pitcher with more than his share of quirks: He drove to the ballpark via the same route each game and made sure he stopped at the last traffic light on his way to Dodger Stadium (stopping even if the light was green); he got dressed the same way before each game; had an exact number of snuff cans in his pocket; wore a towel around his neck in the same style each game; drank the same number of cups of coffee at the ballpark; walked by himself to the bullpen; kept a small lasso in his pocket which he used to rope fellow pitchers' thumbs for good luck; sit in the same contorted position in the bullpen; and warmed up with the exact number and sequence of pitches.

In terms of theatrical gestures, Holton walked to the mound and "screwed himself in" with a 360-degree, counterclockwise routine. Then his Dodger bullpen catcher, Todd Maulding, would match it with a 360-degree walk of his own, which Holton checked out to make sure it was done.

Perfect-game pitcher Dennis Martinez, who spent years throwing effectively in Baltimore and Montreal before moving on to Cleveland, works the big chaw in his mouth, takes the ball from the catcher, spits tobacco juice into his hand, touches the bill of his cap, rubs juice onto the ball, darkens it to just the right shade and enables him to put a drop-hop on his fastball. He's been doing this for nearly 20 years and he hasn't been stopped yet.

SNEAKED PEEKS

Some hitters like to sneak peeks at the catcher — considered poor etiquette or cheating in some circles — to check out the location of the next pitch, or even the type of pitch coming up.

Keith Hernandez, the slick-fielding first baseman for the Mets and Indians, always tried to sneak a peek at the catcher for the pitch setup just milliseconds before the pitcher released the ball. Quick eyes. It paid off to the tune of one batting title and six .300 seasons.

Dave Magadan, Mets and Mariners first baseman, steps out of the batter's box, puts his right foot in the box, straightens his body to line up with the pitcher, then assumes the stance as he peeks over his back shoulder to check out the catcher and possibly steal a sign or glove position.

Cincinnati's Reggie Sanders is another of a growing number of peekers. He quickly moves his eyes to the catcher's glove and then the catcher's eyes to see if he can determine where the next pitch will be. This is really quick as the pitcher is about to go into his windup or stretch.

And we are seeing more and more batters look for this edge and more and more catchers disguise their intentions until the very last moment. Interesting chess game going on at home plate.

HUMAN RAIN DELAYS

As mentioned earlier in this chapter, Carlton Fisk really took his time at the plate. But the king, the original "Human Rain Delay," was Texas Ranger Mike Hargrove. Hargrove's routine has been reported many times, so to briefly describe it: Between each pitch he would step out of the batter's box, think for a moment, take his stance while still out of the hitting area, swing three times, adjust each batting glove, pull up his pants, put one foot in the batter's box, knock the dirt from his spikes, tap the plate with his bat, adjust each sleeve and his helmet — doing all of this slowly as he went over a number of things in his mind. Hargrove said, "It was the key to my concentration. I visualized each pitch, what each pitcher threw me in similar situations, and how I would best swing at his delivery. This gave me an edge."

His edge also gave him five .300 seasons and a career .290 average. It also wasted an enormous amount of time. It was once figured that in his excess of 6,500 trips to the plate, Hargrove wasted some 271 hours — that's *more than 11 days* — just fidgeting.

Today's heir apparent may be the Phillies' Len Dykstra. Dykstra's routine is currently being refined and includes assorted twitches, jiggles and stretches, both in and out of the batter's box, between each pitch. He doesn't quite have Hargrove's time down to a science, nor does he have an exact routine to go into before each pitch, but he's working on it, much to the chagrin of opposing pitchers, fielders and fans who want to make it home before midnight.

The routine he uses most often includes stepping back with one leg pointing to the plate and the other out of the batter's box, resting the bat between his legs, tripod style, adjusting both gloves, adjusting helmet top with his left hand, staring at the pitcher, waiting, kicking dirt in batter's box, taking one practice swing, pointing bat at the pitcher, steping into the batter's box, and getting into his hitting crouch, and setting.

Not bad. Wait until he refines it; he could be up there for hours.

MARQUIS GRISSOM

Montreal Expos speedster Marquis Grissom often steals more than 50 bases per season and really worries about his edge and about pickoffs and jumps. Following each pickoff attempt — the unsuccessful ones, of course, since a successful attempt would have Grissom walking back to the dugout — he paws the dirt in front of the bag with his hand or foot and dig a trench. He feels this will allow him to get lower on a diveback and get under the first baseman's tag.

RICKEY HENDERSON

The most successful base stealer of all-time in the Majors is Oakland-Yankees-Oakland-Blue Jays-Oakland speedster Rickey Henderson. On the bases, he goes into a crouch and stares at the pitcher's eyes, his legs and every movement. He is a real student of pitchers' moves; all good base stealers are.

He is also seen talking to himself, telling himself to concentrate on the pitcher and get a good jump.

But he is most self-talkative at the plate.

Henderson tells himself to be patient, to take the walk, or to look for a pitch in his zone.

And he will often slap himself on the leg as he talks in an effort to drive his point home.

MARTIAL ARTS

In a pregame ritual designed to loosen them up mentally and physically, Dodger pitchers Jim Gott and Kevin Gross went through homegame rituals in which they practiced Hopkido, a Korean form of karate exercise, in an auxiliary clubhouse.

They worked out with local experts and karate champions to help them build their concentration and inner strength. Gott said, "It helps me in relation to how I view the hitters. It gives me things I can use on the mound."

Right. If the curveball doesn't get them, maybe a swift kick will.

TWITCHES AND TICS NUGGETS

Twins batting champ Tony Oliva opened a hole with his left foot and brought his right hand to his tongue for two good-luck licks before every pitch. "It worked that first time," he said, "so I stayed with it for 15 years." He hit .304 for his career with 220 homers.

Rugged Tigers oufielder Kirk Gibson always bends his left ear in half under his batting helmet. And you can tell if he's having a bad day. His missed swings will hit his back, and the bat's dirt and pine tar will create a stain right near his number.

Giants and Rangers first baseman Will "The Thrill" Clark adjusts his batting gloves before every pitch, touches his gloves to the pine tar on his bat, adjusts his helmet with the now-tacky gloves, puts a scowl on his face, squints to the pitcher and pushes his front (right) shoulder of his uniform with his back hand. Then, a mere two practice swings and he's ready to hit away. Clark hit .301 with 29 homers and 116 RBI in 1991.

Former San Francisco slugger Kevin Mitchell tugged his uniform above his back shoulder to get comfy before every pitch. Mitchell hit .291 with 47 homers and 125 ribbies in 1989.

Another ex-Giant, Rick Leach, virtually danced at the plate prior to every pitch. After an exaggerated wiggle of the hips, Leach would employ a seven-step back-front-back-front prance before moving into a closed stance. In Leach's only year with the Giants, 1990, he hit .293 with 2 homers and 16 RBIs.

Like I said before, sometimes it works and sometimes it doesn't.

Other home plate gyrations:

Ex-Yankees, Angels, Padres, Blue Jays outfielder Dave Winfield knocks dirt off his spikes with a healthy bat tap, first the front foot then the rear, followed by a short walk forward in the batter's box, then a quick kick of the dirt around him, followed by a quick practice cut or two before each delivery.

Blue Jays outfielder Devon White is a plate tapper—two to five taps with his front hand only on the bat, followed by two-to-five practice swings before each pitch.

Brad "The Animal" Lesley, a 6'6", 225-pound Cincinnati Reds reliever who gained fame and a cult following in Japan playing for the Hankyu Braves, would work himself into a frenzy and give a loud, gutteral, prehistoric-sounding cavemanesque yell before every tough pitch or "must"-out situation. Following a big out, he would go into his "chain saw" routine and "chop down" the fallen batter in lumberjack pantomime.

Jake "Eagle Eye" Beckley, a Hall of Fame first baseman for the Pirates, Reds and others from 1888 to 1907, hit better than .300 thirteen times during his career. When he was on a hitting tear, which was often, he'd wiggle at the plate, point his bat directly at the pitcher's eyes, and scream out a bone-chilling "Chicakazoola" at the top of his lungs. This unnerved many hurlers who offered up less than their best just to get rid of this intimidating banshee.

Chicago Cubs third baseman Ron Santo, who played the hot corner with prowess (though more hitting than fielding prowess) at Wrigley Field from 1960 to 1973, clicked his heels a la Dorothy of the *Wizard of Oz* after each Cubbie victory in 1969. The team started off hot and the clicking became more frequent, eventually catching on with die-hard Cub fans, who clicked along with him. As the team's inevitable slump occurred late in the season and wins became less regular, the clicking was forgotten.

Wally Joyner, the Angels and Royals first baseman who hit home runs into "Wally World" at Anaheim Stadium during the 1980s, taps his spikes three times after every pitch. It helps him think of taking three good cuts.

Big Mel Hall, the fierce-looking slugger with the Cubs, Yankees and Indians before taking his act to Japan in 1993, would stare down the pitcher, then take three or four big chews on his gum or seeds. During a clutch situation, he'd spit out whatever he had in his mouth, watch where the ejected material landed, and give another stare to the pitcher. It helped him get 134 homers in America and put fear in the hearts of many young pitchers.

Kevin Maas, a two-year wonder with the Yankees — 21 homers in 79 games in 1990 and 23 dingers in 148 games in 1991 — stepped up to the plate and checked out the "X" he inscribed on the bottom of his bat. (The "X" is for "X-Maas" — a combination of his last name and Christmas.) Then, after each pitch, he would step out, swing, adjust his collar, hike up his pants, slap and adjust his shoulder, adjust his helmet, and go back to his collar before going into a really uncomfortable looking sit-down-style crouch, which looked tough to hit out of for a guy 6′3″, 195 pounds. Well, it worked for two years, anyway.

CHAPTER FIVE

Fashion Fanatics

"Clothes make the man."
—ANONYMOUS

"We are by nature all as one, all alike, if you see us naked; let us wear theirs and they our clothes and what is the difference?"
—ROBERT BURTON

Time was that teams had uniform codes of behavior and dress for their players. Players rode on trains and dressed in white shirts, dark suits and subdued ties. On the field, they all wore their stirrup socks the same length, their hair the same length, and their unis in the same manner. But with the emergence of individuality, the term "uniform" has shrunk, and players go their own way in garb on and off the field.

For many ballplayers, whatever is the current rage is the way to go. High-top shoes or low-cut? Stirrups pulled so high they look like pinstripes or worn low like "the real ballplayers wore them in the 1930s and 1940s?" Shirts buttoned or unbuttoned?

Off the field, it's usually the same. Are Western garments hip? Is long hair or close-cropped brushed-back the "in" do? Is grunge in? For many players, that's the only look they feel comfortable with. Baggy or tight fitting? Tailored to the extreme with European styling or T-shirt and jeans? Pastels? Loud prints or subdued businesslike conservativism?

It's all up to the individual player, and usually, the choice is less than a stylish one.

Few ballplayers have appeared on the cover of *GQ*. Fewer still make any of the "best-dressed" lists. And even fewer are invited to offer fashion tips to the Court of St. James. Still, baseball players have their own style when it comes to attire, and often, it is used as a means to capture that elusive butterfly of luck.

As we've seen in past chapters, players use clothing in a routine manner, believing that the lucky socks or tie worn during a hitting streak will continue the streak. Again it is conveniently forgotten that the same apparel was worn during an 0-for-20 slump earlier that year, but a game-winning homer was belted the same day I wore this striped tie with that plaid jacket, the argyle socks and the polka-dotted shirt, so that's what I'll wear to the park every day from now on.

Fashionable, no. But fashion conscious, or conscious of what was worn regardless of fashion, is what stands out in the minds of many players. It may indeed provoke a "Your mother dresses you funny" response, but if the player is hitting or pitching well and the team is winning, what do you care if the fashion police have a warrant out for his arrest?

Try these on for size.

CASEY STENGEL

The Old Professor was a mentor of the New York Yankees. Case guided the Bronx Bombers to ten pennants and seven World Championships in 12 years (from 1949-1960). He looked old and weathered by the time the Yanks got him. He was 59 in 1949 but looked older than his years. In 1952, when a young Mickey Mantle was tutored by Stengel on how to play caroms off the Yankee Stadium walls, The Mick was astonished that his skipper had been a ballplayer. Stengel growled, "I wasn't born old."

Still, when Stengel was in his late 60s and Tony Kubek came to the club (in 1957), Casey had the look of an ancient mariner with a knot the size of an apple on his leg, the aftermath of an accident he absorbed years earlier when a taxicab hit him and knocked him to the pavement.

Fashion? Well, this old, spindly legged, bowlegged man with a spare tire around the middle wore a tight-fitting red union suit for warmth in the opening weeks of the season. If the team started out well, he'd keep the ratty long underwear on throughout the year.

Picture this wrinkled old man with bowed, toothpick legs, a knot above his ankle and a well-rounded belly. Billy Martin used to get his manager's goat by doing an impression of Stengel. Martin would put on a too-tight union suit, pad his middle with towels, stick a baseball under the suit on his leg, and walk around like a cowboy who had spent too much time in the saddle. The players howled, Casey growled, but the old man kept wearing his good-luck longjohns nonetheless.

Kubek remembered that even in July, with the temperature soaring above 100 degrees, Stengel would wear the old underwear, though it had tears in the knee and fabric pills throughout the thing.

The players would plead with Casey to throw it out and buy a new one, and he'd decline. Then they'd plead with him to take the thing off because it was too hot and they worried about his health. That's when Ol' Case would make a concession; he'd leave the rear trap door open "for ventilation."

But the suit stayed on, through hot weather and cold — and the Yankees kept winning.

SCOTT ERICKSON

The ace of the Minnesota Twins staff, 6'4", 225-pound righty Scott Erickson, is a vision of darkness on the mound. When it is his day to pitch, his teammates call it "The Day of Death," as Erickson arrives at the ballpark dressed entirely in black and continues that theme when he takes the mound.

He likes black and disdains white, so he covers all of the lighter color he can before he takes the hill.

He pulls his dark stirrup socks down to cover his white sanni socks, then uses black tape to cover any white that shows.

He pastes lamp black on his shoes to eradicate the white trade name on his footwear, which is custom-made without the traditional white stripes.

His glove is black, the striping on the glove is black, and a batter can only see that big black oblong, behind which are his dark, glaring eyes, as the glove covers all the rest of his face.

Erickson puts himself in a zone on the mound, as well as during pregame warm-ups. Fortified with a good-luck spaghetti dinner, he heads for the park to blacken his gamewear. Once he begins his stretching, he begins to talk — or even yell — to himself. "I don't like anyone touching me or talking to me," he says.

He psyches up and becomes "The Darkman."

Of course when you throw a 92 mph fastball, it hardly matters whether you wear black, white or pink on the mound. But Erickson likes black, so he'll stick with it.

Note: His bark may be worse than his bite. Erickson employs one more ritual that belies his darkness. Before each start, before he begins his warm-ups in the bullpen, he calls his mother. After listening to Stephanie Erickson's critique of his last start—"She really knows how I pitch and analyzes my motion and location as well as anyone in the game," says Erickson—Erickson waits for the words he longs to hear: "Good luck."

Then, with Mom on his side and dressed in his all-black attire and demeanor, he can get on with the game at hand.

His black art has worked well to win him 20 games one season but lose 19 in another.

OTHER DARK MEN

Two others who are using black as their diamond color of choice are San Diego Padres pitcher Trevor Hoffman and Atlanta Braves shortstop Jeff Blauser.

Hoffman, taking a page from Erickson's black book, dyed his glove and spikes completely black. He wears a goatee that is black, too.

He says, "I don't have black anger; this only gives me focus. I wish I could get angry and look like a mean, unapproachable ogre, but just because I look like death doesn't mean I intimidate anyone." Hoffman went 4-6 with a 3.90 ERA in 1993. He apparently didn't intimidate many hitters.

Blauser wears a pair of dyed black, old-style spikes. Using the Erickson method, he paints over the white stripes on his footwear with black polish. His isn't a focusing technique; his is a protest of the shoe company. He says, "They don't give me new shoes when I ask, and when I do get new shoes from them, they're always the wrong size, so I'm not giving them free publicity."

"DIRTY AL" GALLAGHER

Al Gallagher had the longest name this side of Calvin Coolidge Julius Caesar Tuskahoma "Buster" McLish. Gallagher's given name was Alan Mitchell Edward George Patrick Henry Gallagher, but he earned the nickname "Dirty Al." He played third base for the Giants and Angels from 1970 to 1973, hustling on every play he was involved in, but seldom looking like a stylish pro athlete.

Gallagher's uniform was seemingly always in need of a good washing. Dirty doesn't do the uni justice. Gallagher really didn't care about cleanliness, just playing baseball—in the dirt. He wasn't interested in anything but sports and competing hard. Once in college, he was dressed up—with clean clothes—and a greased pig contest was held. Gallagher wasn't entered, but decided to catch the unctuous porcine anyway. Gallagher caught the thing, snuggled it, had a drink with it, danced with it, and then, after he put it down, began asking Santa Clara debutantes to dance. They declined due to noxious pork smells rising from Gallagher's clothes.

On another occasion in college, he went on a 22-game hitting streak, and true to baseball tradition, did not wash his uni for fear of stopping the streak. As Santa Clara played only about three games a week, this unwashed uniform went eight weeks between detergent baths. He admits to keeping unwashed and unchanged jockstraps, socks, sanitary socks, undershirt "sleeves" and sweatshirts, as well as the actual uniform shirt and pants. Gallagher didn't want to wash out any hits.

He kept that demeanor as a pro, and even his teammates would refrain from hanging around his locker on hot August afternoons.

DICK "DIRT" TIDROW

Dick Tidrow, a key pitcher for the Yankees and other teams from 1972 to 1978, was nicknamed "Dirt" by his teammates. It comes from his usual disregard for a clean uniform. Before games, usually during batting practice, he and other Yankee pitchers would play games of "flip," in which a handful of players get together and knock the ball to each other using only their gloves. Sort of like a Harlem Globetrotters pregame "Georgia Brown" drill, only with baseballs and gloves. Tidrow was very competitive and was often seen diving in the dirt and grass to make the plays in this contest. This left his uniform filthy, and while other players would change, Tidrow stayed in his and often took the mound later during the game, with smudges all over himself.

"SLOPPY" THURSTON

Hollis Thurston was a pitcher from 1923 to 1933, going 89-86, mostly for the White Sox and Dodgers. He liked to finish what he started—he led the league in complete games with 28 in 1924—

but he didn't much care how he looked doing it. From the time he was a child, spilling milk on his clothes, through his adulthood, when he spilled food, drink and anything else he got his hands on on his uniform and clothing, Thurston was generally seen in disarray.

His father owned a restaurant in Arizona called "Sloppy's Place," and the family used to feed soup and sandwiches to tramps and hobos who came around the back door.

CHRIS "STYLES" SHORT

Chris Short, an ace pitcher for the Philadelphia Phillies from 1959 to 1972, was the opposite of stylish. He gained the reputation for being the worst-dressed and worst-kept player in baseball. He was generally attired in baggy sweaters and shirts and trousers that were either too long or too short, but nearly always too tight. On road trips, his clothes traveled, not in a suitcase, but in a cellophane bag or rolled up inside newspapers.

Teammate Tim McCarver often tells of the 6'4" Short entering the Phillies clubhouse wearing an expensive new powder blue suit . . . with coat sleeves about four inches too short and trouser cuffs four inches above his ankles.

VADA PINSON

Classy outfielder Vada Pinson, who played for 18 years (1958-1975) mostly for Cincinnati, knew the value of shoes: He stole 305 bases and beat out 2,757 hits during his 2,469 games. Pinson spent hour after hour shining shoes in the clubhouse. He'd sit, think about the upcoming game, and shine his baseball footwear until his face reflected in the leather. He said, "Before I left the game, I got everyone shining their shoes. Frank Robinson started doing it, but he was so lousy at it, he stopped."

He shined his shoes before every game in the Majors—"I learned the process in the Pacific Coast League in 1958"—and continues the ritual as a coach and scout. He's still shining shoes today—his and those of any player who comes to him for the work.

Pinson's shoe leather observations include the following: "Warren Spahn and Lew Burdette of the [Milwaukee] Braves used to spit on their shoes to make them dirty."

And the polish of choice for the man who's been shining, playing and coaching in the Bigs for nearly 40 years? Pinson said, "There's no comparison. Kiwi black. Gotta be."

PASCUAL PEREZ

The Dominican enigma Pascual Perez was a better pitcher than his 67-68 record revealed. In 11 years from 1980 to 1991, punctuated by drug suspensions, stints on the disabled list, and multiple occurrences of getting lost on his way to the ballpark, he was alternately a relied-upon staff ace who won the big games and a disappointment who lost games he should have won.

Perez made several fashion statements along the way. He wore pounds of gold chains, which jumped up and down as he made his characteristic sprint to and from the mound. He wore long, curly hair and pulled his baseball cap down so low you couldn't see his eyes.

Imagine being a hitter, expecting a fastball from this 6'2", 162-pounder from the Dominican Republic, and fearing that he can't even see home plate, let alone the hitter.

Perez said, "I pull down the cap so I can only see from the batter's waist to the ground. This way, I can't throw it high and my pitches have to be low — at the waist to the knees."

Another time Perez said that a batter couldn't see his eyes or his intentions with his cap pulled down.

HANK AARON

Another player who used his cap as a focusing tool was baseball's all-time home run leader, Hank Aaron.

When Hammerin' Hank was slumping or not seeing the ball well, he'd take off his cap and hold it over his face — not at the plate, of course, but when he was on the bench or in the on-deck circle.

Then Aaron would look through the air holes on the top of his cap and stare at the pitcher, his release, and the ball as it traveled to home plate. Aaron reasoned that following the flight of the ball through the tiny holes would isolate the sphere with all else blocked out. Then, when Aaron would stand at the plate and see a bigger ball against a wider background, he said he could see it better and the ball would appear larger to him.

It worked to the tune of 755 home runs and a .305 average.

AL KALINE

Classy Detroit Tigers outfielder Al Kaline employed the Aaron technique, but with a different piece of equipment. He'd sit on the bench and hold his glove up to his face. He wasn't hiding from the public; he was simply focusing on the ball through the open space where his glove's webbing was attached to the body.

He could then isolate the ball and see it better at the plate.

Often, after getting a good read on a pitch from the dugout, he'd place his glove on top of his head — a sort of glove-cap.

Neither practice seemed to hurt. Kaline knocked out 3,007 hits and 399 homers during his 22-year career.

PAUL GIBSON

Lefty reliever Paul Gibson, the 47th player to play for both the Yankees and Mets (although he spent most of his career with the Tigers), wore an upside-down number 48 on his baseball garter when he pitched for Detroit and put on a Michigan State University T-shirt after every win and a Michigan University T-shirt after every loss. He also carried two silver dollars with him wherever he went — even on the mound. Both were given to him by his grandfather, one in 1973 and the other in 1974 just before his grandfather passed away.

DENNIS COOK

Reliever and spot starter Dennis Cook, who spent his first six seasons throwing for four different organizations, had the ugliest, grungiest baseball cap in the Majors. His headwear was always sprinkled liberally with rosin. He'd take the rosin bag before every game and pat the white powder onto his cap. He claimed it was done so he wouldn't have to bend down during a game to pick up the rosin bag and all he needed to do on the mound was go to his cap.

At 6'3", I guess he figured it was a long way down.

"SILK STOCKING" SCHAFER

Harry Schafer, a third baseman for Boston of the National League from 1876 to 1878, was as dapper as they come. He wore silk stockings wherever he went, and some teammates even accused him of wearing the hose under his baseball socks. It didn't help. He hit .257 with no homers in 105 games.

SCOTT LEWIS

Here's a fashion note that may belong in the Bad Hops chapter of this book: It's bad luck for a pitcher to wear a hitter's uniform.

On March 13, 1992, California Angels pitcher Scott Lewis was trying to make the club when, before a scheduled spring training game in Tucson against the Indians, the 6′3″, 178-pound right-hander lost his uniform.

Angels batting coach Rod Carew, a Hall of Fame hitter who stands 6′0″ tall and weighs 185, gave the pitcher his uni to wear on the mound.

Lewis initially declined the offer, saying there were too many hits in Carew's uniform — 3,053 of them in a 19-year career that saw him hit .328. But eventually he relented, though Lewis should have stuck with his instincts. He gave up seven runs in three innings as the Indians beat California 10-2.

Lewis claimed that the ill-fitting uniform put his arm angle off.

TOUGH GUY

David Wells, the 6′4″, 230-pound Toronto lefty pitcher who defected to Detroit, never wears long-sleeved shirts (baseball sleeves). No matter how cold it gets, Wells cuts off his sleeves. He says he likes his freedom and his tough guy appearance. Of course he does wear an earring in his left ear.

BATTING GLOVES

Third baseman Gary Gaetti (Twins, Angels, Royals) goes through more than 200 batting gloves a year. If he goes hitless with a glove on, he'll throw it away immediately. After a strong career start, he's been throwing away more and more gloves as he goes on.

Slugging outfielder Jessie Barfield (Toronto, Yankees, Yomiuri Giants, et al.) also went through 200 batting gloves a year because he liked them to fit tight. If they feel OK, he'd stick with them through hitting streaks or slumps. But if they felt loose, they got lost.

Another slugger who found his way to Japan, Rob Deer, who also belted bombs for the Giants, Brewers and Tigers, goes through 200 gloves per year as well. His gloves must feel absolutely perfect before he'll use them in a game. He's thrown out whole boxes of batting gloves that didn't conform to his standards. Even if he's homered with the handwear on, if it's not comfortable, it's tossed. He likes them tight and not stretched out. Don't we all?

The champion of all champions in the batting glove department is five-time batting champ Wade Boggs. Boggs, the Boston Red Sox phenom of Fenway who moved on to Yankee Stadium to play for the Yankees, admits to going through *1,000* batting gloves a year. One hit, one swing, one practice swing, or maybe just a look or two in the package is all Boggs needs to determine if the gloves are keepers or tossers. If everything isn't just so, it's a new glove out of the package and another on the scrap heap. Boggs isn't just a glove man, he also goes through about 70 bats a year — they have to feel perfect in his hands or its bye-bye batty. Yet the feel can change from one at bat to another . . . but maybe that's why he hit better than .300 in 11 of his first 12 seasons.

RUNNING GLOVES

Just like some Yuppies don't really wear the sweaters they tie around their necks, so some players don't really wear their batting or sliding gloves; they just like to carry them.

Oakland A's outfielder Scott Brosius learned in his rookie season (1992) to carry two batting gloves in his left hand while he runs the bases. He hit .249 and stole six bases in 70 games in 1993. Maybe three gloves would allow him to get on base more often . . . or four.

Boston Red Sox slugging first baseman Mo Vaughn carries both of his batting/running gloves in his right hand when running the bases. With nine stolen bases and 46 homers in his first three seasons, Big Mo (6'1", 240 pounds) shouldn't care what he wears on the base paths and only pay attention to keeping that powerful swing sweet.

New York Yankees second baseman Pat Kelly also carries his batting gloves while touring the base paths, and he stole all of 22 bases his first two Big League seasons. Funny, but Rickey Henderson wears his gloves while on base, and he's stolen more than 1,100 bases in his career.

One-time Cleveland Indians speedster Alex Cole, who wears sliding gloves and carries extras in his hands and pockets, stole five bases in a game against Kansas City on August 1, 1990. His teammates taped the name "Willie Mays Hays," the fictional stolen-base king from the movie *Major League*, and five sliding gloves to his locker after the performance. Cole took the hint and stole two more the next game and finished the season with 40 thefts.

And Florida Marlins catcher Benito Santiago (who is a leader in numerical fashion, thanks to his choosing the number 09 to wear on his uniform—the only zero to appear before another number in Major League history) is also a player who comes prepared with gloves for practical as well as adornment use. Santiago wears his two black batting/running gloves on his hands to grip the bat well, prevent blisters and save his hands on headfirst slides. But he is also a member of the "let's also keep extra gloves in our back pocket brigade." Santiago places a black glove in each rear pocket, with the fingers protruding from the pocket top. They flop up and down when he runs and give the appearance of waving good-bye as he tours the bases. Style, man, style.

TURN BACK THE CLOCK

On June 19, 1991, the Baltimore Orioles promoted "Turn Back the Clock Day" as a tribute to their 1966 squad that won the World Series for the first time in Baltimore's history.

Tickets were sold at 1966 prices, the public address system played 1966 music, and players wore 1966-style uniforms.

The O's held a 4-3 lead in the ninth when closer Gregg Olson was called in to save the game. Olson, a 1990s kind of guy, couldn't get into the 1960s spirit. He gave up five runs, four hits and two walks. He threw three wild pitches and committed a throwing error to lose the game 8-4.

He stormed into the locker room and ripped off his 1966 uniform. He threw his shirt, pants, stirrup socks, sannies and shoes into the garbage.

He said, "I will never, ever wear anything associated with any 'Turn Back the Clock Day' as long as I live."

FASHION PROFIT

John Kruk, the Phillies slugger, has worn a number of numbers since he came to play for Philadelphia in 1989, including 11, 19, 28 and 29.

He switched from the first two numbers because he didn't feel comfortable in them. He was happy with 28 until Mitch Williams came to town and asked for it. Williams had had that number before, and his wife even had jewelry with 28 on it, so Williams asked Kruk to make the switch. Kruk did it willingly. "He gave me two cases of beer for the number," says Kruk, who says he'd gladly give up 29 for some beer or a couple of good dinners.

NUMBER SALUTE

Rocket Roger Clemens, the fastballing right-hander for the Red Sox, uses numbers to show his respect for other ballplayers. Clemens, familiar to his fans as the man with number 21 on his back, has worn number 14 to pay homage to former teammate Jim Rice and number 24 to salute ex-teammate Dwight Evans.

He has also worn patches on his uniform with number 34 on them to show his admiration for a fellow Texas pitcher, Nolan Ryan.

On the day Seattle pitcher Randy Johnson became the 12th pitcher to notch 300 strikeouts in a season (September 26, 1993) by whiffing 13 Oakland A's, he wore uniform number 34 instead of his usual 51 to pay tribute to Ryan, who had retired a few days earlier.

San Diego Padres slugging first baseman Dave Staton put up some big Minor League numbers and was expected to do the same in The Bigs. He selected number 28 when he was called up by the Pads in September 1993, but changed to number 31 in 1994 as a salute to Dodgers catcher Mike Piazza. Staton's reason: "Mike Piazza was a great Minor League player and a tremendous Major Leaguer already — Rookie of the Year in 1993. If I wear his number, maybe I'll hit better." As 28, Staton hit .262 with five homers in 17 games for San Diego after being called up in 1993, but was slumping big time with his 31. Staton slumped badly in the first quarter of 1994, with an average under .200 and was eventually sent back to the minors. Piazza, who said Staton hit the longest home run he had ever seen in the minors — when Staton was with Las Vegas and Piazza was with Albuquerque in the AAA Pacific Coast League — said Staton didn't need anyone's number to do well; all he needed was time to iron out his swing. Easy for a Rookie of the Year to say . . . especially since he's already *got* his number.

MINOR LEAGUE NUMBER SALUTE

In 1989, playing for the Phoenix Firebirds, slugging superstar Matt Williams wore number 10. He was off to a horrible start and threw that number on the scrap heap and switched to number 9. Using number 9 in San Francisco, Williams has become a major star and one of the most productive hitters in the National League.

In 1990, the Firebirds assigned number 10 to Kash Beauchamp, son of former Major Leaguer Jim Beauchamp. Kash had hit better than .500 in spring training for the AAA club, but when the season started and he put on his Phoenix 10, his average plummeted 150 points. Told of Williams's troubles with the number, Beauchamp threw it on the scrap heap, declaring, "If Matt Williams can't hit with that number, I sure can't." Beauchamp became number 6, and his average became more respectable.

Note: The number 10 was also stayed away from in South Dakota when numbers began being issued in the 1920s. Ballplayers in South Dakota refused to wear the numeral because the name of the pub in Deadwood, South Dakota, where Wild Bill Hickock was shot in the back and killed in 1876 was "The Number Ten Saloon."

RON GANT

Former Atlanta Braves outfielder Ron Gant entered the 1991 World Series with an aphorism printed where only he could see it. On the inside bill of his Braves cap, Gant inscribed, "I-Will-I-Can-I-Am."

In the 1991 Series, he didn't, he couldn't, he wasn't. He went 0-for-9 in the final two games at Minnesota's Metrodome, to finish the series with a .267 average and no homers. The Twins won it in seven games.

JIM LEFEBVRE

When Jim Lefebvre was manager of the Seattle Mariners (1989-1991), he was on a graph of constant improvement, bringing the team from a 68-93 mark the year before he took over, to 73-89 his first season at the helm, to 77-85 his second year, and a team-record 83-79 his final year.

That final season, he had some fashion help. The Mariners started 1991 ignominiously, losing their first five games. At 0-5,

Lefebvre searched for something to change his club's luck. A friend gave him a bilious hot pink-and-black, tiger-striped bodysuit. He thought seriously about putting the loud suit on and walking out in front of his players and telling them, "You've got to relax and have a good time." Instead, he hung the brightly colored wear on a hanger in his office locker, touching it for luck.

The Mariners won their next eight games and kept winning to finish the season above .500 for the first time in their 15-year history.

Fashion note: The same day Lefebvre got his lucky bodysuit, team owner Jeff Smulyan put on a good-luck, striped tie. He wore the neckwear during the entire winning streak and went back to it periodically during the season. Team officials estimated that Smulyan wore the tie close to 100 times that season. It was hoped he had it cleaned. One hundred games represents a lot of hot dogs, mustard and peanut shells splattering a single necktie.

FASHION BATTLE: THE BABE VERSUS A BABE

On September 26, 1992, an auction was held in Bend, Oregon, at which a number of celebrity items were sold to the highest bidders.

Among the items up for bid was the jersey actor John Goodman wore while playing Babe Ruth in the feature film *The Babe*.

Another piece of memorabilia on the table was the uniform worn by rock star Madonna in her baseball movie *A League of Their Own*.

The Goodman/Babe jersey went for $1,600.

The Madonna uniform was sold for $9,000.

Apparently people would not pay as much to get into Babe Ruth's movie shirt as they would to get into Madonna's pants.

ANOTHER FASHION BATTLE

In the 1991 World Series between the Atlanta Braves and Minnesota Twins, a battle of the good-luck styles took place.

When the Braves needed runs or defense, the players on the bench would wear their "shark" rally caps, putting the bills of the caps on the back of their heads and pointing the bills skyward.

The Twins and their fans, in the same situations, used "Homer Hankies" and waved the cloths in a plea for success.

The hankies wrapped up the sharks in seven games.

And in a Series note, Braves catcher Greg Olson (no relation to then-Orioles pitcher Gregg Olson) played the Fall Classic while wearing a T-shirt emblazoned with a caricature of Twins star outfielder Kirby Puckett. Olson explained that the shirt got him (and the Braves) to the World Series and kept Toronto (Minnesota's play-off rival) out. When both Puckett and Olson homered in the game played on October 12, Olson laughed as he showed off his T-shirt. An examination in the Twins' locker room showed that Puckett did *not* wear an Olson T-shirt. He homered anyway.

MORE T-SHIRT MAGIC

Knuckleball pitcher Charlie Hough wears a T-shirt with a picture of Elvis Presley on it under his uniform top when he's on the mound. Hough has a collection of "The King" shirts and has been wearing them for years. Some of his best-luck shirts bear the slogan "Elvis Lives."

When Angels and Royals first baseman Wally Joyner is on a hot streak, he'll turn his T-shirt inside out and wear it that way until his hot streak is over.

Pittsburgh pitcher Bob Walk color coordinates his T-shirts, and also uses them for advice. The T-shirt under his black-and-gold Pirates jersey is also black-and-gold and reads: "Work fast. Throw strikes." He tries to take his clothing's advice to heart.

WRISTBAND MAGIC

A Yankee who reveres the tradition of the Bronx Bombers is center fielder Bernie Williams. Williams wears the numbers 3, 4, 5 on his Yankee wristbands in tribute to three great Yanks of the past: Babe Ruth (3), Lou Gehrig (4) and Joe DiMaggio (5). He says he does it not so much for luck, but more to keep tradition alive. He'd need wristbands on each wrist, leg, and several other areas of the body to pay homage to all the men whose numbers the Yankees have retired (13 in all): Billy Martin (1); Ruth; Gehrig; DiMaggio; Mickey Mantle (7); Bill Dickey and Yogi Berra (8); Roger Maris (9); Phil Rizzuto (10); Thurman Munson (15); Whitey Ford (16); Elston Howard (32); Casey Stengel (37); and Reggie Jackson (44).

A different way of using wristbands was displayed by outfielder Shawn Abner, most notably when he was with the Chicago White Sox. Abner was a weight lifter who shaved his arms to better show off his bulging muscles. Did he wear wristbands on his arms? No. He wore them above his ankles. Abner said, "They're not wristbands; they're anklets." He said he was inspired by teammate Frank Thomas, who wore wristbands on his legs one day and hit two home runs.

No matter where he wore those things, he never approached the numbers put up by Thomas. A combination of wristband placement and talent might accomplish more.

FASHION STRATEGY PAYS OFF

The 1952 Denver Bears of the Western League, under manager Andy Cohen, wore white uniforms with dark patches to coincide with the strike zone. A dark blue shoulder pad set up from the armpits to the neck and another dark blue zone from the knees to the bottom of the pants outlined the hitting area and would seem to be beneficial to umpires and opposing pitchers. The hitters hated the idea and vetoed the notion the following years.

But in 1952, Denver won the Western League title, and Bear slugger Bill Pinckard led the loop in homers with 35.

Nowadays, with the shrinking strike zone, every team has a darkly colored strike zone on their uniforms . . . it's called a belt, which is just about the height and depth of the zone.

FASHION NUGGETS

Frugal New York Yankee lefty Ron Guidry wore the same stirrup socks throughout his entire 14-year career. "Louisiana Lightning" won 170 games and lost only 91 in 368 games with those tattered leggings.

Thurman Munson caught his entire career with the Yankees (1969-1979), 1,423 games, wearing two batting gloves under his catcher's mitt. And, as discussed briefly in the preceeding chapter, he always wore a batting helmet on which the "NY" logo was off-center. He was a working-class guy who didn't want to look stylish. Also, he homered the first game he wore the nonsymmetrical headgear and stayed with it from then on.

Yankee skipper Billy Martin added religion to fashion. He wore a tiny crucifix pin between the two "forks" of the "Y" on the "NY" logo on his Yankee caps. He said he wanted to remain close to God. Presumably that was also the case when he was arguing with umpires or opposing managers.

In 1992, the New York Mets' kangaroo court fined Vince Coleman $16 for letting his buddy, Willie McGee of San Francisco, use Coleman's glove during the Mets-Giants game. McGee caught eight Mets fly balls — the fine was $2 per catch — with Coleman's glove. McGee's own leather was stolen.

Dodgers catcher Mike Scioscia would turn his protective helmet around on all foul balls he'd chase after, then turn it around again when he got down behind the plate. Scioscia also mistreated his batting gloves. He spit on his right glove, then rubbed his two gloves together before every at bat. Can you say hygiene?

Tigers bombing first baseman Cecil Fielder needs sanni socks with "life" in them. Only Fielder knows what that means, but he'll stay with a "lively" pair and toss away all "lifeless" impostors.

Longtime Houston Astros reliever Dave Smith changed shoes after each blown save and kept wearing the same shoes after each successful save. With 216 saves, he kept the same shoes quite often. With blown save after blown save that put him out of baseball in 1993, he also became the Imelda Marcos of the bullpen.

Cincinnati Reds outfielder Deion Sanders had a problem on another field in 1992. While playing cornerback for the Atlanta Falcons of the National Football League, he was "forced" to leave a game for a series of downs when his earring fell out. He had to find the team's equipment man to put the jewelry back in. Suppose that happened in the seventh game of the World Series. Would he leave the game for a fashion pit stop?

When pitcher Tim Crews threw for the Dodgers from 1987 to 1992, he was prematurely gray before he was 30. In 1991, on advice from his mother, Crews, who had given up the game-winning hit in relief in three consecutive appearances from July 15 to 19, dyed his hair and trimmed and colored his moustache. In his next half dozen appearances, the now younger-looking and neater Crews pitched scoreless ball and soon became a bullpen stopper.

Former Dodger manager Leo Durocher was a fashion plate . . . and plate was the operative word. "Lippy" would occasionally reward his players by buying them suits and was known for his own sartorial splendor. He dressed as though he were going out on the town every night — and he might have — and was always prepared. He kept a tux handy and always carried spare false teeth — his two front teeth were not the ones he was born with — in a jeweled cuff link box. He was not shy about his looks or his abilities.

One player who is shy about both is Yankees pitcher Scott Kamieniecki. Kammie stays humble about his beginnings in the game and keeps a fashion reminder with him to keep in touch with his roots. Kamieniecki hangs his AAA minor league cap, from the Columbus Clippers, in his locker to remind him from where he came and that he could be sent back if his work and work habits aren't up to par.

Kamieniecki's teammate, Wade Boggs, known for many other superstitions and rituals, wears an owl's foot around his neck for luck and to remind him of *his* roots. Boggs wore one around his neck on a string when he was a child and it brought him luck; when it was stolen, his father hunted for a year to find another one. Boggs takes good care of this one . . . owls are hard to find in the Bronx, and it helps him remember his younger days.

Former New York Yankee Media Relations Director Jeff Idelson bought special ties that he felt were lucky. Once a tie went on, it stayed on until the Yanks lost. Then the tie was retired and a new lucky tie was sought. He went through a lot of ties and found that his luckiest one, a piece of neckwear he brought back from time to time when the club needed a win, was emblazoned with an Egyptian design depicting the Tut exhibit. When in trouble, he was tied to his mummy.

CHAPTER SIX

You Are What You Eat

"Moe, Larry . . . the cheese."
—JEROME "CURLEY" HOWARD

Some of these delicacies are best served at French restaurants named Chez Stadium, Willie Maison or Chateau du Ruthbuilt. As with fashion, where no one can tell a ballplayer how to dress, in food, no one can tell a ballplayer how to eat.

Babe Ruth used to mix pickled eels with chocolate ice cream and down a quart of beer at the same time. Wade Boggs ate nothing but chicken for nine years, until his batting average slipped under .350. And Gates Brown ate hot dogs on the bench until he was summoned to pinch hit, had to stuff the beef sticks in his uniform, doubled to center, and slid into second base as mustard covered his chest.

As those gentlemen were headline players, we've come to another area in which players will do, in these cases eat, whatever got them there. If a guy had leftover pizza for breakfast one day and he went 4-for-4, he'll eat pizza for breakfast for the next three weeks regardless of the fact that he went 0-for-30 the previous seven times he ate breakfast pizza. Convenient memory again serves to override natural cravings for different foods. That one day in the sun is what is remembered, and you wind up having players think, *Hmm, I went to this bratwurst place in Milwaukee the day before I pitched that one-hitter. Let's go there again so I can pitch well against the Brewers every time I hit town.*

While some of these dietary habits are rather harmless, some players go overboard at the table with gut-busting regularity.

Taste these morsels. . . .

"SWEETBREADS" BAILEY

Abraham Lincoln Bailey, a pitcher from 1919 to 1921 with the Cubs and Dodgers, was known as "Sweetbreads." He absolutely loved the delicacy and insisted on chowing down on them before every start. Oddly, he won only one of his six starting assignments in the Majors and picked up his three other career wins in relief.

"OIL CAN" BOYD

Dennis Boyd was an enigmatic pitcher with a lot of promise who threw for 10 years, going 78-77 from the early 1980s to 1991 with the Red Sox and Expos. He exhibited excellent control on the hill — often issuing fewer than one walk every four innings — but little of it outside the white lines.

While pitching in his hometown of Meridian, Mississippi, where beer is called "oil" and cans of brew are called "oil cans," Boyd earned a reputation for downing six-packs of oil after games.

He also got to the point, in the minors and in the Major Leagues, where he consumed his oil cans before games, often taking the mound with three or four cans in him, then finishing the game and downing another six-pack. Amazing for a 6'1", 150-pounder.

TONY OLIVA

Cuban-born Pedro Oliva y Lopez, known as Tony Oliva, was a sweet-swinging lefty outfielder for the Twins from 1962 to 1976.

Tony O. won three batting titles and was as superstitious as they come.

For batting strength, Oliva would eat mangoes whenever he could get them. "The luckiest mangoes," he said, "were in New York by way of Cuba. Whenever we were in town to play the Yankees, I'd go to the barrio section — from 198th Street to 118th Street — and stop by ex-Major Leaguer Julio Becquer's brother Orlando's place. Orlando would bring me mangoes he had brought in, illegally, from Cuba. Invariably, after eating one or two, I'd have a big night. I swear by mangoes."

In the Minor Leagues, however, he and fellow Cuban and Minnesota Twin Sandy Valdespino would eat meat loaf and apple pie every single day. Oliva said, "Whether we were in Tacoma or

Salt Lake City, it didn't matter. We'd order meat loaf and apple pie and eat the same food at exactly the same time every day. It worked. We both got to the Major Leagues."

BEN McDONALD

Louisiana native Ben McDonald, a first-round draft choice pitcher for the Baltimore Orioles, claims to have a favorite country dish—squirrel heads. He and his father seem to enjoy the same parts of the animal. No, not the white meat or dark meat. McDonald and son fight over the brain and tongue.

JOSE CANSECO

Texas slugger Jose Canseco loves tortoises, not to eat, but to collect. He owns a dozen of them, the largest of which weighs more than 40 pounds. He says he owns them because "fans, especially kids, can relate to animals." What makes this a food story is the tortoises' diet. Canseco's animals have a fondness for shoes, and one of them chowed down on teammate Willie Wilson's shoes when the two played for Oakland. Wilson was not amused.

TOM LASORDA

Los Angeles Dodger skipper Tom Lasorda is an eater's eater. In 1991, L.A. pitcher Kevin Gross rolled a 100-pound watermelon up to his manager's office and bet the Dodger-Blue bleeder that he couldn't eat the entire thing in 24 hours. Lasorda, who once won a bet by choking down 100 oysters in Houston, finished all but the rind and pits. He won, but his team went on a five-game skid.

DALE MURPHY

Atlanta Braves outfielder Dale Murphy was a model of consistency in the early 1980s, hitting 36, 36, 36, 37, 29 and 44 home runs from 1982 to 1987. He also had a recipe for bread that he baked and ate whenever he was in a slump. Watching Nathalie DuPree's cooking show on television, he observed her technique as she baked and prepared a bread meal, then developed his own recipe, which included garlic, herbs, cheese, Greek olives, mozzarella cheese, ham, pimientos and tomatoes.

The first time he tried the bread meal, he emerged from a deep slump by hitting two homers and driving in six runs—the begining of a sustained hitting tear. He swore by the meal thereafter.

RANDY JOHNSON

Seattle Mariners ace left-hander Randy Johnson has a food and music ritual before every start.

The big pitcher gets up at 9 A.M. and motors directly to the nearest International House of Pancakes for a big stack of flapjacks with extra maple syrup. While eating, he will read the entire local newspaper except for the sports page. Then he goes home, plays his drums for an hour, and drives to the ballpark. It has been worth two strikeout crowns and as many as 19 wins in a season.

JAKE KAFORA

Frank Jacob Kafora, a catcher from 1913 to 1914, was called "Tomatoes." He ate the red fruit with every meal, convinced that eating tomatoes would give him strength and speed. Kafora played in just 22 games with the Pirates. He never hit a Big League home run and never stole a Major League base.

"TACKY TOM" PARROTT

Thomas William Parrott, a pitcher from 1893 to 1896, went 39-48 with four saves in 115 games for the Reds, Cubs and Cards. He was an odd duck on many levels including the area of food. He seemed to delight in playing his cornet in the middle of the night, disturbing fellow boarders in his boarding house. He loved to ride his bicycle to the ballpark and once took a 25-mile ride before a game, losing track of time and arriving at the park just minutes before he was to take the field. He still had enough energy left to throw a complete game victory, though he gave up 15 hits in the process.

Parrott's food fetish deals with an opponent's luck against him. In an 1893 game he pitched for Cincinnati, Hall of Fame slugger "King" Kelly, who was ending his career with the Giants, managed to go 4-for-4 versus Parrott, despite being mired in a severe slump.

After the game, Parrott asked the aging icon what he had eaten for breakfast that morning, and Kelly told him it was a platter of ham and eggs. That night, Parrott stopped at a delicatessen and picked up a dozen eggs and a whole ham. He proceeded to eat that breakfast before every game he pitched for the rest of his career.

"T-BONE" KOSKI

William John Koski was a 6′4″, 190-pound reliever who lasted one year in the Majors, with the Pirates in 1951. Koski, who walked 28 batters in 27 career innings, obviously had a control problem.

As a growing, healthy and hungry 19-year-old rookie, rooming with Pittsburgh hurler Vern Law, he had finished dinner and ordered a second T-bone steak dinner. When sportswriter Les Biederman saw the rookie chow down on steak number two, he told him that if he could down a third, he'd pick up the check. Koski completed the assignment, and the sportswriter paid the tab.

Good appetite and poor control equal a short career.

OYSTERS

Tommy "Oyster" Burns, an outfielder who played from 1884 to 1895, mostly with the Dodgers, loved oysters. He ate them as often as he could find them and often swallowed handfuls of them before ball games. He said the mollusk increased his virility and stamina and made him strong. We don't know about the first two, but he did hit 66 home runs.

"Oyster Joe" Martina, a pitcher in 1924 for Washington, had a long, storied career in the minors, winning 349 games—No. 2 on the all-time Minor League list—and occupying the second spot all-time in bush league strikeouts with 2,770.

A wild fireballer, Martina was fond of the bivalve and began eating them when he was growing up in New Orleans. He was tagged with the nickname, however, when he was traded in the minors for two barrels of oysters.

CIGARETTES

They aren't food, but they *do* show up in the mouths of many ballplayers. One player uses tobacco sticks to calm his frayed nerves.

When pitcher Bryn Smith was in St. Louis with the Cardinals, he sweat out all of his victories. And with the sweat came a few puffs and then a few more puffs and then a few more puffs.

He says, "I did whatever it took. I smoked six, seven, eight, nine cigarettes. I lit them forward, backwards and in the middle." Shaky relief pitching will do that to a starter.

And one player who used to *eat* cigarettes was the enigmatic Joe Charboneau, the Cleveland Indians' 1980 Rookie of the Year who marched to his own drummer and who burned out quickly — three years and out. Charboneau, who had an act in which he'd open up a beer bottle with his eye socket and drink that beer through his nose, once ate five filter-tipped cigarettes on a dare. Of course he also ate bottles and anything else he was dared to consume.

YOU'RE NO MR. COFFEE

A player who will never get to do a Mr. Coffee commercial is infielder Julio Franco.

Franco suffered chest pains in 1993 as a member of the Texas Rangers. The second baseman was diagnosed as having ingested too much caffeine. Franco, who likes to have a cup or three before each game and more in the morning and in the evening, also had a negative reaction in 1990.

He cut back on the java but it was a tough act for him to take. Coffee's his life, man.

FOOD NUGGETS

Los Angeles Dodger outfielder Raul Mondesi took six years to make The Majors following his signing in 1988. The muscular 5'11", 210-pounder wasn't always that big. He works out with weights twice a week but reported that when he began as a pro, he was skinny. Coming from San Cristobal, Dominican Republic, Mondesi says he didn't eat well and good food was scarce. He says, "Then I came to the Dodgers camp in the Dominican Republic and started piling down great food, and my arms and chest filled." He says food made him a Major Leaguer. During his first Minor League season in America at Great Falls (Pioneer League) in 1990, he once ate 22 slices of pizza at a single sitting. "I was hungry," says Mondesi. Think how muscular he'd be if he ordered pepperoni.

Much has been written about Wade Boggs's addiction to chicks — make that chicken. The fowl has been credited with helping the third baseman find more than 2,000 hits and five batting crowns. When Red Sox teammate Tom Brunansky stumbled into Fenway Park in an 0-for-34 slump in 1991, he searched for a cure. Boggs invited Bru home to a dinner of lemon chicken, and the outfielder responded with a three-hit game. With averages of .229, .266 and .183 in the years since the chicken dinner, the career .246 hitter may want to make a standing date with the Colonel before every game.

Boggs, of chicken fame, emulates Joe DiMaggio in one pregame ritual. It was no mistake the Joe D. became a spokesman for Mr. Coffee. "The Yankee Clipper" would sit at his locker before every game and slowly drink two, three or four cups of coffee while he would relax and meditate before taking the field. Boggs, too, must have his two or three cups of joe before every game. Can Mr. Coffee commercials be far behind?

Melido Perez, Yankees pitcher, is a rice and beans man. He'll wolf down the dish at home at precisely 2:30 P.M. so he can be at the ballpark at 3:00 for a night game. Same routine before every start.

Legendary freethinker Jay Johnstone, an outfielder who played for many clubs, most notably Dodgers and Phillies, had to have a tall stack of pancakes, but only when he was to play in a day game.

Los Angeles Angels behemoth slugger Steve Bilko christened the Halos' first spring training camp in Palm Springs in 1961 by drinking beer virtually nonstop throughout the camp. His roommate, rookie catcher Bob "Buck" Rodgers, recalled that Bilko hired a bellhop to keep the slugger's bathtub filled with ice and beer. Bilko's procedure was to sit on the toilet, drink several cans of beer, and run hot water over the iced bathtub, creating a steam room effect. Rodgers says Bilko reasoned that he would sweat off all the beer he drank as he was drinking it. The 33-year-old first baseman was about 6'1" and close to 260 pounds, but still managed to hit .279 with 20 homers while appearing in 114 games that season.

Los Angeles Dodgers outfielder Brett Butler admits to drinking 20 cups of coffee per game. No wonder he's stolen close to 500 bases in his 14-year career. Caffeine rush. Perfect for a leadoff hitter.

It is a tradition in St. Louis for Cardinals players to store cabbage leaves on ice and put them under their caps to ward off the heat when the temperature in Missouri rises above 100 degrees.

Washington Senators ace pitcher of the 1950s, Camilo Pascual, ate chopped onions for breakfast, saying it gave him strength. He had enough strength to win 174 games in 18 years for some very poor teams.

Hall of Fame shortstop Walter "Rabbit" Maranville was known for his superior acrobatic fielding, his love for alcohol and pranks, and his ability to make people laugh. He also started the fad of swallowing goldfish in the 1920s, a full decade and a half before Harvard student Lothrop Wirthington began the college trend of piscine gobbling in 1939.

Pittsburgh Pirates star outfielder Andy Van Slyke has a sunflower seed routine. Before every game, he'll take a full bag of seeds and pat the bag 40 or 50 times, then shake, rattle and roll the cellophane before opening and devouring the seeds, dropping them from the bag to his mouth — without using his hands. Like any good seed pro, Van Slyke cracks the seed, scoops out the nutmeat with his tongue and spits out the empty shell all in good form, one seed at a time despite having a mouthful of the kernels.

San Francisco Giants star Will Clark ate a Clark bar June 1, 1991, and waved it to the camera during the televised game of the week. He hit the game-winning homer to beat Atlanta. There is no comparable story to link Reggie Jackson with Reggie bars, Henry Aaron to O Henry bars and Babe Ruth to Baby Ruth bars. Only the Reggie bar was named after the player, but only Clark ate his namesake confection and homered.

In 1991, following two tough losses in Toronto by the Boston Red Sox, Boston outfielder Mike Greenwell grabbed a banana, and in front of the whole team, crushed it and rubbed it on his face and head. He said to his fellow BoSox, "I stink, but if I go 3-for-4 tomorrow, I'll do this after every game." He only went 2-for-4 and never squeezed and mashed a banana again. For 2-for-4, there's a thousand guys who'd wear bananas in their ears every game.

Yankee catcher Yogi Berra, a Hall of Famer at the plate, behind the plate and near the plate, had a habit of going to the clubhouse dining table wearing only a T-shirt. While eating with his hands, he would scratch himself, grab his nether regions, and pick things off his body before grabbing more food. The Yankees of that era made sure they ate before Yogi did . . . or not at all.

CHAPTER SEVEN

Not Your Best Role Models

"Imitate him if you dare, World-besotted traveler ..."
— WILLIAM BUTLER YEATS

(Baseball players are) "Little tin Gods on wheels."
— RUDYARD KIPLING

The guys in this chapter should come with manufacturers' warning labels stitched on their uniforms or be rated not for human consumption or perhaps come equipped with disclaimers that read "Kids, don't try this at home." These gentlemen — and I only use the term because they apparently came out of a room marked "Gentlemen" — are the kinds of guys you don't want your kids to play with.

Maybe basketball's Charles Barkley was right when he said he didn't want to be anyone's role model and that athletes should not be thrust into that position. Still, in America, from the time of The Babe and Shoeless Joe through the DiMaggio era, the Jackie Robinson epoch, and the dynasties of Mantle, Mays, Aaron, Seaver, Reggie and Ryan, the kids in this country have emulated their baseball idols.

While many diamond heroes deserve the accolades and idolatry, not all have had such wholesome images as Stan Musial, Don Mattingly, Al Kaline, Ernie Banks, Roberto Clemente, Dale Murphy, Brooks Robinson, Tony Gwynn, Jim Abbott, Cal Ripken, Jr., and Kirby Puckett, to name a few.

While we think of ballplayers as being the larger-than-life bonhomies of the good-guy network, we often confuse on-the-field athletic exploits with personal behavior ... much as we trust politicians, lawyers and other people who say, "Trust me," until we get to know them better.

Well, perhaps we've gotten to know some of the following players too well—well enough to cheer their abilites, yet jeer their
atrocities.

Call them the kids you would like on your team, but whom
you'd never take home to meet Mom.

Since owners have seldom been held up as role models, we
have passed on including the dubious masterstrokes of such lumi-
naries as Marge Schott (racial slurs), George Steinbrenner (character assassination and "my way or the highway" management
style). Ray Kroc (apologizing on the public address system during
the game for his team's performance), and all of the good-old-boy
owners and baseball leaders who kept baseball segregated until
1947 (Adrian "Cap" Anson and Kenesaw Mountain Landis, to
name just two). Instead we have opted to cover a few of the boys
in uniform who get their faces on the bubble gum cards and their
autographed pictures under the pillows of the juvenile hero-
worshippers.

And since this book is for fun, and little fun can be found in
drug abuse, we will refrain from including those who threw the
dream away by using narcotics.

Although drug abuse has a place on the rap sheet our first anti-
role model.

DARRYL STRAWBERRY

Outfielder Darryl Strawberry is smooth, graceful and has power,
speed and talent to burn—and he has burned it. His on-the-field
and off-the-field behavior are worthy of a "don't grow up to be
like him" tag.

His talents: a home run title and 280 home runs in his first
nine years with the Mets and Dodgers (1983-1991), an average of
92 RBIs per year over that span, and a member of the 30-30 club
with 39 homers and 36 stolen bases in 1987.

But the 6'6" "Straw Man" had a dark side.

In addition to his other transgressions, Strawberry wanted to
leave New York and in several press conferences told the world
he wanted to leave The Big Apple for Los Angeles by 1990. His
days on the Mets were punctuated with missed practices, walk-
outs, shoves, fights, and threatening remarks made to teammates
Lee Mazzilli and Wally Backman. Straw then punched Keith Hernandez during a team photo shoot March 2, 1989. Yet, while a

member of the Dodgers in 1993, Strawberry said, while being interviewed during devastating fires that charred Los Angeles, "Let it burn down."

He came full circle on April 3, 1994, when he missed the team's final spring training game and was not located until that night, when he gave team General Manager Fred Claire a "flimsy excuse." The next day he admitted to having a substance abuse problem as the team placed him on the disabled list, but it took more than a week for Strawberry to check into a chemical dependency care program.

Soon, he was gone from L.A., and he took his apparently cleaned-up act to San Francisco.

On to your average poor-role-model superstar. . . .

TY COBB

Tyrus Raymond Cobb, "The Georgia Peach," was arguably the greatest hitter in baseball history. His .367 career average ranks No. 1 among all ballplayers, and his charter selection to the Hall of Fame was a sure thing, as he retired holding 90 Major League records. He was also a swift, daring runner and an excellent fielder with a strong arm during a 24-year career spent largely with the Tigers. Cobb was a master of gamesmanship, was one of the most competitive men in the game's history, and has been called the meanest man ever to play the game — he always got the upper hand and was relentless in all he did, once beating nearly to death a man who had no arms.

He sharpened his spikes and purposely slid high, intending to skewer any fielder who got in his way. He slashed Frank "Home Run" Baker's arm in 1909.

In 1911, vying for the AL batting title against Shoeless Joe Jackson, he played with Jackson's mind, ignoring the young player who wanted to be friendly, then yelling at him and insulting the naive hitter until his average *dropped* to .408 while Cobb won the crown at .420.

On May 15, 1912, while playing against the New York Highlanders, he attacked a fan in the stands, Claude Lucker, who had been insulting Cobb. The ballplayer beat the man senseless and had to be pulled off him. Cobb's victim had lost one arm and part of his other in an industrial accident, so was ill equipped to defend himself. Cobb struck him, spiked him and kicked him. As Cobb kicked the man's head, a bystander yelled, "Don't kick him. He has no hands." Cobb growled, "I don't care if he has no feet," and continued his assault.

The fan was actually lucky. Cobb generally carried a boot dagger, a hideout knife [hidden blade of small dimension] and what he termed "a weapon of good caliber."

On September 24, 1919, Cobb, player-manager for Detroit; Tris Speaker, player-manager for Cleveland; and Indians outfielder Smokey Joe Wood allegedly agreed to fix a game that gave the Tigers third place.

Cobb was also one of many players of that era who opposed the inclusion of black ballplayers in the Major Leagues and often went out of his way to spike and injure black opponents during barnstorming games. During one such tour, Cobb refused to room with Babe Ruth because he had heard a rumor that Ruth had a black ancestor.

But one of the meanest, most egocentric schemes he pulled was on a young power hitter—a plan that destroyed a Big League career.

Hanging on for one final year with the Philadelphia A's in 1928, an aging Cobb was put in the background as young stars Jimmie Foxx, Al Simmons and Joe Hauser garnered the headlines. Cobb couldn't mess with the heads of Foxx and Simmons, but he found a man he could manipulate in Hauser. Hauser, who hit 27 homers for the A's in 1924—second only to Babe Ruth's 46—before breaking his leg and missing a year and a half, was coming off a 20-homer Minor League campaign in 1927 and was tearing up the American League early on in 1928—when Cobb got to him. Cobb had complained to the press that "That kid Hauser is getting all the press." Soon after Cobb's offensive, the press stopped coming around.

Hauser felt sorry for the 41-year-old Cobb because no one else would talk to him. Bad move. Hauser was hitting .365 and was in double figures in homers for the first 40 games. Cobb took the powerful lefty with a sweet pull-hitter's swing aside and insisted that he stopped pulling the ball and use the entire field. Advice is advice, but Cobb was fanatical about it. He bellowed at Hauser during ball games: "Stand closer to the plate. Keep the bat higher." He screamed at Hauser as the young star was about to swing at a pitch. Hauser recalls, "I was up with two out and the tying run at second. George Pipgras threw me a fastball, and as he released it, I heard Cobb, in the on-deck circle, yell, 'Get in on the plate. Hit behind the runner. Hit off your back foot.' "

When that wasn't enough, he'd call Hauser in the middle of the night, restricting his sleep, and yell instructions to him. Wherever he went, whatever he did, he saw Cobb and heard Cobb's instructions. Pretty soon Hauser was not Hauser at the plate anymore, hitting .250, and was out of the Majors.

It took two years for Hauser to regain his swing, which he did by hitting 63 home runs for Baltimore of the International League in 1930 and 69 roundtrippers for Minneapolis in the American Association in 1933. Hauser hit 399 career blasts in the Minors but never did get back into the Majors — thanks to the man Hauser calls "the meanest bastard who ever lived."

Even after Cobb retired, he played with people's heads.

In a 1947 Old Timers' game, Cobb warned catcher Benny Bengough to back up so he wouldn't get hit with the old-timer's bat. When the catcher moved back, Cobb laid down a bunt and beat it out for a hit.

BABE RUTH

George Herman "Babe" Ruth did everything to excess — hit homers, pitch, eat, drink, smoke and enjoy women. His larger-than-life persona single-handedly saved baseball when it was near extinction following the 1919 "Black Sox" scandal. Ruth hit more homers himself than other whole teams did. He was the epitome of the big-money player and may have been the only player ever to be bigger than the game itself.

But that didn't make Babe worthy of being the idol of millions of American kids of the 1920s. If Ruth's off-the-field behavior had been subjected to today's bare-all media scrutiny, parents would have likely kept their kids away from their radios and the sports pages.

He was known for chasing showgirls, in various stages of undress — both he and the showgirls were scantily clad — through the coach cars of team trains.

Teammate on the 1927 Yankees Mark Koenig said of Ruth, "Babe never went in for reading. He didn't know the difference between Robin Hood and Cock Robin. He was just interested in girls, drinking and eating." Add to that, cigars.

Another Ruth teammate, Jimmie Reese, who saw it all in his nine decades in the game as a Minor League player, Major League second baseman and coach, recalled a story in which he and Ruth were sharing a room.

Reese remembered, "I didn't see Babe much because he was never in the room, always out on the town or with some girl."

It seems Ruth had a ritual of lighting up an expensive Cuban "victory" cigar after finishing each sexual conquest.

One day as Reese left the hotel room to go downstairs for breakfast and a newspaper, he looked in the foyer, glanced down at an ashtray and saw that Babe had crushed out two stogies. Babe declined an offer of breakfast, saying he was "busy."

Reese came back a little while later to get Babe and go to the ballpark and saw five cigar butts in the glass container. He yelled into Ruth's bedroom, "Hey, Babe, we'll be late for the game."

Ruth growled, "Come back in half an hour. I'm still busy."

When Reese opened the door 30 minutes later, a provocatively and briefly attired woman ducked out of the door past the startled second baseman. Ruth was dressing for the ballpark. Reese looked down at the ashtray and spied seven crushed-out perfectos in the dish and another in Babe's mouth.

"ART THE GREAT" SHIRES

Charles Arthur "Art The Great" Shires was a cocky, hard-hitting first baseman of the 1920s and 1930s who made a career out of feuding with managers and umpires. He chose his nickname himself and also called himself Art "Whattaman" Shires. His great love for himself, however, didn't carry over to others.

On May 31, 1928, Shires, playing first base for Waco of the Texas League, threw a ball into the Negro section of the grandstand at Shreveport, Lousiana's Biedenharn Park, striking baseball fan William Lawson in the face, fracturing his jaw. Shires claimed that he had heard remarks directed at him from that section of the bleachers. He reacted angrily and fired the ball into the stands.

The game was not interrupted, though Lawson was taken to the hospital. Following the game, Shires was rushed by incensed fans who wanted him arrested. They chased him, and Shires sought the aid of a passing motorist who whisked him out of town.

A week later, Shires was fined $50 by the Texas League for the attack, and several months later, Lawson, who had been injured so severely that he never regained health, died. On January 11, 1930, Shires was ordered by federal court to pay Lawson's widow $500 for the act.

In the spring of 1929, Shires, then with the Chicago White Sox, took a punch at skipper Lena Blackburne, a popular manager who invented the procedure of rubbing down baseballs with special mud he discovered on his land in New Jersey. The altercation took place when Shires refused to take off a red felt hat he wore to the plate. A few weeks later, Shires popped Blackburne as the two squared off in the Sox clubhouse, sending the skipper down for the count. This battle occurred after Blackburne found Shires drinking bootlegged whiskey.

After the 1929 season, Shires was suspended by the ChiSox for slugging Blackburne, the team's road secretary and several hotel employees.

After a short career as a professional boxer, Shires returned to the diamond, and in 1949, former Texas Leaguer Hy Erwin was killed in a fight with Shires.

Two deaths, illegal booze, a punched manager, and an ego the size of a ballpark. Now there's a royal flush to pattern your life after.

LEN DYKSTRA

Len "Nails" Dykstra is certainly the spark that ignites the Philadelphia Phillies. His spirit and hard-nosed play inspire the Phils as much as his ability to hit, run, field and throw. But off the field, Dykstra's behavior might be less than inspiring to those who want their kids to emulate sports heroes. True, he does donate $100 for every hit (about $20,000 since he began the practice) to Children's Hospital of Philadelphia, but donations alone do not a role model make.

The spark plug signed a four-year $24.9 million contract, and while that might be a bargain for the Phillies, money, success, field leadership and talent don't overshadow the missteps. Here's the rap sheet:

In the mid-1980s, a waiter at a Los Angeles restaurant, the Pacific Dining Car, reports that Dykstra profanely abused and insulted the staff while eating there and falsely accused the waiter of stealing his credit card. While Dykstra's meal buddies apologized for the action, Nails never did. He just cursed and walked out.

In 1988, he punched the wall in the team video room and broke his right hand.

On May 5, 1991, he broke his ribs, cheekbones and collarbone in a drunk-driving accident that left teammate Darren Daulton injured as well. After drinking at Smokey Joe's, a Philly night spot, for four hours, Dykstra took his red 1991 Mercedes-Benz sports car and, with Daulton in the passenger seat, lost control and crashed into two trees off a main intersection.

On at least two occasions, he was ticketed for excessive speed — at least 80 miles per hour.

He has been investigated by Major League baseball for gambling practices; he claims to have lost $78,000 in high-stakes poker games. But he says he never ever gambled illegally.

On December 22, 1993, Dykstra, drinking in a crowded restaurant, yelled profanities and got into a loud, off-color exchange with Pennsylvania state Senator Earl Baker, who maintained his own cool and acceptable public language. At the swanky Strafford Inn, Dykstra is reported to have been dressed in the grunge look and was loudly spewing forth four-letter words in locomotive fashion. After the senator leaned over and softly asked the ballplayer to watch his language, Dykstra responded with a louder, more profane demonstration. Another urging brought the 30-year-old Dykstra to louder, more abusive language and a challenge to fight the 53-year-old legislator.

Sports agent Alan Meersand fired Len Dykstra. When have you ever heard of an agent firing a meal ticket? Meersand terminated the 13-year relationship, saying, "I'm not going to condone or defend his behavior anymore. This guy is completely out of control."

Maybe he just shouldn't be allowed out of the ballpark. A helluva player, he just may need to practice his human fundamentals as much as he practices his ball field fundamentals.

REGGIE JACKSON

Reggie Jackson, the Hall of Fame slugger who always seemed to rise to the occasion when he was in the spotlight, had legendary power and an ego to match. He was a champion of equal rights who disdained bigotry—except once when he fell victim to espousing the same stereotypes he scorned.

In spring training with the California Angels, his club faced the Milwaukee Brewers, who had brought in 36-year-old Japan League star pitcher Yutaka Enatsu for a tryout. Enatsu, one of the all-time greats in the Far East, had won 206 games for the Hanshin Tigers, Hiroshima Toyo Carp and Seibu Lions, setting strikeout and victory records in the process, and was the highest-paid pitcher in the Japanese game in 1984.

Enatsu, with a career full of his own highlights, was slated to pitch against the Angels and paid Reggie a compliment by saying that throwing to Jackson was the highlight of his 18-year career.

Reggie responded by saying, "I don't need some cook from Benihana's to tell me that facing me will make his career. Let him go back where he came from."

Reminded by a writer that the slur would be akin to having Enatsu refer to Reggie as "some fry cook for Colonel Sanders," Reggie flew into a rage and yelled some things that would be unprintable in English as well as Japanese.

BRET SABERHAGEN

New York Mets hurler Bret Saberhagen displayed some washday ugliness July 27, 1993, on a day he wasn't even the pitcher of record. Following a game against the Florida Marlins, reporters flocked around hard-luck, record-breaking loser Anthony Young, who is in the record books for losing 27 consecutive games over two years.

Angry? Mischievous? Dumb? All three? Whatever the reason, Saberhagen took umbrage at the media, grabbed a container of bleach, and sprayed it at the group. The bleach splashed onto Dave D'Alessandro of *The Record* of Hackensack, New Jersey, and Mark Herrmann of *Newsday*.

Saberhagen was fined one day's salary—$15,384. At the request of the Baseball Writers Association of America, the money was donated to the Eye Research Foundation of Central New York because you can put an eye out that way.

The league cleaned Saberhagen, too, suspending him without pay for the first five games of the 1994 season. He should have known you don't bleach writers. They're drip dry.

The incident was Saberhagen's second attack on the media that season. Earlier he tossed a lit firecracker into a crowd of reporters to watch them scatter after the explosion. Not smart. Just ask teammate Vince Coleman about throwing explosive devices near people. Coleman's escapade injured a young girl outside Dodger Stadium in Los Angeles and resulted in a lawsuit, a suspension and a trade. Maybe Bret wanted to escape from New York, too.

TOM LASORDA

Before Tom Lasorda was the fiery skipper of the Los Angeles Dodgers, he was a pitcher — and a pretty good one, too, though most of his best years were spent in The Minors. His 125 career wins in the International League place him among the all-time IL leaders. In 1948, while pitching for the Schenectady Blue Jays of the Canadian-American League, Lasorda struck out 25 batters in a 15-inning win over the Amsterdam Rugmakers. He was also the 1958 IL MVP, going 18-6.

In what some might call bad role model behavior — although some might call it good competitive spirit — Lasorda, playing for the Los Angeles Angels, touched off a brawl in the Pacific Coast League on August 24, 1957. After pitching to Hollywood Star second baseman Forrest "Spook" Jacobs, Lasorda gave the batter a rolling football block to keep Jacobs from reaching first base on a bunt attempt. Jacobs got up, charged Lasorda, traded fists first with him and then Angels second baseman George "Sparky" Anderson and shortstop Bobby Dolan. The bench-clearing melee lasted half an hour, after which Lasorda resumed his work on the hill as though nothing had happened.

STAN WILLIAMS

One of the most feared pitchers in baseball from 1958 to 1972 was fireballing righty Stan Williams, who won 109 games for the Dodgers, Yankees, Indians and others. Williams was one of those pitchers in the Early Wynn-Don Drysdale-Bob Gibson mold who figured they not only owned the inside part of the plate, but the entire plate and the the batter as well.

He openly admitted to throwing at batters, for any reason. And when the 6'5", 230-pounder fired his high hard one, he didn't care whether he was facing Hall of Famers, such as Willie Mays, Henry Aaron or Mickey Mantle, or backup utility players, such as Casey Wise or Bob Christian.

Once, Williams fired a fastball off Henry Aaron's helmet, sending the Braves' slugger reeling and dazed. Williams walked up to Hammerin' Hank and said, "I'm sorry I hit you in the helmet." When Aaron graciously accepted the pitcher's apology, Williams barked, "I meant to hit you in the neck."

Williams practiced hitting Aaron; he even had a picture of the home-run hitter in the locker room and threw baseballs at it to get in the mood. And he kept a journal to record each player he faced and whether they were on his hit list. Four stars by a player's name meant he was targeted for a beaning.

And once on the list, a player never was taken off—even if it meant tracking a guy down in batting practice, at an old-timer's game or at a picnic. Williams usually made good on his chin music.

Williams said his goal was to see two (batter's) feet sticking up in the air with the hitter on his back.

DICK DONOVAN

Dick Donovan was another tough pitcher who hated hitters even before they came to bat and showed them just how much in a display of violence of which Mom would never approve. A 6'3", 190-pound right-hander with a mean slider, good fastball and nasty disposition, he won 122 and lost 99 during a 15-year career from 1950 to 1965, spent mostly with the White Sox, Indians and Braves.

Toiling in the Minors for nearly a decade must have made him mean, because when he finally got to the Majors to stay in 1955, he made the most of it and took no quarter.

He once knocked a batter down who was just standing in the on-deck circle. His reply, "It took me a long time to get here, and I'm not leaving. I'm not letting any batter get me out of here."

He hit Cleveland Indians hitter Vic Power so hard in the back that Power had the baseball's stitch marks embedded near his spine for a week. Donovan hit Power because Donovan's manager, Al Lopez, mentioned he didn't like Power.

It was said of Donovan that his out pitch was his slider, but his knockout pitch was the fastball.

Asked once if he enjoyed tatooing opposing hitters, he replied, "I don't care one way or another, but it does make an interesting sound when the ball hits them."

EARLY WYNN

Perhaps the toughest and nastiest pitcher of Donovan's and Williams's era was Early Wynn, a Hall of Fame right-hander for the Senators, Indians and White Sox from 1939 to 1963 who won 300 games on his fastball and grit alone. Wynn was said to be the meanest player of his time, calling the pitching mound his "office" and home plate his "territory." He boasted he'd knock down his grandmother if she dug in against him.

During one pregame batting practice, his 15-year-old son, Joe, stepped in to take a few swings against dear old Dad. The senior Wynn watched his son hit two long drives. On the third pitch, Dad came in at the kid's head. The younger Wynn was eating dirt while the elder Wynn glared.

Once, after Mickey Mantle lined a Wynn fastball up the middle and through Wynn's legs for a base hit, the pitcher ordered his first baseman to stand directly behind Mantle at first. Wynn fired fastball after fastball directly at the Mick in an effort to hurt him rather than pick him off.

A man with a long memory, if a batter knocked one through the pitcher's box one season, he would someday be a target for Wynn's duster, even if it was years later. And if a hitter took Wynn deep, sooner or later Wynn would get him in his sights and blast him with a fastball.

"SHUFFLIN' PHIL" DOUGLAS

Phil Douglas was a spitball pitcher from 1912 to 1922, mostly with the Cubs and Giants. He went 93-92 and threw 20 shutouts, due largely to his good control and great wetball.

Phil liked to get wet, too, stopping for drinks whenever he could get his hands on them. His seemingly omnipresent state of stupor kept him staggering to the mound. The uncertain gait appeared to be a shuffle—hence the nickname.

Douglas took frequent rests from the game to dry out, and other departures from the lineup were due to binges. In 1922, he took a tongue-lashing from Giants skipper John McGraw and, in response, went on an alcoholic binge. While intoxicated, he wrote a letter to St. Louis Cardinals outfielder Les Mann, explaining that he didn't want his Giants to win the pennant. For "goods," Douglas wrote, he would be willing to quit the Giants and let the Cards win the flag.

Baseball czar Judge Kenesaw Mountain Landis was given the letter and used it as grounds to banish Douglas from baseball for life.

JOE "DUCKY" MEDWICK

Joe "Ducky" Medwick, the St. Louis Cardinals Hall of Famer who patroled the outfield and hit up a storm (.324) from 1932 to 1948, was a great man to have in your lineup. But he was no joy to be around otherwise. A bad-ball hitter, he was also a bad-ball kind of guy.

While with the Brooklyn Dodgers, he fought with Cardinals pitcher Bob Bowman in an elevator, questioning the pitcher's manhood. Bowman retaliated in the next game by beaning Medwick within an inch of his life.

But Medwick wouldn't back down. He played every game as though it were his last and fought every guy as if it were his last fight. It didn't matter to him whether you were friend or foe. You were just another sparring partner for Medwick.

One time in 1935, a fly ball dropped in front of him and Cards pitcher Ed Heusser accused him of not giving it his all. Medwick ran to the mound, knocked out Heusser with one punch, forcing his Cardinals to bring in a cold reliever to replace the knocked-cold starter.

He fought teammate Dizzy Dean on a regular basis and did the same with other dugout buddies. When teammate pitcher Tex Carleton was taking batting practice before a game in 1933, Medwick barked at him to get out of the batting cage so the regulars could hit. The 6'2", 180-pound Carleton took another cut, and the infurated 5'10", 185-pound Medwick jumped into the cage and knocked Carleton unconscious. Manager Gabby Street ran out to the field in his undershorts to see what the commotion was about, and Medwick said nonchalantly, "You'll have to go with another pitcher." The regulars had to hit.

PITTSBURGH PIRATES EXECUTIVES

In a case of poor judgment at best, and spitefulness and meanness at worst, a 1990 Pirates triumvirate of team president Carl Barger, general manager Larry Doughty and manager Jim Leyland sought to exert control over two outspoken players, Barry Bonds and R.J. Reynolds.

The Pirates' brass fined the two ballplayers each $1,500 for missing a team-sponsored charity auction. On the surface, you can identify with the club and say to heck with the players.

But Bonds missed the event to stay home and take care of his nine-month-old son, who had been sick for a week and was nursing a high fever.

And Reynolds, a community do-gooder who attended dozens of good-cause functions each year, objected to the party, at which fans were charged an admission fee plus additonal funds for each autograph they obtained. Reynolds said he would never charge a kid for an autograph. "I don't play that game."

The Pirates execs said the function was mandatory and had been voted on by the players. Neither player — nor others on the team — could recall a vote, but Bonds had a history of verbal run-ins with management and Reynolds was said by some in the Bucs' hierarchy to be "too independent." Reynolds was gone at the end of the season, and Bonds left for the greener pastures of San Francisco two years later.

NEW YORK METS PLAYERS

On March 27, 1992, the New York Mets players announced they were ending all communication with the news media. This was in reaction to the constant scrutiny by the press regarding off-field behavior and investigations of sexual harassment charges — later dropped — against pitcher David Cone, as well as countless articles concerning Mets drinking, sleeping, eating and carousing habits.

They apparently weren't too pleased either with the press accounts of their previous season's performance — fifth-place finish with a 77-84 mark.

The world went on, the sun rose and set, and Major League baseball survived, even without Mets talking to the press. The commissioner's office protested and complained and pressure was put on the players to talk. Within a few weeks, the media ban was lifted and the press was able to enlighten the world on Mets' comings and goings, which was really important, in light of the club's second straight fifth-place finish and a 72-90 record.

ROLE MODEL NUGGETS

Rick Bosetti, an outfielder for the Toronto Blue Jays in 1979, was on a quest. It was to make the Hall of Fame or lead the league in batting; Bosetti publicly stated that it was his life's work to urinate on every outfield in the Majors. He claimed he had christened every park in the American League and hoped he'd be sent back to the National League because "To water the lawn at Wrigley Field would be a dream come true."

John Lowenstein, a clutch hitter for the Orioles, Rangers and Indians from 1970 to 1985, had his own tune to which he marched. In June 1980, he pretended to get knocked out while hit with a thrown ball on the base paths and waited until the stretcher came for him to "regain consciousness," while all in attendance were concerned about his health. He chose to use the situation as an opportunity for a prank. And any time a birthday cake or celebration confection was sent to the clubhouse, Lowenstein examined it and more often than not would destroy the dessert with several hard smashes from his bat.

Still, Lowenstein's cake routine was kinder and gentler than the ritual employed by Yankee reliever Sparky Lyle. Lyle, the enigmatic southpaw closer, chose to sit naked on any cake that found its way into the Yankee clubhouse. Very few desserts were eaten by the Bronx Bombers during Lyle's tenure there (1972-1978). He was also responsible for taking sleeping teammate Jim Mason out to a public pool, stripping him, tying him to a chair, and calling police to tell them that Mason was a potential suicide. Lyle then told all his teammates to come see the deep-slumbering infielder naked at poolside. But Mason awoke, worked himself loose, saw the police and ran, thinking the cops were after him. The police chased the shortstop for three hours before they found out it was a joke.

Lyle, a slider-throwing Cy Young Award winner who saved 238 games during his 16-year career from 1967 to 1982, was also known for calling up the Queen of England or ordering Chinese food from mainland China while using the bullpen telephone, nailing teammates' shoes to the floor, or utterly destroying players' clothing as they showered. Fun guy to be around, but a tough choice to bring home to Mom, especially if it's her birthday and you've bought her a cake.

Bert Blyleven, the fun-loving hurler from the Netherlands who toiled for half a dozen teams over 22 years, finishing with 287 wins, was a supreme practicer of practical jokes. From writing obscenities on cherished memorabilia—they were usually doubles and he returned the pristine originals later—to destroying clothing, and messing with a player's toiletries, Blyleven was the self-proclaimed "King of the Hotfoot." No one and no shoes were safe from fire if Blyleven was on the scene. Shoelaces, socks, shoes, and an occasional rear end or two were no match for Blyleven's matches, fuses and alcohol fuel. A lot of teammates walked around barefoot after seeing their favorite shoes go up in flames, falling victim to the big righty's arson.

Infielder Tony Fernandez, winding down a solid career, fell on tough times, being moved to third base from his traditional shortstop, being benched, and being paid like a young, marginal player, rather than as an experienced all-star. In 1994, playing for Cincinnati, he stormed out of the locker room on several occasions, threw equipment in the clubhouse and screamed at teammates. On May 10, at Jack Murphy Stadium in San Diego, Fernandez snapped after being heckled by fans. He fired a warm-up throw over first baseman Hal Morris's head and into the stands near the hecklers. He later went over to sign autographs in the section where the taunters were sitting. He said the throw was unintentional. Let's see . . . a warm-up throw, thrown by an all-star with a great arm, sails 50 feet past the intended target . . . hmmm.

CHAPTER EIGHT

Capricious
Purple Hearts

"The scars of others should teach us caution."
—ST. JEROME

We think of diamond warriors as being a tough lot, able to play with pain and grind it out day after day. And we think of these graceful athletic specimens as people who only get injured in battle—crashing into fences, crunching into opposing fielders, diving, running, sliding, getting their legs broken because they stood their ground to complete the double play, or getting their heads dented because they wouldn't back out in the face of a high-and-tight 100-mph fastball.

Heroes all. Impervious to pain. Invulnerable to the wussy types of clumsy injuries that befall mere mortal men.

Wrong, Band-Aid breath.

It turns out the baseball players are just as clumsy off the field as are nonathletes. And they are just as wimpy about playing in pain when they have to face a tough left-hander as you were when you had a math test in school.

Many injuries are legitimately caused. Many more are unfortunate on-the-field juxtapositions of ill fate. Even more are off-the-field, maladroit miseries that make the rest of us look graceful by comparison. And still more are of dubious nature, as in "Ryan's pitching? I think I have a tight hammie. I'd better sit this one out."

Injuries aren't exclusive of the season or spring training, though Will Rogers said of preseason work, "Baseball teams go south every spring to cripple their players. In the old days, they only stayed a couple of weeks, and they couldn't get many of them hurt in that time. But nowadays [1930s], they stay till they get them all hurt."

Injuries can and do happen anywhere any time to these multi-millionaire athletically inclined klutzes.

And in case sitting on that spot on the bench has strained your best attribute, we've included a few injury cure-alls to help facilitate your speedy recovery.

Don't get hurt. Find a soft chair and check out these boo-boos, and you may find yourself saying you're not nearly as clumsy or as wussy as these guys.

RON GANT

A candidate for the Bad Luck chapter is Ron Gant, who broke the Jim Lonborg rule. Lonborg, a Boston Red Sox pitching hero and Cy Young winner in 1967, blew his knee out while skiing in the off-season of 1968. His win total dropped from 22 in 1967 to six in 1968 and pretty much wiped out the promise of a spectacular career, though he did hang around until 1979. Since then, owners have put hobby and activity provisions in players' contracts to keep them from partaking in hazardous and potentially injurious events.

In the midst of a nonguaranteed contract that would have paid him $5.5 million, Gant was coming off a multimillion-dollar year—personal bests of 36 homers and 117 RBIs, along with 26 steals and 113 runs scored for the NL West pennant winners, the Atlanta Braves. In the off-season, though, Gant took his career and bank account on a dirt bike ride with him February 3, 1994, in suburban Atlanta. One crash and one double right-leg fracture later and Gant was through for at least half a year and out of the Braves' plans completely. Gant was stripped of his contract and sent packing with only $906,593.40 in severance pay—not bad severance pay, but still $4.6 million in the hole.

JOSE CANSECO

Big, strong, matinee idol, Madonna companion Jose Canseco, the Oakland A-turned-Texas Ranger outfielder, seems to have Hall of Fame power, dubious fielding prowess, great speed for an athlete who's a solid 6'4" and 240 pounds, and a flair for controversy.

Canseco put up marquee numbers several times during his first eight years in the Majors (1986-1993), hitting 40 or more homers twice (30 or more homers five times), driving in more than 100 runs five times, and becoming the founding member of the

40-40 club (40 homers and 40 stolen bases in the same season) with his 42 homer-40 steal year in 1988.

So why risk a $5 million player with a history of back and shoulder problems on a silly, egocentric whim during a lost ball game? Why, indeed.

Canseco now admits that his right elbow and shoulder had been hurting him for two years, yet, on May 29, 1993, with his Rangers being blown out by the Red Sox at historic Fenway Park—final score 15-1, Sox—the outfielder talked manager Kevin Kennedy into letting him pitch the eighth inning.

Canseco was hardly the reincarnation of Babe Ruth. The slugger threw 33 pitches, gave up two hits and three walks while surrending three runs for an ERA of 27.00. But he also blew out his right elbow and soon needed surgery to replace a torn ligament. The injury limited Canseco to only 60 games and 10 home runs.

This injury came just four days after Canseco's biggest headache—a header over the fence. Making highlight reels around the country, a fly ball off the bat of Cleveland first baseman-third baseman Carlos Martinez, headed Canseco's way in Cleveland, hit him on the head and bounded over the fence for a home run and two dents—one to Canseco's skull and one to his ego.

SHAWON DUNSTON

From the mid-1980s through the early 1990s, Cubs shortstop Shawon Dunston was in the elite company of Ozzie Smith and Ozzie Guillen—one of the best shortstops in the game.

The rangy athlete could make all the plays and pick up anything hit his way. Then he made a mistake; he picked up something that wasn't hit his way—his daughter Whitnie.

Dunston injured his back lifting his baby out of her car seat in 1991. Although he averaged 145 games a year the previous four seasons, Dunston was too hurt to play more than 18 games in 1992 and seven in 1993.

Oww. The guy signed a four-year, $12 million contract before the 1992 season. He can afford to hire a nanny to lift the kid.

BAD TIME TO HURT YOUR LEG

On July 13, 1953, Al Ware, a slugger for Waterloo of the Three-I Minor League, belted a pitch some 400 feet during a game at Evansville. What would normally have been a triple with a chance for four bases turned into an out when he was thrown out at first on a relay from the right fielder to the second baseman to the first baseman. Following his big swing, Ware tore ligaments in his right knee and collapsed in the batter's box. He was still laid out near home plate when the out was recorded . . . the final out of the game, won by Evansville.

ATTACK GEAR

San Diego Padres manager Greg Riddoch fell victim to a protective helmet, July 2, 1991, during a hometown loss to the Dodgers before 31,543 fans.

In the sixth inning, with the Pads trailing, catcher Benito Santiago grounded out to end the frame. As few paid any attention, a helmet came whizzing toward the dugout at high speed — Santiago had angrily fired the headgear after the recorded out. The flying helmet caromed off the ground, grazed pitching coach Mike Roarke, and struck manager Riddoch on the side of the forehead, cutting him and inflicting a concussion that had him brought off the field with dizziness and nausea. He missed the rest of the game.

That year, 1991, might be known as the year of the equipment attacks — at least in this paragraph — as another gear-related injury occurred on August 9 during the Pan American Games in Havana. A melee during the sixth inning — a very injurious inning — broke out in the game between Canada and Mexico that left Team Canada's coach John Upham with an angina attack, catcher Dave Krug with a broken nose, and Team Mexico's manager Antonio Pollerena with a four-stitch gash in his forehead as a result of a swing and a hit by Canadian catcher Alex Andreopoulos, who used his mask to make contact. The Mexican team took off after the Canadians with swinging bats and inflicted some half dozen injuries. The Canadians, using fists, caused a half dozen of their own. Mexican team members said they reacted to a racial slur. Mexico won the game 7-5, and the North American Free Trade Agreement was signed by both countries two-and-a-half years later with no provision for free trade of insults or baseball gear.

DIAL "I" FOR INJURY

Milwaukee Brewers prospect pitcher Steve Sparks, a righty who had a shot at making the Big Club after seven years in the bushes, ran out of ammunition when he suffered a motivationally inspired injury. In spring 1994, Sparks attended a seminar by Radical Reality, a motivational group. Visualizing success, he attempted to tear a telephone book apart with his bare hands. The book won, and Sparks suffered a dislocated left shoulder. Sparks's team trainer, John Adam, helped aid his injured pitcher, but became vexed when he had to look up a phone number later in the mangled book.

It's in the yellow pages under "H" for "Hospital" or "L" for "Lawsuit."

"VOICELESS TIM" O'ROURKE

Third baseman Tim O'Rourke, a player for six teams from 1890 to 1894, was hit in the throat by a bad hop and was left with a whisper of a voice. His throat was apparently a magnet for bad hops; it has been reported that this errant grounder was the third ball to strike the player's neck.

"RIP" SEWELL

Truett Banks Sewell, the originator of the eephus pitch, or blooper ball, pitched from 1932 to 1949, mostly with the Pirates, going 143-97. He began his career as one of the dominant pitchers in the league, with good control and good movement on his pitches.

In 1940, he had part of his foot shot off in a hunting accident that left buckshot in both legs. The pain and partial foot forced him to develop a new pitching style that included tossing a pitch with backspin that made the ball fly 20 to 30 feet high before coming down to cross the plate. Using the pitch and his still potent fastball, he won 21 games in 1943 and 21 again in 1944.

Ted Williams blasted the lob for a home run in the 1946 All-Star game, the only time that pitch was ever clouted for a four-bagger. Williams called the thing a "sissy" pitch and pleaded with Sewell not to throw it, adding that it was a disgrace to the game.

The pitch got its name from Sewell's teammate Maurice Van Robays, an outfielder, who said, "Eephus ain't no word, and that ain't no pitch."

BOB OJEDA

Bob Ojeda, the gutsy finesse pitcher for the Red Sox, Mets, Dodgers, Indians and Yankees for over a decade and a half, has had his brilliant moments. But one of them wasn't that September 1988 afternoon in New York when he decided to trim the hedges outside his house.

Ojeda was 10-13 with a good 2.88 ERA for the Mets when he picked up his electric hedge clippers. Before he knew it, he was cutting off the tip of his middle finger.

Ojeda's wife, Ellen, drove the pitcher and his dangling, bloody finger to the hospital. Doctors suggested they just cut the useless thing off, but Ojeda would have none of that. He instructed them to perform microsurgery and reattach the digit. Doctors told him the finger would be of little benefit, but would he want it attached straight or slightly bent? Ojeda opted for the bent model so he could grip the curveball.

"Bent-Finger" Ojeda came back to go 13-11 for the Mets in 1989 and was 12-9 for the Dodgers in 1991.

CECIL FIELDER

The Tiger behemoth known as Cecil Fielder was coming off his best year, a 51-homer, 132-RBI campaign for Detroit in 1990 and had ballooned up 30 pounds heavier than his reported 230 pounds the prior season.

Fielder had a variety of aches and pains in spring training of 1991 and missed the first half of the Grapefruit League when he strained ligaments in his left knee doing something very strenuous: He slipped getting out of bed.

He worked on his debedding technique and recovered sufficiently to hit 44 homers in 1991 with 133 RBIs. He didn't miss a game during the regular season. Must have gotten a lot of bed rest.

OLIVER "GHOST" MARCELLE

One of the greatest-fielding third basemen in Negro League history was the graceful New Orleans native "Ghost" Marcelle.

Marcelle, known for his clutch hitting and fierce temper, was also fiercely proud of his good looks. That, and an incident, hurt him and took him out of the game.

In 1928, playing Winter League ball in Cuba, Marcelle got into a monster fight with teammate Frank Warfield over a game of dice. During the combat, Warfield bit off Marcelle's nose. The lack of the facial appendage forced the infielder to wear a black patch over the hole, and he soon became so self-conscious that he refused to play ball in public. He played in five games for the Brooklyn Royal Giants in 1930, then called it quits before his 33rd birthday, for ego's sake, not for loss of skill.

HE'S A PITCHER WITHOUT CONTROL

New York Mets relief pitcher Mike Maddux had been in The Bigs since 1986 (with the Phillies) and should have known better. While his brother Greg (Cubs and Braves) may have garnered most of the headlines by twice being a 20-game winner, Mike had been a steady middle-relief man with a two-to-one strikeout-to-walk ratio.

But control? None. At least not on April 26, 1994. Called on to save a Mets victory against the San Diego Padres, Maddux surrendered two runs on three hits in the ninth inning to lose an apparent victory.

Angry at his performance, his pitch choices and himself, Maddux slammed into the dugout and kicked the floor so hard he split his big toe—a hairline fracture that made him the second Mets hurler in a week to injure a great toe. Dwight Gooden, who wasn't mad, just unfortunate, hurt his toe a week earlier and was out more than a month.

It would be wise for Mets pitchers to be on their toes in the future and learn some control.

HE'S A PITCHER, NOT A HITTER

In the reverse of Jose Canseco's hitter-turned-pitcher injury, New York Yankees pitcher Melido Perez strained a hip flexor muscle in his final spring training start versus Atlanta in West Palm Beach, Florida, March 31, 1993. Perez was running out a sacrifice bunt in his only hitting appearance of the spring. American League pitchers don't bat at all, so if ever an injury was needless, this it is. Perez missed the first two weeks of the season and never did get in stride, going 6-14.

CATCH THIS!

On August 5, 1939, the San Francisco Seals of the Pacific Coast League held a "Celebration of Baseball Day" extravaganza at the Golden Gate Exposition. With a blimp hovering 800 feet overhead, an official dropped a baseball, and Seals catcher Joe Spring attempted to catch the falling object. The ball struck him in the face, and Spring suffered a compound fracture of his jaw, lost eight teeth, and cut and thickened both his lips. Cruel teammates charged him with a passed ball.

HAPPY MOTHER'S DAY

Two-time defending Cy Young Award winner Greg Maddux, of the Atlanta Braves, was sailing along in pursuit of his third consecutive Cy, with a 5-2 record and microscopic 0.94 ERA, when he was minding his own business on Mother's Day 1994.

Maddux was sitting in the Braves' dugout along the first-base line, when Montreal Expos hitter Cliff Floyd fouled off a line drive that struck Maddux on the left cheek, causing a deep bruise and a lot of stars.

It was the first time all year Maddux had been knocked out of the box.

INJURY ATTRIBUTED TO DESERT STORM

In September 1991, California Angels second baseman Luis Sojo sustained a season-ending injury that teammate Lance Parrish took the blame for, but it was America's troops that were to blame.

During Operation Desert Storm, America's foray into the Middle East to take on Iraq and free Kuwait, some California Angels personnel visited Camp Pendleton in Southern California to show support for the families of marines in the Gulf. As a token of appreciation, a marine sergeant visited Anaheim Stadium and presented pitcher Jim Abbott and first baseman Wally Joyner with ceremonial knives with their names inscribed on the blades.

Joyner's knife was mounted on a plaque, and Angel catcher Parrish turned the knife around so he could read it. He jousted with teammate Sojo and jabbed the butt end at him in jest. Sojo threw up his hands in fearful self-defense and sliced his left thumb and little finger to the tune of seven stitches in the thumb and three more in the pinky.

It ended Sojo's season. Parrish accepted the blame, though Sojo tried to protect his buddy by saying he cut his fingers on a drinking glass.

Not so. It was a marine's gift. A sharp gift that drew blood.

MOST ACCIDENTS OCCUR AROUND THE HOME

In real life, it has been determined that most accidents happen around the house. In the baseball world, many diamond warriors have shown that they are just as susceptible to household injuries as the rest of us.

In August 1990, Mariners outfielder Tracy Jones was placed on the disabled list after his knee locked up while he was driving home. His wife had to help him crawl into his house after he squeezed himself out of his vehicle.

A month later, Oakland A's slugger Jose Canseco needed a cortisone shot in his jammed middle finger after he slammed it in his refrigerator door at home. Been there. Done that.

Even coaches fall to the evils of homelife. In August 1990, Dodger coach Joe Amalfitano required 22 stitches behind his ear after falling in his bathtub.

In 1991, Boston Red Sox right fielder Tom Brunansky lost four days of work when he jammed his toe in his backyard.

And Yankee outfielder Jesse Barfield missed a couple of games after burning his arm and spraining his left wrist during a fall in his sauna at home.

Dodgers pitcher Mike Morgan got hurt for Mom. In 1991, he was moving his mother's television set and injured muscles in his upper leg and groin. After working out with a boxing therapist in Las Vegas, he reported to training camp in good enough shape to be named to the All-Star squad in July.

Another Dodger who moved something he shouldn't have was infielder Alfredo Griffin. Griffin cut his toe while helping a carpet shampooer move his couch. He missed two weeks in May 1991.

Also in 1991, Angels catcher Ron Tingley switched uniform numbers—from his normal number 41 to the departed Chili Davis's number 24—and inherited Davis's back problems. Davis, who had had pain in his back the previous year, left the ball club for greener pastures, and Tingley, who got Davis's old uni, injured his own back while clearing some trees near his Nevada home. He was unable to take batting practice for two weeks.

The winter of 1991 was a tough one for ballplayers at home. Cleveland Indians first baseman Keith Hernandez moved some furniture in his apartment and sustained a back injury that put him behind schedule for much of spring training.

And later that year, Dodger outfielder Brett Butler tore the skin off the little toe on his left foot while chasing two of his three daughters up some steps with his three-year-old son on his back. Butler was pretending to be a shark, and he crashed into a wall. Land shark?

And one of the final home-related injuries of 1991 occurred when Atlanta's save leader that season, Juan Berenguer, injured his forearm when he hit a table while wrestling with his children.

Man, those kids are tough. Baseball players ought to stay away from them.

GOLF IS DANGEROUS TO THE METS' PITCHERS

On April 26, 1993, New York Mets ace Dwight Gooden reported an injury that kept him from starting a game against the Dodgers. Gooden had been struck on the shoulder blade that afternoon by Vince Coleman's practice swing with a new golf club he had brought into the clubhouse.

Earlier that spring, pitcher Sid Fernandez was on the golf course and was blindsided by a golf cart driven by another Mets player, Terry Bross. Fernandez injured his left knee and was saved from further injury when teammate John Franco sprinted and dove to catch him before he fell in the lake.

BREAKING UP (FIGHTS) IS HARD TO DO

On August 9, 1990, Mets outfielder Kevin McReynolds suffered back spasms following his breaking up of a bench-clearing brawl between the Mets and Phillies.

Balitmore Oriole first baseman Glenn Davis suffered a broken jaw while breaking up a fistfight while on a rehabiliation assignment to AAA Rochester: He ran to help teammate Randy Ready who was outnumbered in a bar altercation, and Davis took one in the mouth.

SLOPPY MANICURE

Ben McDonald was scheduled to debut in early 1991 when he was scratched from the lineup due to bad weather and a bad manicure. McDonald admitted he had clipped a fingernail on his pitching hand a little too close and injured himself.

JUST CLUMSY

California Angels third baseman Jack Howell needed three stitches in 1990 to close a cut on his right index finger that put him out of action for a week. He sliced the finger on a staple that was securing the top of a box of bats he was opening.

In September 1990, Twins first baseman Kent Hrbek sprained his left ankle while running through the clubhouse in a bit of postshower horseplay. His shower clogs didn't support him very well.

In spring training 1991, San Francisco Giants rookie catcher Steve Decker sprained his left foot while running to avoid an autograph seeker who had jogged onto the field during practice.

Another spring 1991 injury befell Cleveland Indians speedster Alex Cole, who dislocated his right shoulder when he tripped coming out of the batter's box during an exhibition game in Phoenix. After hitting a line drive to right, Cole turned to run to first, tripped, and landed on his right shoulder. Maybe he tripped over the foul line.

In spring 1992, Cardinals utility infielder Geronimo Pena broke his collarbone while shagging flies in the outfield. The 24-year-old reached for a ball, tripped over his glove, and fell on his left shoulder.

And during the season, Cardinals left fielder Bernard Gilkey suffered two chip fractures and a dislocation on his right thumb when he tripped over the bullpen mound in San Diego and fell into a wall.

IT'S WISE TO CURB YOUR TEMPER

In 1991, Angels pitcher Scott Bailes sprained his right foot when he jumped in the air in frustration after losing a Ping-Pong match in the team's game room.

And Cubs slugger George Bell threw a tantrum, a shoe and an ankle when he stomped and kicked after a 5-4 loss to the Phillies at Wrigley. Bell was 0-for-2 and felt he should have done better, so he kicked the dirt and found the confines weren't friendly to his foot.

Dodgers center fielder Brett Butler lost some games and points off his average in 1991 when he suffered a thumb injury in August. He hit a trash can in anger after a poor game and thrashed his digit.

SNIFFING

California Angels reliever Joe Grahe sniffed himself into pain in 1993. He was clearing his nasal passages when he pinched a nerve in his neck that made it uncomfortable for him to throw. His cold and cruel teammates started calling him "Neckersley" after his neck injury.

WORKOUTS MAY BE HAZARDOUS TO YOUR HEALTH

San Diego Padres lefty pitcher Atlee Hammaker fractured a finger on his throwing hand in a weight-lifting accident and missed the start of the Padres training camp in 1991.

Minnesota Twins infielder Gene Larkin was out of the Twins' 1990 lineup for a few days after injuring his left ring finger while exercising.

And Angels right-hander Mike Fetters strained a hamstring muscle during conditioning drills in 1991. The injury put him on the shelf for a week.

TONY OLIVA

Tony Oliva, the great-hitting outfielder for the Twins in the 1960s and 1970s, broke into professional ball by batting .410 for Wytheville of the Appalachian League in 1961. Recently he was reading a book on baseball superstitions, *The Incomplete Book of Baseball Superstitions, Rituals and Oddities*, and came to a story about a fellow Cuban, pitcher Luis Tiant, who rubbed marijuana and honey on his arm as an injury cure-all for his arm. Oliva said, "Yeah, marijuana and honey works, but only on your arm. For your leg, you've got to rub tobacco and rum on the injury."

Oliva also swears by his "miracle lady."

In 1969, Oliva tore the ligaments in his shoulder while playing against Baltimore in the American League Championship Series—he still hit .385 in the play-off. When he went to Mexico to play winter ball and couldn't play through the pain, he was sent by local fans to "The Miracle Lady in the Mountains." She rubbed his arm and shoulder with special water and oil and told him not to throw for five days. From that point on, Oliva says, he never had another arm problem.

In 1976, he took two Cuban pitchers down to see his miracle lady. She saved their careers as well.

In 1978, Oliva advised the Detroit Tigers to send Mark "The

Bird" Fidrych, who was a shadow of his 1976, Rookie-of-the-Year self, to see the Miracle Lady. Oliva said it wouldn't cost the Tigers a cent. No money, just travel expenses for Fidrych, and they'd have their star back. The Tigers didn't take Oliva up on his offer, and "The Bird" was finished.

Oliva also reports that whenever Red Sox Hall of Fame outfielder Ted Williams had a sore shoulder, stiff neck or tight arms, he'd go out to rural Boston and shovel snow during the spring and dirt during the summer, to loosen up. It seemed to work for "The Splendid Splinter," and there must be two dozen teams out there willing to dump snow outside their ballparks to see if it works for their hitters.

There are as many cure-alls as there are injuries and believers in the power of potions and salves. . . .

INJURY CURE-ALLS

August Weyhing, a pitcher who won 264 and lost 235 for more than half a dozen clubs from 1887 to 1901, was nicknamed "Rubber-Winged Gus." He had everything but control, having hit 286 opposing batters and walked 1,566, eighth on the all-time list.

Weyhing got his nickname from his ritual of soaking his arms—every day—in hot water and never letting his team trainer touch him. He maintained that his regimen kept his "wing" loose. He claimed never to have gotten a sore arm during his career, despite pitching 4,234 innings over his 14-year career.

Nolan Ryan threw with speed and effectiveness for more than a quarter century in The Bigs, far longer than any power pitcher ever dreamed of performing in The Show. Perhaps it was due to his cure-all. He soaked his fingers in pickle brine when he was a rookie with the New York Mets in 1966 and went back to it whenever necessary throughout his 27-year, record-setting career.

Roger Clemens, the Red Sox fireballer, strengthens his fingers by exercising them in bowls of uncooked rice.

Another fireballer, reliever Rob Dibble of the Cincinnati Reds, avoids injury to his hands by refraining from shaking hands. He also has cut back on his autograph signing. "I won't sign many autographs," he says, "because I have to take care of my arm." But he doesn't mind throwing the baseball, and that includes firing it at opponents running to first base, as he did at Doug Dascenzo in 1992.

In 1992, the Los Angeles Dodgers feared the mental game was getting the best of them, so they enlisted the aid of a team psychiatrist, Dr. Herndon Harding, who traveled with the team on the road. He even wore a Dodger uniform and patrolled the outfield during batting practice looking for a few good minds. Hey, wait a minute . . . this isn't a cure-all. The Dodgers finished dead last in 1992 with a 63-99 record. The doctor was not asked back in 1993.

INJURY NUGGETS

Note from the American Medical Association: In 1992, it was determined that 16 percent of the 1,109 Major League players on the 40-man rosters suffered from mouth sores directly related to tobacco—rough cut, snuff or other variations.

In December 1991, Toronto Blue Jays left-hander Jimmy Key broke his right ankle outside his Tarpon Springs, Florida, home. Key was at the top of a 12-foot ladder changing a security light bulb when the ladder wobbled and the pitcher jumped to "safety," landing awkwardly in a grassy area. How many lefties does it take to screw in a light bulb?

Los Angeles Dodger catcher Steve Yeager was speared in the neck by a bat shard following a foul by teammate Bill Russell on September 6, 1976. Yeager, who was in the on-deck circle, had nine splinters removed from his neck. The injury inspired team bullpen coach Mark Cresse to invent a safety flap that hangs down from the bottom of all catchers' masks.

In a less serious splintering, California Angels outfielder Tim Salmon was struck by the jagged edge of teammate Stan Javier's broken bat June 8, 1993. Salmon was in the ever-dangerous on-deck circle when Javier was handcuffed, sending the broken bat sticking into the triceps area of Salmon's left arm. Salmon recovered nicely enough. He was the 1993 American League Rookie of the Year.

New York Yankees second baseman Billy Martin went to spring training in 1952 secure that he'd be a Bronx Bomber starter. Helping our buddy Joe DiMaggio, who was in his first year as a television commentator, Martin agreed to appear in a spot in which he would demonstrate sliding for the audience.

Martin's first two slides were great for the camera: a headfirst dive and a classic hook style. DiMaggio asked for one more, a hard breakup slide into second. Martin jumped, stuck out his leg and . . . broke his ankle on camera and was out of action for a month.

A far less serious "injury" happened to far less of a gamer, Florida Marlins infielder Bret Barberie, in 1994. Barberie complained that his contact lenses were causing him discomfort. Jerry Browne was penciled in to replace him in the lineup until the boo-boo subsided. Kind of reminds you of "The Iron Man" Ripken.

Steve Foster was recalled from the Minors to give the Cincinnati Reds some relief pitching in 1992. On his way to rejoin the club, Foster injured his shoulder throwing his suitcase into his truck on his way to the airport.

Cleveland Spiders right fielder Lou Sockalexis, a Penobscot Indian from Maine who is thought by many to be the first Native American to play Major League baseball (1897-1899), suffered an injury in 1897 that severely hurt his fielding skills, which had been considered exceptional prior to the accident. According to reports of the day, Sockalexis fell victim to "a pale-faced maiden." Following an exaggerated lovemaking marathon and an abundance of "the grape," his right-field play became punctuated with stumbling, fumbling and humbling performances. It didn't affect his bat, however, as he hit .338.

Lawton Walter "Whitey" Witt, an outfielder for the A's and Yankees in the 1920s, was a drinking buddy of Babe Ruth. During the game in which the Yankees captured the 1922 pennant on the last weekend of the season by defeating the St. Louis Browns, who finished a game back, a fan threw a bottle from the stands and conked the Yankee on the head, rendering him unconscious. As the St. Louis crowd grew unruly, American League President Ban Johnson sought to diffuse the rising anger and ruled that Witt had stepped on the bottle, after which it flew in the air and struck him on the head. Was Ban Johnson part of the Warren Commission? He'd have loved the "Single, Magic Bullet Theory."

One man who did conk himself was Ed Stewart, an outfielder for the Minor League Vancouver Canadians of the Western International League. On May 10, 1939, Stewart swung at and missed a fastball and knocked himself unconscious when his follow-through allowed the bat to crack against his head. It was only strike two, but Stewart was out . . . cold.

Another Minor Leaguer who "dogged" it was an outfielder named Hill who played for the Binghamton Bingoes in 1899 against the Cortland Wagon Makers. Hill loped after a long foul fly, and as he reached for the ball, he was bitten on the leg by a vicious dog who apparently didn't want the fielder to make the play. The serious injury led to surgery and prevented Hill from playing ball for three months. When he returned to the lineup against his old nemesis, Cortland, the dog was gone and so was Hill's injury. He returned with a bang and hit a grand slam to lead Binghamton to the victory.

After Cincinnati Reds manager Lou Piniella lost his third consecutive game to Atlanta to put the Reds out of the 1991 pennant race, Piniella said, "I really don't know what to say. I really don't. I've got a headache."

SPECIAL CITATIONS

Capricious doesn't do justice to this man of grit. Sylvester Adam Simon, a right-handed hitting and throwing third baseman from Evansville, Indiana, played 1,072 games in The Minors and 23 in the Majors (for the St. Louis Browns in 1923-24) from 1920 to 1932. A career .320 hitter in the bush leagues, Simon had most of his thumb and the three inner fingers of his left hand severed in 1926 in an industrial saw injury at the factory in which he worked in the off-season. Left with a thumb stump and his little finger, Simon devised a special glove and a mechanical grip for holding the bat. He responded by hitting .360 for Ft. Wayne (Central League) in 1928 and .338 with a career high of 30 homers for Erie (Central League) in 1929. His career-best batting average of .364 was achieved in 1930, back with Ft. Wayne.

And who says it is the grizzled veterans who have all the grit? A college player with grit and electric personality who doesn't let a shocking injury get him down is Ryan Whitaker, a pitcher for Arkansas University. On March 28, 1993, in a game at Fayetteville, a lightning strike knocked out the scoreboard. Whitaker, who was raking the mound as teammates rolled a protective tarpaulin on the field, felt the shock wave and was blasted 10 feet in the air returning to earth with a thud. He was taken to a hospital and checked out and returned in time to pitch scoreless ninth and tenth innings to give Arkansas a 5-4 victory.

Whitaker said, "I felt the electricity come up through my spikes in my right leg and I went up . . . and down. I took my spikes off but couldn't put any pressure on my leg at all. I wasn't knocked out . . . but I wasn't all there, either."

He was all there in the ninth and tenth and got the win.

Positively electric.

INJURY WARNING

Outfielder Andy Van Slyke of the Pittsburgh Pirates, talking about Atlanta Braves ace pitcher Steve Avery who had put together a string of 16⅓ scoreless innings in the play-offs, talked about disease and future illness. "If Avery is in the league much longer, I'm going to develop a new disease: Averyitis. That's what we [Pirates] have: Poison Averyitis. If he's in the league five or six years, I might poison him."

CHAPTER NINE

Nicknames From Hell

*"What's in a name? That which we call a rose
By any other name would smell as sweet."*
—WILLIAM SHAKESPEARE

"Oh, call it by some better name. . . ."
—THOMAS MOORE

Warning: This chapter contains ethnic slurs and archaic and objectionable sterotypes and inappropriate language used to degrade or define players under the language and mores of the day. Ballplayers, it seems, were never politically correct.

They just don't build nicknames like they used to. Of course, in this era of political correctness, maybe it's just as well.

Gone are many of the great names of the past for various reasons — kinder and gentler stereotypes for one — and it is arguable that some players minus their nicknames become bland by comparison, their on-the-field accomplishments notwithstanding.

And, of course, the language has changed as has the way we describe things. In baseball of yesteryear, ailing pitchers had sore arms. Today, they have impingements, rotator cuff tears and ligament inflation. Bad wheels were a result of charley horses. Today, they are cruciate ligament strains. Batters who could knock in a run or two, but were terrible on defense were called "good hit, no field." Today, they are "designated hitters." Pitchers who couldn't go the distance were "six-inning" wonders. Today they are referred to simply as "millionaires."

Baseball has moved on with the times.

Through baseball history, the most popular baker's dozen nicknames (in alphabetical order) have been "Babe," "Buck," "Bud" (and "Buddy"), "Butch," "Chief," "Cy," "Doc," "Dutch," "Kid," "Lefty," "Red," "Rube" and "Whitey." Those who plead for political correctness are cetainly happy that many of these nicknames, as well as many more that weren't as popular, have disappeared from the baseball landscape. Attitudes and changing times have seen a diminishing of these chestnuts of the past.

Gone is the nickname "Whitey," except in the locker room or the parking lots of inner city ballparks after the games. So the classy Yankee Hall Of Fame lefty becomes Eddie Ford, Lefty Ford, or his inside nickname of "Slick." Player, manager, exec "Whitey" Herzog has another nickname to move to, and anyone who has ever seen his haircut knows that "The White Rat" is appropriate for all days and eras.

In 1927, perhaps the most feared lineup in baseball history was assembled in New York: The Bronx Bombers. Murderer's Row. The highest team slugging percentage in history—.489. One hundred ten victories to win the pennant by 19 games. The awesome lineup of center fielder Earle Combs (.356, 231 hits—tops in the league), shortstop Mark Koenig (.285, 11 triples), right fielder Babe Ruth (.356, 60 homers, 164 RBIs), first baseman Lou Gehrig (.373, 47 homers, 175 RBIs), second sacker Tony "Poosh 'Em Up" Lazzeri (.309, 18 homers, 102 RBIs, 22 steals), left fielder Bob Meusel (.337, 103 RBIs, 24 stolen bases—second in the league), followed by third baseman "Jumpin' Joe" Dugan (.269), and catcher Pat Collins (.275). Awesome, yes. But Murderer's Row? Today that would be unacceptable. Today, that Yankee lineup might be called "Guns and Roses" or "The Terrorists" or "The Patriot Missiles" or maybe even "The Mighty Morphin Power Rangers." Can you imagine Babe, Lou and Lazzeri et al. on a poster with Power Ranger attire as they morph into feared sluggers?

Calling someone a "bum" is homeless-bashing, so the Brooklyn Bums become the Brooklyn Homeless, or the Brooklyn Domestically Challenged.

"Giants" is a slap at those with glandular irregularities, so the New York/San Francisco Giants become the San Francisco Vertically Enriched.

A weighty problem is flab. "Fat Freddie" Fitzsimmons, the 5'11", 240-pound pitcher for the Giants and Dodgers in the 1920s, 1930s and 1940s, and "Fat Jack" Fisher, a pitcher in the 1960s for the Mets at 6'2", 220 pounds, as well as "Fat" Freddy Gladding, the 6'1", 240-pound pitcher for the Tigers and Astros in the 1960s, might be "Calorically Advanced" Fitzsimmons, "Metabolically Challenged" Fisher and "High-Density" Gladding today. How come these "Fat" guys are all pitchers? I guess it's because you wouldn't call Gates Brown, 5'11", 240-pound slugger for the Tigers, "Fat." Or Cecil Fielder, 6'3", 260-pound behemoth for the Tigers. At least not when they held a bat in their hands. And to follow up on Gates Brown, William James was called "Gates" by his mother when he was five years old for his propensity for hanging out at the family farm's gate. (The moniker was not hung on him, as is commonly thought, because he spent time in prison before being signed by the Tigers. The term refers to the family farm, not the big house.)

The Cleveland Indians were named after their popular Native American team member Lou Sockalexis, thought to be the first full-blooded Native American to play in the Majors, so they really should be correctly renamed the Cleveland Sockalexi. As for the Boston/Milwaukee/Atlanta Braves, the Atlanta Native Americans might be better, but it might be better just to tomahawk-chop the whole thing and rename the club for something they're more "fonda," like the Shape-ups or the Videos.

Back to Native Americans ... you'd never get away with "Chief" Bender or Allie "Superchief" Reynolds today. Those two fine pitchers—Bender with the Philadelphia A's and Reynolds with the Yankees—would be candidates for other sobriquets today, dealing with their skills and not ethnicity. The same goes for "Chief" Meyers, "Chief" Yellowhorse, and "Chiefs" Aker, Blatnick, Bowles, Cheeves, Chouneau, Eaves, Harder—a misnomer, because he was not Native American, only a great pitcher for Cleveland—Harrelson, and more than a dozen others. It's amazing how many "Chiefs" were pitchers ... just as many of the "Mooses" were first basemen. "Moose" Skowron, "Moose" Dropo, "Moose" Alexander, "Moose" Grimshaw and "Moose" Werden were all big and hulking first-sackers. "Mooses" Clabaugh, Marshall, Moryn and Solters were big, lumbering outfielders; "Moose" Farrell was a small but slow-footed second baseman, and "Mooses" Earnshaw and Haas were slow-moving, huge pitchers. "Chief" may only be used with reservation these days, but "Moose" won't put you on the horns of a dilemma ... it stands the test of time.

And two nicknames for the less-than-fleet-of-foot went to "Slow" Alejandro Pena, a pitcher, mostly for the Dodgers, who began his career in 1981 and who won't speed up his game or his pace for anyone, and "Slow Joe" Doyle, aka Judd Doyle, a pitcher for the Highlanders during the first decade of this century, who was also guilty of taking his own sweet time on the mound. This nickname, as well as others devoted to slow-moving ballplayers, doesn't make it in the politically correct 1990s, in which it is gauche to make fun of the velocity challenged.

Another name that is out is "Shorty," as in outfielders Glenn "Shorty" Crawford and Robert "Shorty" Randman and catcher John "Shorty" Shea, all of whom were 5′9″. Today, such men are vertically challenged and not to be made fun of.

One old-time moniker with an alteration that still works belongs to the Waner brothers. Though their nicknames, Paul "Big Poison" and Lloyd "Little Poison" Waner, were the Brooklynese mispronunciation for "person," as in "Here comes that Big Person (poison)," calling a player "Big Poison" might sell a slew of posters.

And to update an old one, Charlie "King Kong" Keller might be "Barney" Keller or, for something less purple, "Velociraptor" Keller.

Hall of Fame shortstop Phil "Scooter" Rizzuto got his moniker in reference to the way he scooted after balls hit near his position. Today, though, there are few scooters around and Phil might be "Skateboard" Rizzuto or "Rollerblade" Rizzuto.

Some noms de guerre just don't make it today and must be changed to fit the times.

"Shoeless Joe" Jackson once played in a Minor League game in South Carolina sans footwear. It seems that the all-time great hitter had blistered his feet the day before while breaking in a new pair of cleats. Today, "Shoeless" connotes someone down and out, and we can't have that, so a natural for a career .356 hitter on today's playing field might be Joe "It Must Be the Shoes" Jackson.

Mickey Mantle, was simply called "The Mick." Yankee PR director Red Patterson tried to tie in Mantle's hometown and his speed by calling him "the Commerce Comet," but it never stuck. Today, Mantle might be "Dr. Homerstein."

Willie Mays was "Say Hey" because of a phrase he greeted people with. Today he'd either be "Yo," or "Wha' s'up." But maybe "Magic" Mays is more suitable.

Sorry, Dwight Gooden, but Sandy Koufax would be "Dr. K" if he pitched today.

You'd never be able to get away with "Dizzy" Dean or "Daffy" Dean today — it indicated mental illness and we don't do that with our heroes today. So you'd probably settle for Jay Dean and Paul Dean, but you might see "Downtown" Dean or "Mean Jay" Dean.

Chicago Cubs faithful who are called "the Bleacher Bums" could be updated in a musical vein — "10,000 Maniacs."

JOE DiMAGGIO

Joe DiMaggio, the graceful "Yankee Clipper," might be "The Italian Stallion." It's poster material. DiMag was good enough to earn five nicknames — the good ones need more than one way to properly describe them. He got "Yankee Clipper" in reference to a swift and graceful sailing ship, "Joltin' Joe" jolted the ball out of the park, "Joe D." was all anyone had to say about the man, and his teammates called him "The Big Dago" to put him ahead of any other Italian athlete who bore the ethnic epithet "Dago." After two decades of television commercials, he is now also known as "Mr. Coffee." That's sad.

Joe set the Major League mark for longest hitting streak at 56 games. He said he had been contacted by the Heinz Company and its 57 varieties of food products, and if he had hit in 57 straight games in 1941, he would have made $25,000 for endorsing "Heinz 57." Then Joe would have been "Mr. 57."

TED WILLIAMS

Ted Williams was also great enough to have five fitting sobriquets tossed his way: "Teddy Ballgame," "The Splendid Splinter," "The Kid," "Big Guy," and "The Thumper." All of these nicknames were descriptive of his ability, stature, and penchant for taking control of a game. Today, he might be called, not "The Thumper," but "The Rapper." Or, a name similar to Charlie Keller's prehistoric moniker, "The Raptor." Or something musically fearsome, "H.W.A." — "Hitter With Attitude." Or "The Thumper" could change musically to "Smashing Pumpkins" or perhaps the more-baseball-appropriate "Smashing Apples."

"PEPPER" MARTIN

Johnny Martin reluctantly answered to the name "Pepper" during his "Gas House Gang" career with the St. Louis Cardinals (1928-1944). He got the name for his aggressive pepper-pot play. Martin hated the sobriquet. But he also had the longest nickname in baseball history : "The Wild Hoss of the Osage." Martin picked up that nom de guerre during his football-playing days for the Homing Indians team of Oklahoma in 1924. As a halfback, he galloped like a stallion for the team sponsored by the Osage Indians. Today, that name would reflect current climate, and Johnny Martin might be called "The Wild Jogger of the Ghetto" or "Swift Feet on the Street."

MORDECAI "THREE FINGER" BROWN

One of the standards of yesteryear that gets amputated from today's language is the publicizing of a player's handicap. Mordecai Brown was a Hall of Fame righty for the Cubs in the early part of this century. Brown, whose work as a coal miner earned him a better nickname, "Miner," lost his right index finger below the second joint, when, as a seven-year-old, he caught his hand in a corn shredder on his uncle's farm. His index finger was amputated, his middle finger mangled and crooked, and his little finger stubbed. This debility led Brown to develop an unorthodox delivery and grip, producing unnatural break on his curveball, making it extremely tough to follow, let alone hit. Still, the sobriquet "Three Finger" seems cruel in the current era of enlightened behavior.

Consider Jim Abbott, the sterling left-hander who signed off the U.S. Olympic Baseball team to pitch for the Angels and Yankees. Abbott was born without a right hand, but learned to throw lefty and field his position well by switching his glove to his throwing hand after releasing the pitch, fielding the ball, then taking off his glove and throwing. You wouldn't call him "One Hand" Abbott; that would be cruel.

And in an eerie similarity to Brown's dilemma, there is Yankee right-hander Bob Wickman. "Wick" lost the tip of his right index finger in a farming accident, when, as a two-year-old, he caught his digit in a compressor. The stump of a finger causes Wickman to grip and throw the ball irregularly, which, in turn, causes the ball to break and move irregularly. But you wouldn't call him "Three Finger" Wickman today; that would be cold. So by today's standards, "Three Finger" Brown would be as politically incorrect and downright mean as calling John Kruk, a victim of operable testicular cancer, "One Ball" Kruk.

Not that ballplayers have ever been a kind lot.

"DUMMY" HOY

William Ellsworth Hoy was a fleet outfielder for a number of teams around the turn of the century. The diminutive 5'4", 148 pounder spent 14 years in The Bigs, and though he was a good ballplayer — 2,054 hits and a .288 average — he was not one of the greats. His legacy has endured for more than a century because William Hoy was a deaf mute. Meningitis caused his disability when he was three. Ballplayers referred to him as "Dummy" because he was deaf and dumb. Hoy actually liked the name and preferred that to William. His legacy is that of signals. Umpires used to call all plays and balls and strikes, but for Hoy they would signal the calls by hand, which became standard practice. His coaches could not yell code words to him when he was in the field or at bat, so they used an elaborate series of gyrations to signal their instructions. That, too, became standard operating procedure. And no dummy, Hoy liked to have fun. Once in The Minors, playing for Oshkosh, he jumped on a horse and rode it to deep center to catch a fly ball. To show their appreciation of his play, fans would wave white handkerchiefs rather than cheer.

I can think of a few ballparks where handkerchiefs would be much more appreciated than the language and crowd noise.

Other "Dummy"'s included William Deegan (pitcher, 1901), Ed Dundon (pitcher, 1883-1884), George Leitner (pitcher, 1901-1902), Matt Lynch (pinch hitter, 1948), Herbert Murphy (shortstop, 1914) and Reuben Stephenson (outfield, 1892). Clearly Hoy was the best "Dummy" of the lot, and while certain of today's players have earned that title emotionally, not physically, it's nice to see that this abusive pseudonym hasn't been hung on anyone since 1948.

"BEANS" REARDON

John E. Reardon was one of the more colorful umpires of his era (1926-1949). He earned a reputation for his heavy drinking and abusive language and his friendship with Mae West—he appeared in five of her films.

He was a friendly man and often talked with fans in the stands before, during and after games. His slogan: "Never too busy to say hello."

Many think his nickname came from his being raised in Boston; he was a Boston bean. Others report that when Reardon was a teenager, he was playing baseball at a railroad station and one of the Pullman car painters yelled, "Come on Baked Beans, old boy, hit one now." The crowd heard the cry and yelled "Come on Beans." And the name stuck.

But according to Hall of Fame slugger Ralph Kiner and many others who squatted next to or stood within hearing distance of the umpire, Beans earned the nickname for doing thunderous and aromatic impressions of The Great LePetomaine. Or, to put it mildly, Beans had the granddaddy of all flatulence problems. He apparently was able to expel gas on cue. A belch was a ball and an outburst from a lower elevation was a strike.

The noise and the fumes caused more than one hitter and dozens of catchers to break out laughing or quickly bolt upwind.

Many ballplayers greeted Reardon with the singsong ditty, "Beans, beans, the musical fruit, the more you eat, the more you toot."

Speaking of fruit. . . .

NICK CULLOP

Players can be mean, if descriptive. Heinrich Nicholas "Nick" "Tomato Face" Cullop was one of the greatest Minor Leaguers of all time. He did spend five years in The Show in the 1920s and 1930s—.249, 11 homers—but he was a mainstay on the farm, playing for 24 years (1920-1944), appearing in 2,484 games, compiling a .312 average, driving in a Minor League career-record 1,857 runs, and belting 420 home runs—No. 3 on the all-time Minor League list.

The muscular, 6'0", 200-pound outfielder had a chameleonic face. His muzzle had a ruddy complexion, and when he was exerted or angry, his features would turn bright red . . . and round, hence "Tomato Face."

On his bad days, maybe he should have had a "V-8 Face."

"PEACHES" DAVIS

Ray "Peaches" Davis, a Cincinnati pitcher in the late 1930s, came by his name when, as a child, he sneaked into a nearby orchard and picked a ripe peach. He sat down to eat it and inadvertently rested his rear on a red ant hill. They covered his tender derriere and bit him, and the youngster began yelling. Saved by his mother and brother, his sibling laughed and said, "You like peaches so much, that's what we're going to call you from now on."

Other "Peaches" players included George "Peaches" Graham, (catcher, 1902-1912) — fans called him "a peach of a catcher" — and John "Peaches" Werhas (Dodgers-Angels, third base, 1964-1967) — a fight in college against a team from the Marine Corps inspired the military men to yell, "Are you all right, Peaches?" His college coach at USC, Rod Dedeaux, liked the taunt and hung it on the player for good. Ty Cobb was "The Georgia Peach" because he was from Georgia and he'd fight you if you just called him "Georgia."

OTHER FRUIT

Andy "Apple" Lapihuska, a Phillies pitcher duing the war years, ate a lot of apples and threw them, as well as baseballs, in menacing fashion.

"Strawberry Bill" Bernhard, a pitcher, mostly with Cleveland, in the first decade of this century, was a redhead and detested the name "Red." He preferred the nickname "Bernie," but sportswriters gave him "Strawberry Bill" in reference to his strawberry-red locks.

VEGETABLES

Luke Hamlin, a pitcher in the 1930s and 1940s, mostly for the Brooklyn Dodgers, got tagged with the observational "Hot Potato" Hamlin name when a New York sportswriter covering the Dodgers watched the pitcher bounce the ball gingerly from hand to hand between pitches, as though the ball was a hot potato.

Oscar "Spinach" Melillo, a second baseman from 1926 to 1937, mostly with the St. Louis Browns, had Bright's disease, which affected his kidneys. As he was put on a spinach-only diet for several months as treatment, fellow players let that nickname grow on him. Had he hit more homers—his best year was a five-spot—he could have been "Popeye" Melillo.

Moving from big vegetation to bigotry. . . .

"NIG" CLARKE

Jay Justin "J.J." "Nig" Clarke was one of the first Canadians to make it in The Bigs for a long career—nine years, mostly for Cleveland, in the first two decades of this century. The catcher, long admired for his defensive prowess, was an average hitter—.254 and six homers in 506 games—but he had a day to end all days in The Minors on June 15, 1902, in Ennis, Texas, when his Corsicana Oilers destroyed the Texarkana Tigers 51-3 in a Texas League game. While his teammates all had great games—53 hits among nine players—Clarke had the greatest day of all time. He went 8-for-10 and blasted eight home runs, driving in 14 runs. All of his hits were off Texarkana pitcher-owner C.B. DeWitt, who refused to come off the mound and pitched the entire game. Still, Clarke's day was incredible.

But back to his nickname. Clarke was a Wyandotte Indian, but was not called "Chief." He had a very dark complexion, and in those days, anyone who was swarthy, and not Negro, was called "Nig," an obvious racial slur encompassing a vulgarism for Negroes. The name "Nig" was given to scores of dark-complected athletes—most of whom were catchers or second basemen—including Joe Berry (Giants, second baseman, 1921-1922), George Cuppy (Cleveland [NL], pitcher, 1892-1901), Charles Fuller (Brooklyn, catcher, 1902), John Grabowksi (Yankees, catcher, 1924-1931), Gerard Lipscomb (St. Louis [AL], second baseman, 1937), John Perrine (Washington, second baseman, 1907), and Frank Elmer Smith (White Sox, pitcher, 1904-1915). Smith was also called "Piano Mover" and "Piano Legs," a reference to his stubby legs, stocky build and his off-season job.

Harlond Benton Clift, known as "Nig" Clift, was a power-hitting third baseman from 1934 to 1945. He got his nickname, not for his skin color, but for his name—a St. Louis Browns team-mate Alan Strange thought Clift's first name was "Harlem." Clift was also called "Darkie," also in reference to the Negro community of Harlem, New York. Charles Niebergall (catcher from 1921 to 1924) saw his last name bastardized into the moniker.

Notice that none of these guys and, as far as we can tell, no other players carried this derogatory name after Jackie Robinson broke the Major League's color barrier in 1947.

Those nicknames have disappeared, thank goodness, and today, all these players would be in search of ESPN's Chris Berman, "King of the Nickname Givers," who has bestowed some 700 monikers on athletes. As most deal with either food, music or celebrities, some of these men — with apologies to Berman — might be called "J.J. Clarke Bar," "Harlond Montgomery Clift," "Joe Chuck Berry," "Charles Fuller Brush Man" and "John Valerie Perrine."

And combining pure admiration for a remarkable athlete with jealousy and the vulgaristic bigotry of the day, we have one of the all-time greats, with the greatest collection of nicknames. . . .

BABE RUTH

George Herman "Babe" Ruth was given, and deserved, more nicknames than have ever been given to any ballplayer in Major League history—more than 30, possibly as many as 40. He was the man who saved the game. Even his home ballpark, Yankee Stadium, was given a Ruthian nickname, "The House That Ruth Built." He was "The Sultan of Swat," "The Bambino," "The Man Who Saved Baseball." He was bigger than life and so were many of his noms de guerre. But some would never make the cut today.

First, take "Babe." When Ruth attended St. Mary's Industrial School in Baltimore, he was just a kid who wanted to play ball with the older guys. They told him no, that he was "just a babe." Ruth himself wrote that when he played ball with the Minor League Baltimore Orioles in 1914—Ruth was 19 at the time, signed by owner Jack Dunn—a coach named Steinman told reporters, "Here's Jack's newest babe." A no-no for female ballplayers today, this one doesn't make it for males either. How about "The Kid," "The Natural" or "Dr. Ruth"?

But Babe is just the tip of the Ruth iceberg. While some names were complimentary, some were downright vicious, mean-spirited and crass.

His closest friends often called him "Jidge," a New England takeoff on his first name, George. Ruth himself referred to that name as "Jedge," a nickname used often by Yankee catcher Benny Bengough. Yankee owner Col. Jake Ruppert called Babe "Root," but that stems more from the brewery owner's German accent than anything else. He was also "Lefty" because, well, he was left-handed.

Sportswriters came up with an astonishing, but oft-deserved, string of cognomens including "Bambustin' Babe," "Manlin Mandarin," "The Great Gate God," "High Priest of Swat," "Colossus of Clout," "The Slambino," "King of Klout," "Battering Bambino," "Bustin' Babe," "King of Diamonds," "Caliph of Clout," "Caliph of Crash," "Potentate of the Pill," "Big Boy Blooie," "Behemoth of Bust," "Behemoth of Biff," "Behemoth of Blast," "Mightiest of the Maulers," "The Wizard of Whack" and "The Man."

Opposing players called him such crude names as "The Big Baboon," "The Big Monk," "Monkey," "Nig," "Nigger" and "Nigger Lips."

The simian epithets referred to his bulk and manners — he was 6'2" and weighed 200 pounds with huge biceps and few social graces whatsoever. He was, as Dodger broadcaster Vin Scully has said, "perhaps the biggest animal, in all manners of the word, the game of baseball has ever seen."

The dark-skinned invectives aimed at him seem to refer to several things: his appearance; the rumor started by jealous white players that Ruth had Negro ancestors; and as a swipe at Ruth for playing in barnstorming games against Negro teams and players. As Ruth was pure in his desire to play ball against all comers — skin color didn't matter to him, he just wanted a good game against the best competition — prejudiced men of the day likened that to baseball blasphemy and publicly said, Ruth must "be one of them" or at least a "Nigger lover."

Base comments aside, this king of the nicknames also bestowed plenty in his time. It was said that Ruth really couldn't remember people's names, so he gave them names he could remember. Many folks were called "Kid" or "Pops" by Ruth, who also called Yankee teammates such appellations as Lou "Buster" Gehrig, Myles "Duck Eye" Thomas, and Julian "Flop Ears" Wera. And to combat teammate Leo Durocher's profane riding of the Babe — he often called Ruth "Nigger Lips" — Babe got even with a descriptive nickname, calling Durocher "The All-American Out."

Even Babe's bats had nicknames. His dark bat, "Black Betsy," helped him hit 59 homers in 1921, and when he broke that, the two pieces of lumber he used in her stead, to break the mark with 60 in 1927, were named "Big Bertha" and "Beautiful Bella."

GARLAND BUCKEYE

So Babe Ruth had some 30 nicknames, Joe DiMaggio and Ted Williams had five nicknames, Stan Musial had three — "Stan The Man," "The Donora Greyhound" and "Stash" — and Sandy Koufax one — "Sandy." So maybe there isn't a direct relationship to degree of talent and number of nicknames, but you sure aren't going to be in Babe's lofty stratosphere without being in his talent range.

It seems to follow that you can get a name or two — or even three — without displaying a great deal of talent, but you couldn't surpass Joe D. or Teddy Ballgame unless you were really a baseball legend. Right? Wrong, "Wild Horse of the Osage" breath.

Garland Buckeye, who played football for the Chicago Cardinals of the NFL in 1921 to 1924, was a huge southpaw pitcher for the Senators, Indians and Giants from 1918 to 1928. The six-footer was bigger in physical presence than he was in talent, as a 30-39 record, 3.90 ERA, and 622 hits given up in 564 innings would indicate.

But Buckeye went nose to nose with Ruth — he gave up a homer to Babe in 1927 — in terms of nicknamery. Garland Buckeye was the recipient of nearly 30 sobriquets himself, generally given him by teammates and the press. Among his also-known-as's are "Gob," from his days in the U.S. Navy, "Great Lakes Dreadnaught," "Indians Bologna," "Indians' Bambino," "Ponderosa," "Hooks" and "Lefty," most of which described his girth, his pitching ability, and his home team of Cleveland.

His girth also earned him such names as "Dining Car Addict," "Mastodon Moundsman" and "Pitching Pachyderm," as well as a reported two dozen other digs.

Some less-cruel, more complimentary descriptions can also take on dramatic, illustrative visions. . . .

"DEATH TO FLYING THINGS"

Jack Chapman, an outfielder from 1860 to 1876 with the Philadelphia Athletics and Brooklyn Atlantics, played barehanded and thrilled fans with his long-running, one-handed catches. He seemed to snare anything out of the air that was hit his way, thus the moniker "Death to Flying Things."

Sharing the accolades and the nickname is Robert Ferguson, a leading ballplayer from the 1860s to 1880s. The infielder for the Brooklyn Atlantics — Chapman's teammate — and several other teams was equally adroit in the field. He was baseball's first switch-hitter but was a better fielder than hitter. He and Chapman teamed to help the Brooklyn Atlantic defeat the "unbeatable" Cincinnati Red Stockings in 1870, handing Cincy its first loss in two years.

Ferguson, who later became an umpire, was elected president of the National Association of Professional Baseball Players in 1872 and openly sought to raise the questionable morals and honesty of the athletes who were thought to be in league with gamblers. His fight for honest baseball led to the organization of the National League in 1876, raising the perception of ballplayers and the game as being honest and trustworthy.

LIPMAN PIKE

Staying in baseball's predawn era of the 1870s, we come to Lipman Pike, who is the answer to three baseball "firsts."

Among the firsts attributed to him: He is thought to be the first player to be paid (along with Jimmy Creighton), the first Jewish ballplayer in professional baseball, and the first professional ballplayer to hit a home run.

Lip Pike, who played for the Troy Haymakers, the Lord Baltimores, the Hartfords and St. Louis from the 1860s to 1875, was a remarkable athlete who played the outfield and was quick enough as a center fielder to run foul line to foul line to catch balls that would have eluded his slower fieldmates. He was a real "Death to Flying Things," though that name was never pinned on him.

The name he got was "The Iron Batter." In those days, iron was considered the strongest, toughest metal around. Even 60 years later, "Iron" was tacked onto Lou Gehrig, "The Iron Horse," and several "Iron Man" types (including George Davis, Joe McGinnity, Ray Mueller and Joe Oeschger — who pitched a 26-inning complete game May 1, 1920, for the Brooklyn Dodgers against the Boston Braves, whose pitcher, Leon Cadore, also completed the 1-1 tie). "Iron" was always complimentary until Chuck Hiller got "Iron Hands" for making too many errors at second base.

Pike was "The Iron Batter" for several reasons. He apparently hit the ball extremely hard and it supposedly took someone of iron to do that, and Pike was one of the first players to employ the macho posturing of not rubbing a spot after being hit by a pitched ball. Pike got hit a lot and never rubbed. He was made of iron.

Nice legacy. This black-and-blue badge of courage has lasted 130 years. Now, from complimentary to biting commentary. . . .

CARL "SKOONJ" FURILLO

Carl Furillo was a Brooklyn hero from 1946 until the team's move west in 1958. He stayed with the transplanted Dodgers through 1960. The strong, 6'0", 200-pound outfielder had a powerful swing—26 homers in 1955—and a strong arm—151 assists in his career. He preferred the nickname "The Reading Rifle," a nom de guerre he earned while playing for Reading, Pennsylvania, in the Eastern League, where he threw out six runners at first base from right field on hits that should have been singles.

He also got some nicknames he detested. He was called "Rock" and "Rock Head" for his lack of education, and the name that stuck the longest among his teammates and opponents in The Bigs was "Skoonj," which is short for the Italian word *scungeli*, or snail. It was a reference to his Italian heritage linked to the observation that he was as slow as a snail on the bases. Escargot anyone?

BABE RUTH'S LEGS/MICKEY MANTLE'S LEGS

When you're a superstar legend, as were Babe Ruth and Mickey Mantle, you not only get nicknames yourself, but they are also bestowed upon those who fill in for you.

Sammy Byrd, an outfielder from 1929 to 1936, mostly with the Yankees, got the tag "Babe Ruth's Legs" due to his primary role with the Bronx Bombers, that of being a pinch runner or late-inning replacement in the outfield for the Bambino . . . to save Babe's legs. He was also called "Babe Ruth's Caddy" because of his golfing ability. Byrd was one of the finest golfers of his day, arguably the best of that time to ever play baseball.

Jump ahead 25 years and on the Yankees from 1961 to 1963, you have Mickey Mantle needing pinch runners and late-inning replacements in the outfield to save his legs. And you also have Jack Reed, "Mickey Mantle's Legs." Reed played 222 games, yet only went to bat 129 times. He was also called "Mickey Mantle's Caddy," probably because Mick took the young man golfing with him on several occasions during the season. It was the least the Mick could do for the guy who saved his legs.

Staying with body parts. . . .

"THE ARM"

Tom Hafey, a third baseman from 1939 to 1944, had an unusually strong and accurate throw from third to first. Losing time out to the war effort, Hafey got in only 78 games for the Giants and Browns, hitting .248 and committing eight errors—presumably fielding and not throwing miscues.

"BOOTNOSE"

Fred Hofmann, a catcher from 1919 to 1928, mostly with the New York Yankees in their dynastic beginnings, had a long nose that curved in such a fashion that it looked to some like a boot. If he was Italian, he may have been called "The Nose of Italy" because it was also described as looking like a map of that country. He was a backup backstop, but his face took a back door to no one.

"BURRHEAD"

Baseball has had two "Burrheads." The most famous was Ferris Fain, a clutch-hitting and slick-fielding first baseman from 1947 to 1955. Fain won back-to-back batting crowns in 1951 and 1952 for the Philadelphia A's and was considered the finest-fielding first sacker in the league until Vic Power came up with Philadelphia in 1954. He was a tremendous contact hitter with a great eye and in 1,151 games drew 903 walks while striking out only 261. He hit .290.

While playing in the Pacific Coast League in the 1940s, Fain's roommate, Win Ballow, called him "Burrhead" in reference to a really bad haircut. He also got the name "Cocky" as a mispronunciation of cockeyed. It seems that his trainer didn't think Fain's eyes were in synch.

The other "Burrhead" was Joe Dobson, a pitcher from 1939 to 1954, who threw 12⅔ innings without allowing an earned run for Boston in the 1946 World Series against St. Louis. He was a steady pitcher who won 18 games in 1947 and went 137-103 in his career. Dobson got the name in reference to his tightly curled hair. He also was a candidate for another nickname, as he lost his thumb and left forefinger while playing with a blasting cap at age nine. He could have been another pitching "Three Finger" in addition to Mordecai Brown.

"CORNS"

Hugh Bradley, a first baseman from 1910 to 1915, mostly with Boston in the American League, had terrible feet that hurt his play. His corns were notorious, and he had to soak his feet for hours before and after games. The pain limited his action to 277 games, never more than 118 in a season.

"THE HEAD"

How can you do this to a player who was godlike to others? Well, players can be cruel, so even a Hall of Famer such as Brooks Robinson can't escape their wrath. Brooks, the perennial all-star third baseman for the Baltimore Orioles from 1955 to 1977, earned his more commendatory nickname of "The Human Vacuum Cleaner" for his ability to sweep up any ball hit his way. Robinson played 23 years, appeared in 2,896 games, and was a 16-time Gold Glove winner. Considered by many the finest-fielding hot-corner player in the history of the game, Robinson, one of the game's nice guys, was readily recognizable on the field for his play and off the field for his receding hairline.

With his scalp thinning since his early years in the game, Robinson was called "The Head" by playful teammates who swore they could see more of Robinson's skull every day.

"RIBS"

Frank Raney, a pitcher from 1885 to 1890, was not called "Ribs" because of his appetite for baby backs. Just the opposite, it was for his lack of appetite. When he was a teenager, he stood 6'4" and weighed only 150 pounds, and whenever he played ball without his shirt on, teammates could see his ribs poking out.

"SCHNOZZ"

Noses are a popular item to pick on in baseball. And one of the most popular players with a prominent proboscis was Ernie Lombardi, a catcher from 1931 to 1947, mostly with Cincinnati and the Giants. A two-time batting title winner, Lombardi caught in 1,542 games and was behind the plate for both of Johnny Vander Meer's no-hitters in 1938. An Italian from Oakland, he was also called "Sausage Nose" in Italian by his buddies, but "Schnozz" was the name that hit it right on the nose. He was a big man with big skills and a big nose.

Leaving human bodies for piscine ones. . . .

JIM "MUDCAT" GRANT

Jim Grant was a steady pitcher from 1958 to 1971, toiling mostly for the Indians and Twins, for whom he won 21 games in 1965 to make him the first black American Leaguer to win 20 in a single season. Grant got his nickname due to an error by a teammate. While playing for Fargo-Moorehead in the Northern League in 1954, his buddy Bartow Irby thought Grant was from Mississippi, the "Mudcat State," and called Grant "The Mississippi Mudcat" and then "Mudcat." The moniker stuck, though Grant protested. He is from Lacoochee, Florida, not Mississippi.

It's a good thing he didn't think Grant was from Louisiana, otherwise Irby might have called him "Louise."

"CATFISH" HUNTER

Jim Hunter was one of the classiest pitchers to take the mound from 1965 to 1979 with the Royals, A's and Yankees. The Hall of Famer won 20 or more games five seasons in a row en route to a 224-166 record. He was a gamer. He also had a bogus nickname. When Kansas City A's owner Charles Finley signed Hunter out of high school in 1964 for a $50,000 bonus, the publicity-minded Finley called a press conference to announce the deal. Deciding that Hunter needed a nickname, Finley hit on the idea that if Hunter was from Hertford, North Carolina, then he must be a backwoods fisherman. And if he was a backwoods fisherman then he must catch catfish. So Finley introduced his new find as "Catfish" Hunter. The supposition was apocryphal. Hunter never caught a catfish in his life, and as soon as he was able, he left Charles Finley's employ, suing him for breach of contract in 1974, becoming the first big-salary free agent in base-ball history by signing a five-year $3.75 million contract with the Yankees.

Another misnomer, if you bring this story ahead 100 years, is the story of "The Only" Nolan.

"THE ONLY" NOLAN

Edward Sylvester Nolan was a pitcher for five teams in five years from 1878 to 1885, during which time he won 23, lost 52, but gained prominence by pitching as a teenager in his home state for the New Jersey Olympics, an amateur team that was nearly unbeatable. At 16, he played with skill against players 10-15 years his senior.

In 1878, at age 19, he was signed by Indianapolis for the princely sum of $2,500. Heading north from their spring training site in New Orleans, Indianapolis won 11 consecutive exhibition games, six by shutout, and Nolan was the team's only pitcher. Nolan was the only hurler they used, and he became "The Only" Nolan.

He went on to go 13-22 that year and didn't last long.

One hundred years later, with Nolan Ryan pitching for 27 years, winning 324 games, striking out 5,714 batters and throwing seven no-hitters, many felt he should be called "The Only" No-lan, but it never stuck, and "The Express" remained Ryan's most fitting sobriquet, describing his 100 mph fastball.

Speaking of misnomers, how about "Home Run" Baker?

"HOME RUN" BAKER

Frank Baker was a solid third baseman who played from 1908 to 1922 with the Philadelphia A's and New York Yankees. He had power in the dead ball era and did lead his league in home runs four years in a row (1911-1914) with totals of 11, 10, 12 and 9. Hardly Ruthian numbers, but enough at the time to warrant praise. Still Baker's career total of 96 four-baggers in 13 years seems a bit light to support such a nickname.

Baker was given the name, however, for two home runs hit in the World Series—kind of like Reggie Jackson being called "Mr. October" largely on the strength of his three-home-run perform-ance in game six of the 1977 Series against the Dodgers. For Baker, it was the 1911 World Series against the New York Giants.

Baker hit a game-winning blast off Rube Marquard to win game two and hit one in the ninth inning of game three against Christy Mathewson to tie the game and send it into extra innings. His A's won the Series in six games.

The baseball world was so thrilled by Baker's performance that they hung the name on him and began calling home runs "Bakers," much the way homers are now called "dingers," "taters" or "knocks."

Another misnomer. . . .

"THE GAY RELIEVER"

Baseball may have come to terms with the 1990s, but few diamond heroes have come out of the closet. So before you jump to sexual orientation conclusions, this nickname has nothing to do with male-male relationships. In the old days, "gay" meant light-hearted and party-animal behavior.

Joe Page, who from 1944 to 1954 was one of baseball's best relief pitchers for the dynasty Yankees, was also called "Fireman" for his ability to put out fires, or opponents' rallies, late in the game. He preferred that as well as "Smokey Joe," an accolade for his good fastball.

But Page also liked the nightlife. He was a free spirit who could party in New York until dawn and come out throwing smoke again the next day. It was this fun-loving behavior that saw him, through the vocabulary of the day, called "gay." Hence, he was "The Gay Reliever."

The closet remains closed.

Or maybe not. Consider the nickname "She". . . .

"SHE" DONAHUE

Charles Michael Donahue was an infielder for the Cardinals and Phillies in 1904, playing 62 games and hitting .219 while committing 38 errors. The Oswego, New York, native was also given a nickname that stuck so closely that few knew his given name was Charles; they just thought he was "She."

"She" Donahue was a mild-mannered ballplayer and acquired the name by fitting one of the following criteria of the day for calling a male "She." (This particular nickname had several meanings and reasons behind the tag.) The person either had to be of different sexual orientation, have feminine characteristics, or be a nonsmoker, nondrinker, nonswearer. Donahue, apparently, fit at least one of the standards.

On to a more widely regarded ballplayer with known manly tendencies, but also the bestower of a feminine nickname. . . .

"SATCHEL" PAIGE

Leroy Robert Paige was, without argument, one of the finest pitchers of his era, a reign that covered five decades. As a pitcher in the Negro Leagues, semipro leagues, barnstorming tours and leagues in Mexico, Canada, Cuba and the Dominican Republic, it is thought that Paige pitched in close to 3,000 games.

Playing in the Negro Leagues for such franchises as the Birmingham Black Barons, Chattanooga Black Lookouts, Cleveland Cubs, Pittsburgh Crawfords, Kansas City Monarchs, Philadelphia Stars and Baltimore Black Sox, Paige drew capacity crowds to watch his skill, guile and charisma.

He was finally allowed to play in the Majors after Jackie Robinson broke baseball's color barrier in 1947. On July 7, 1948, starting for the Cleveland Indians, he became, at 42 (though some reports had him as old as 48), the oldest rookie in Major League history and the first black to pitch in the American League. Paige lasted five years with Cleveland and the St. Louis Browns. He also made a token appearance in 1965 for the A's.

Paige got his nickname "Satchel" while working at a train depot in Mobile, Alabama, as a youth. He took a pole and some ropes and rigged a system to tote suitcases, three or four at a time, to earn money. Other kids, amazed at his ingenuity, but amused by the look of this tall, skinny kid lugging satchels with a rope and two poles, said he looked like "a satchel tree." Soon all of his friends and neighbors called him "Satchel," and the name endured. Paige later remarked, "That's when Leroy Paige became no more and Satchel Paige took over. Nobody called me Leroy, nobody, excepting Mom and the government."

He was as big a hero in his circles as Babe Ruth was in his— big enough to name other players, as well as his own tools. Paige named his pitches, and they became known far and wide by his descriptions. His best fastball was "Long Tom"; "Little Tom" was a medium fastball; "two-hump blooper," a moving change-up; "smoke at the yolk," a fastball at a batter's head; "pea at the knee," a fastball low; and "hesitation pitch," when he would stop in mid-delivery before continuing on to the plate.

"NANCY"

John "Buck" O'Neil was a big, strapping first baseman — good fielder, exceptional bat — who played in the Negro Leagues for 20 years, mostly with the Kansas City Monarchs. He earned his name "Buck" as did many of his contemporaries, by displaying strength and virile, high-spirited behavior as a teen. But his name "Nancy" was given him in a moment of quick thinking by a desperate Satchel Paige.

Playing in North Dakota in the early 1940s, O'Neil roomed with Paige. O'Neil says Paige met a pretty Native American girl named Nancy there and decided to invite her to Chicago, the team's next stop. He set her up in the hotel room next to his and O'Neil's room and spent the night with her.

As a surprise, Paige's fiancée, Lahoma, came to Chicago and went to the hotel. She knocked on the door to Nancy and Satch's room and woke Paige up.

Paige yelled out, "Is that you, Nancy?"

O'Neil, Paige's buddy, heard Lahoma coming and came out to the hallway beside Lahoma and covered his buddy's act by yelling back, "Yeah, Satch, it's me, Nancy. Lahoma's here." O'Neil hurriedly explained that the girlish nickname was Satch's pet moniker for the first baseman.

Satch caught on fast and always made it a point to call O'Neil Nancy whenever Lahoma was around. Soon the name stuck and Satch began calling Buck "Nancy" from then on ... just to be safe.

It's surprising that many of today's ballplayers aren't named "Stacy," "Heather" or "Cyndi."

NICKNAME NUGGETS

Acrobatic New York Yankees third baseman Graig Nettles, who helped lead the Bronx Bombers back into prominence with five pennants in six years from 1976 through 1981 and then spearheaded the San Diego Padres into their only World Series appearance, in 1984, was nicknamed "Puff" by his teammates. Nettles, a man with a keen sense of humor and a keener sense of starting things up so he could watch them develop, was said by fellow Yankees to stir up trouble then be gone in a puff of smoke when all hell broke loose.

Yankee shortstop and utility player during Nettles's era was Fred Stanley. Stanley was called "Chicken" by his teammates, not for lack of courage, but for his appearance. They said he was pale, skinny, and walked like a chicken.

Bill Lee, an enigmatic pitcher for the Red Sox and Expos from 1969 to 1982, was outspoken and marched and pitched to the tune of his own drummer. He was called "Spaceman" because some of his off-the-wall comments made fellow players believe he must have come from outer space or that he was spaced out. One such comment, made upon seeing Fenway Park's 37-foot-high Green Monster wall in left field, was "Do they leave it there during the games?" He admitted to sprinkling marijuana on his corn flakes, and commissioner Bowie Kuhn fined him without proof.

Hall of Fame pitcher Don Drysdale, the workhorse righty for the Dodgers from 1956 to 1969, was called "Big D" for his 6'5", 200-pound frame and "The Sidewinder" for his way of wheeling and dealing his sidearm fastball to wary hitters. But his team-mates called him "Route 66" because of his circuitous route from the pitcher's mound to the dugout after each inning. Drysdale felt it was bad luck to step on bare spots in the infield, so he hopped around and walked where he had to in order to find grass on which to plant his spikes. His long way home was comical to teammates, but not so to opponents, whom Drysdale beat 209 times during his career.

Fireballing strikeout king Nolan Ryan, who was born Lynn Nolan Ryan, was called "Nollie," "No-No" and "The Express" by the press, calling upon his name, his penchant for tossing no-hitters, and the rapidity of his fastball. But his California Angels teammates simply referred to his Alvin, Texas, homestead and called him "Tex."

Josh Gibson, the all-time great slugging catcher in the Negro Leagues from 1930 to 1946, hit some mammoth home runs for the Homestead Grays and Pittsburgh Crawfords, and the press called him "The Black Babe Ruth." Newspapermen of the 1930s also called his teammate Walter "Buck" Leonard "The Black Lou Gehrig," to capitalize on the theme. But Gibson's teammates showed him less respect when they jokingly called him "Boxer," intimating that he caught foul balls as though he were wearing boxing gloves rather than a catcher's mitt. This was really "dissing" his ability. As pitching great Walter Johnson once said, Gibson was "the greatest catcher" he ever saw. Supporting the sobriquet, Negro League foe James "Cool Papa" Bell said, "Gibson was a great handler of pitchers, but terrible on pop-ups." And as he played for many years in Latin American leagues — Dominican Republic, Venezuela and Mexico — his Latino teammates and fans called him *"Chimpance,"* or chimpanzee, as a comment on his appearance and his style of crouching behind the plate.

For the record, other ethnic nickname takeoffs include:

Spotswood Poles — "The Black Ty Cobb." Often called the fastest man in baseball during his era — from 1909 to 1923 — this outfielder played for a number of teams including the New York Lincoln Giants, New York Lincoln Stars and Philadelphia Giants.

Jimmy Crutchfield — "The Black Lloyd Waner." Swift and graceful outfielder in the Negro Leagues from 1930 to 1945 with such teams as the Chicago American Giants, Pittsburgh Crawfords, Newark Eagles and Birmingham Black Barons.

Oscar Charleston — "The Black Ruth." Outfielder-first baseman during a long career from 1915 to 1954 with more than a dozen Negro League teams, including the Indianapolis ABCs, Chicago American Giants, Homestead Grays and Pittsburgh Crawfords.

Charles Dougherty — "The Black Rube Marquard." Negro League pitcher for many teams before the organization of Negro Leagues in 1920. Dougherty played from 1909 to 1918.

Jose de la Caridad Menchez Mendez — "Mathewson in Black." A legendary pitcher of his era, he played in the Negro and Cuban Leagues from 1908 for such teams as the Cuban Stars, All-Nations team and Kansas City Monarchs.

Cristobal Torriente — "The Babe Ruth of Cuba." A power hitter who played the outfield from 1913 to 1938 in Cuba and in the Negro Leagues, he toured with such teams as the Cuban Stars, Chicago American Giants, Detroit Stars, Gilkerson's Union Giants, and the Atlanta Black Crackers.

Ray Dandridge — "Brooks Robinson of the Negro Leagues." Third baseman Hall of Famer who played with grace and skill in the Negro Leagues from 1933 to 1949 for the Detroit Stars, Newark Dodgers, Newark Eagles and Nashville Elite Giants. He retired in 1949, so this is a retrospective nom de guerre.

Mose Solomon — "The Jewish Babe Ruth" and "The Rabbi of Swat." Power-hitting outfielder hit 49 homers for Hutchinson of the Southwestern League in the minors in 1923. Played two games for the New York Giants that same year.

Phil Weintraub — "The Jewish Lou Gehrig." Slugging left-handed-hitting first baseman-outfielder who hit .401 for Nashville of the Southern League in 1934. He played for the New York Giants, Cincinnati Reds and Philadelphia Phillies from 1933 to 1945.

Ron Blomberg — "The Yiddish Yankee." The first man to bat as a designated hitter. The first baseman played with the Yankees and White Sox from 1969 to 1978.

Mike Epstein — "Superjew." A power-hitting first baseman for five teams including the Orioles, Senators and A's from 1966 to 1974.

Sadaharu Oh — "The Japanese Babe Ruth." The man who broke Henry Aaron's all-time pro ball home run record, with 868 lifetime blasts in Japan. He played first base for the Yomiuri Giants from 1959 to 1981 and won 13 consecutive home run titles.

Shigeo Nagashima — "The Japanese Lou Gehrig." He batted fourth in Yomiuri's lineup, behind Oh. Played from 1958 to 1974. The third baseman was arguably Japan's most popular player and was reportedly the highest-paid player of his era.

George Pipgras — "The Danish Viking." Right-handed pitcher for the Yankees and Red Sox from 1923 to 1935. Later on, he became an umpire and once thumbed out 17 players during a St. Louis Browns-Chicago White Sox game.

Mike Chartak — "The Volga Batman." Ex-coal miner who became outfielder and pinch hitter with the Yankees, Senators and St. Louis Browns from 1940 to 1944.

Speedy outfielder for the Detroit Tigers, Ron LeFlore was called "Twinkle Toes Bosco." LeFlore earned this sobriquet from teammates on his Jackson State Prison baseball team when he was serving a 5- to 15-year sentence for armed robbery. He took the American League by storm, when, after being discovered on a prison visit by Billy Martin, he signed with the Tigers and stole (legally) 58 bases for Detroit in 1976 and 97 bases for Montreal in 1980. LeFlore got the nickname because he loved drinking chocolate milk—preferably Bosco—and resembled (to some inmates) the Bosco Bear character in commercials. And he was so fast, perhaps the fastest player in the game from 1976 to 1980, that Twinkle Toes was a natural name for him.

Bob Horner, the slugging third baseman for the Atlanta Braves, jumped from Arizona State University to the Majors in 1978 and was the National League Rookie of the Year. Only injury and weight problems kept him from becoming one of the dominant players of the 1980s, though he did hit 218 homers in only 1,020 games. He had no prominent nickname in America, but when he signed to play ball in Japan for the Yakult Swallows in 1987, he started off on a tear and smacked 11 homers in his first 29 games to earn the nom de guerre "Mr. Ho-Mah." He was also called "Red Devil" by the Japanese press and fans because of his reddish blond hair and the omnipresent serious scowl on his face during ball games.

Charles Grant, a great Negro Leagues second baseman for the Columbia Giants (out of Chicago), Cuban X Giants and New York Black Sox, among others, was serving as a bellboy at a hotel in which the Baltimore Orioles stayed during their spring training of 1901. John McGraw, manager of the club, saw the bellboy play second base and felt he was a great player. As Grant was a light-skinned black, McGraw thought he could sneak him past baseball's color line by announcing he had signed an Indian to play second base. McGraw called his new player "Chief Tokohama," a "full-blooded Cherokee Indian."

The ruse worked in spring training until Charles Comiskey, owner of the Chicago White Sox, blew the whistle on the scam. He recognized Grant from watching him play around Chicago for the Columbia Giants. Grant was never allowed to play in a Major League game.

Since this chapter began with a statement that they just don't build nicknames like they used to, we should include what the late researcher James K. Skipper, Jr., the world's foremost baseball nickname authority, said was the very first baseball nickname ever bestowed. It was a pitcher from 1860 who got the first known "aka."

"UNBEATABLE" JIMMY CREIGHTON

James Creighton, who toured with the Brooklyn Excelsiors in 1860, was considered "one of the best players in the Union" before his death at the age of 21, in 1862, from a heart attack incurred while batting.

Creighton's speedy delivery and wrist snap—delivering the world's first sliders—bedeviled the hitters of the day who were used to underhand and stiff-armed deliveries. He is believed to be, along with Lip Pike, one of the first truly professional players, receiving payment for his ball field skill. He is also credited with throwing the first real fastball and became known as "Unbeatable" Jimmy. His was a legend just beginning in a game that was just beginning. News of his greatness had already covered the known baseball world. Connie Mack likened his exploits to the first shot of the American Revolution: "His achievements were heard around the world."

He was considered unbeatable, and though records are incomplete from that era, it is thought that he may not have lost a game his final two years.

Had "Unbeatable" Jimmy Creighton lived, he might have been remembered as one of the all-time great pioneers of the game instead of garnering little footnotes like this one.

A chapter such as this one wouldn't be doing the job unless it contained what is thought to be the longest nickname known to baseball. . . .

"DON JOSE BLOCKE EL DIRIGENTE DE AQUADILLA TEBORINES"

Third baseman Seymour "Cy" Block played only 17 games in the Majors from 1942 to 1946 with the Chicago Cubs, hitting .302 and committing only two errors. When he came up, he and Stan Musial were lumped together as the league's most promising prospects. After the war was in full swing, however, Block spent three years in the Coast Guard and had little left for baseball. When he played winter ball in Puerto Rico, local fans and media gave him the nickname "Don Jose Blocke el Dirigente de Aquadilla Teborines," which sounds more exotic than it really is.

While it is not as illustrative as Charlie Pabor's (outfielder from 1871 to 1875 with the Cleveland Forest Citys, Brooklyn Atlantics and others) maligning nickname of "The Old Woman in the Red Cap," bemoaning the fact that the player-manager was a complainer, or Pepper Martin's "Wild Hoss of the Osage," Block's Spanish name was meant as a tribute. It means, roughly translated, "The Distinguished Gentleman Joe Block, the Mentor of the Aquadilla Sharks." The name says it all. He played for Aquadilla and was a teacher, coach, mentor and player who taught baseball fundamentals and skills to his Puerto Rican teammates. The name has no other significance other than that it may be the longest such moniker given to a Major Leaguer . . . and one who only played in 17 games.

As this is a nostalgic look at names gone by, it seems appropriate to end with a reflection on the innocence of the past and an outlook that doesn't exist today.

"THE HUMAN EYEBALL"

Bris Lord, a fine outfielder with a deadly arm, was acquired by the Philadelphia A's in 1905 for their pennant run. Signed off the sandlots, the 5'9", 185-pounder was stocky and strong. He hung on until 1913, and after being twice traded, he was reacquired by the A's from Cleveland in a deal that included rights to Shoeless Joe Jackson.

Lord was called "The Human Eyeball," first by his teammates and then by the press in the early 1900s. Colorful name. It wasn't due to his appearance, and it wasn't due to his knowledge of the strike zone. He didn't strike out much, but there were plenty of guys who fit that description. Apparently, he had amazing eyesight, the kind Ted Williams and Wade Boggs are said to have, though Lord's .256 career average indicates he didn't apply the attribute as well — Williams had a .344 career mark, Boggs is near .340. But Lord's teammates were amazed that he could spot a dime on the ground across the street, pick out people seated behind home plate while he was in the outfield, and once noticed a teammate's wife as she entered a hotel while the teammate and his floozy (and Lord) were clear across the ballroom — just in time to save the teammate's hide . . . and marriage.

A nickname saved is a nickname earned. And Ted "The Human Eyeball" Williams has a nice ring to it, doesn't it?

CHAPTER TEN

Just Plain Weird

*"Some of these guys are (mentally) three players
short of a full roster."*
— PAUL WHITE

*" 'Tis strange — but true; for truth is always strange;
Stranger than fiction."*
— LORD BYRON

One man's weirdness is another man's normal occurrence, but
regardless of your definition of weird — we use *Webster's New
World Dictionary*, third preferred meaning: "strikingly odd,
strange, fantastic, bizarre . . . eccentric, erratic or unconventional
in behavior . . ." — it can be argued that baseball diamonds produce some of the most unusual events ever witnessed in public
by paying crowds, and baseball players are themselves a most
peculiar, though entertaining, lot. That said, a chapter like this in
a book like this is a given.

Baseball . . . weird? How else can you explain 50,000 people
waving green wienies? Or chanting absurdly non-Native American war chants while chopping an empty hand as though it were
a tomahawk? Or throwing 20,000 round candy bars — The Reggie
Bar — on a field in an attempt to hit the confection's namesake?
Or watching elderly, overweight men who haven't played the
game in decades — we're talking about coaches here — stuff themselves into bulge-revealing double-knit baseball uniforms and display their out-of-shapeness in front of fans in groups larger than
most cities in America? Or employing and perpetuating a language that is all its own, borrowing its jargon from the Deep
South, Merrie Olde England, poets, engineers, gardeners, aero-
space technicians, ghetto cultures, Ivy League universities, little

kids, old men and everywhere in between? Or players crashing through fences, talking to baseballs, hiding birds under their caps or sitting on cakes? That's baseball. And if you don't find that weird, or at least entertaining, then you must be watching PBS 24 hours a day. Get a life ... a baseball life, and enjoy these strange-but-true offerings.

BILL VEECK

Bill Veeck (as in "wreck") was a showman, innovator, keen baseball mind and eccentric. The former baseball owner — Cleveland Indians, St. Louis Browns and Chicago White Sox — is famous for staging many baseball events and sights, such as sending up a midget — 3'7", 65-pound Eddie Gaedel — to bat in one game in 1952. Some of his more innovative promotions, in an era in which marketing was an underused technique, included giving away a two hundred pound block of ice, live lobsters, livestock, cases of food, beer, cars, money and paint. He had pig races, staged weddings at home plate, and put on fireworks displays. His scoreboard at Comiskey Park in 1960 was the first exploding scoreboard in baseball.

In 1943, he planned to buy the Philadelphia Phillies and stock the team with Negro League all-stars to make them an instant pennant contender, but baseball's antiblack hierarchy beat him to the punch and sold the team before he could make the purchase. The punch line to this was that the man who bought the team to keep Veeck and his black stars out was William D. Cox, who was kicked out of baseball less than a year later for improprieties and betting on Phillies games.

Veeck fought in World War II with the U.S. Marines in the South Pacific, and wounds caused him to have his leg amputated. He had a wooden leg attached, and as he was a heavy smoker, Veeck would often amuse his buddies by taking the limb off to use as an ashtray. A beer drinker as well, before he gave up both vices on the advice of doctors, he joked that he might have a beer cooler put in his leg just under the ashtray. Those who knew Veeck weren't sure if he was joking.

MIKE GRADY

Mike Grady was a horrible fielder at every position — he occupied the catcher's position (you couldn't say he "caught") and also tried to play seven other positions between 1894 and 1906. He was the New York Giants' third sacker in 1899, when on a single play, he booted a grounder to third for error number one, recovered, and threw wildly to first for error number two. As the runner rounded second and headed to third, the first baseman picked up the errant toss and fired to Grady at third to get the runner sliding in, whereby Grady muffed the perfect throw and let it go through him—error number three. The runner gulped for air and headed for home as Grady retrieved the ball and fired home. Alas, that throw, too, was high and the runner scored—error number four.

If baseball had any more bases, this might have gone on all day.

TOM TREBELHORN

When former Milwaukee Brewers manager Tom Trebelhorn applied for the vacant managerial position with the Chicago Cubs, Cubs general manager Larry Himes gave him a psychological test to see if he was right for the job. One of the questions read: "If you were a tree, what kind of tree would it be?" Instead of responding with a traditional or lucid answer such as mighty oak, old hickory, baseball bat ash or towering sequoia, the Cubs manager-to-be responded with "a Cubs tree." Well, that was good enough for Himes, and Treb got the job.

If Colorado gives that test, and asks what kind of road would you be, would Trebelhorn answer "a Rocky road"?

GOOD SCOUTING

Hall of Fame slugger Mickey Mantle was scouted in Oklahoma when he was only 13. His career was followed closely by the Indians, Cubs, Giants, Cardinals and Yankees, and by the time The Mick was 18, he was labeled as "can't miss" by those knowledgeable in the game. The Yankees, realizing that the fleet, graceful and powerful Mantle could be their shortstop of the future to continue the Yankee dynasty, forked over $1,100 as a bonus to secure the switch-hitter's services. Good deal, even after they switched him to center field. Eighteen years of legendary play for a grand advance.

Wise scouts of the same era for the Pittsburgh Pirates saw a 19-year-old New York-born center fielder and signed him out of high school for a $2,000 bonus and sent him to Brunswick of the Georgia-Florida League. The outfielder, Matt Cuomo, played 81 games and hit .244 with one homer before a ball hit him in the head and he became the Governor of New York—under the name Mario Cuomo.

HOME . . . A PLACE TO HANG YOUR CAP

Bobo Newsom is generally thought of as the baseball vagabond extraordinaire for his 17 uniform changes—the Washington Senators five different times—over his 20-year career from 1929 to 1953. His several years of nonactivity and/or Minor League stops along the way put his total uniform-change total to around 25. The pitcher, who won 211 and lost 222, was a free spirit and seemed to be an asset, for a while, for each of the clubs who traded for him. But Bobo is just the tip of the nomadic iceberg when it comes to relocations.

William J. "Bill" Sisler, a 5'6", 150-pound southpaw pitcher from 1923 to 1950, made a Minor League career out of changing cities enough to make a skip tracer change lines of work. Sisler signed contracts with and wore the uniforms of 50 different ball clubs. His stops usually didn't last long—usually five games or less—and he never won more than eight games for any club in compiling a startlingly low total of 36 career wins and 57 losses in 175 games over 27 years. Even his three tenures as a bush-league manager lasted roughly half-a-season each.

Sisler never made the Fortune 500 through his baseball work, but his travel agent may have retired a millionaire.

ROSE, BUD AND BIRD

Eddie Rose, a career Minor League outfielder from Oakland, California, played 2,193 games and banged out 2,517 hits in 15 years from 1926 to 1940, playing mostly in the South Atlantic and Sally leagues. While playing for the New Orleans Pelicans in 1935 against Birmingham, Rose popped one high above the second baseman. There were no pelicans to be found, but a preponderance of pigeons swarmed over the field and the ball struck one of the bewildered birds. The ball and newly dead bird ricocheted near the shortstop, who retrieved both, just in time to see Rose standing safely on first with a single. Then, in a scene that would have made *Citizen Kane* proud, the Pelicans found that to score

Rose, Bud Connolly sledded a drive to the outfield and doubled Eddie in. Rosebud.

FAN REACTION

Fan fanaticism reached great heights and depths during the 1908 pennant-deciding series between the New York Giants and Chicago Cubs. The game of October 8, 1908, in New York decided the pennant, and with the Giants ballpark filled to the rafters, knothole fans clung to every conceivable location in hopes of viewing the contest: standing on people's shoulders, hanging from light posts and telegraph wires, and perched on elevated trains. One fan fell to his death at a train station.

The New York Times reported that the fan who fell was "the only fatality of the day, and his vacant space was quickly filled."

Mordecai "Three Finger" Brown outdueled Christy Mathewson for a 4-2 Cub victory and a winning trip — in five games — to the World Series to face Detroit.

FOR IT'S ONE, TWO STRIKES YOU'RE OUT AT THE OLD BALL GAME

In a sport that doesn't employ an instant replay to check an umpire's decision, the boys in blue must always be right. Right?

Well, the game between the California Angels and Kansas City Royals in Kansas City on June 24, 1993, might change that axiom.

The umpire crew for the night was comprised of Joe Brinkman, Derryl Cousins, Tim McClelland and Gary Cedarstrom, and for four innings, the crew was pefect, and none of the 26,409 fans in attendance, nor the players and coaches, figured anything odd would transpire that night.

In the fifth, Angels pitcher Mark Langston got two outs and then fell behind Kevin McReynolds, two balls and one strike. Langston looked at the scoreboard and the count read two balls and *two* strikes. Langston shook his head, then asked Cedarstrom what the count was. Cedarstrom agreed with the scoreboard.

Langston fired the pitch past McReynolds for a strike. As everyone else ran off the field, McReynolds tapped the dirt off his cleats and waited for the next pitch. Cedarstrom told McReynolds to move, and the hitter refused to leave the batter's box.

Langston and catcher John Orton stood nearby, agreeing with McReynolds, that there were only two strikes. Angels skipper

Buck Rodgers growled, "Get in here (the dugout). Don't broadcast it."

Royals skipper Hal McRae had been thumbed out of each of the previous two ball games and ached to make it three in a row. But when the entire umpiring crew gathered around McRae and began discussing the situation, Rodgers knew the crew had realized its mistake.

Cedarstrom was embarrassed but had to call the Angels back onto the field. To make matters worse, he picked up the ball and fired a fastball to whom he thought was Langston. It wasn't. It was first baseman J.T. Snow, who never saw the toss coming. The ball caromed off Snow's shoulder and into the outfield.

Langston took a full warm-up, just as if a new inning had begun, and one pitch later, McReynolds grounded out to end the inning again.

One inning later, a 31-minute downpour stopped the game.

When it finally resumed, the Royals prevailed 7-1.

TWO BALLS ARE BETTER THAN ONE

In a case of an umpire blowing it big time, there was one play at Wrigley Field in which two baseballs were in play at the same time.

On June 30, 1959, in a game between the Cubbies and the St. Louis Cardinals, Chicago pitcher Bob Anderson had a 3-1 count on Stan "The Man" Musial late in the game. Anderson fired one in the dirt and past reserve catcher Sammy Taylor. Musial raced to first as home plate umpire Vic Delmore called "ball four."

Taylor and Anderson let the ball roll away, and they argued with Delmore that Musial had foul-tipped it. Musial saw the argument and saw the ball, untouched, and ran toward second, as third baseman Alvin Dark sprinted to pick up the ball. As this was going on, Delmore reflexively pulled an additional ball out of his pocket and handed it to Taylor.

Anderson realized Musial was running, grabbed the ball out of Taylor's hand, and fired a fastball to Cub shortstop Ernie Banks who was covering second. At the same moment, Dark grabbed the original loose ball and fired a perfect strike to Banks.

Anderson's throw was wild and ended up in center field. Musial saw the errant toss and headed for third base. He was intercepted by Banks, who had caught Dark's relay.

As Musial was tagged with the original ball, Delmore called him out at second.

Good call, blue. And good call by National League president Warren Giles, who fired Delmore at the end of the year.

THE DAY BABE RUTH HIT RIGHT-HANDED

Babe Ruth was arguably the greatest power hitter in baseball history, and his classic lefty swing was tailor-made for the park that was tailor-made for him, Yankee Stadium. But Babe was actually a switch-hitter, at least a couple of times.

On August 1, 1923, the Yankees were losing to the Indians 5-2 in the ninth when Cleveland manager Tris Speaker decided to try some strategy. With Babe Ruth having a monster season (.393, 41 homers and 131 RBIs) the Tribe's skipper replaced his righty starter and inserted lefty reliever Sherry Smith to face the lefty-swinging Bambino. This infuriated Babe. He cursed at Speaker and Smith and called them every name in the book associated with lack of courage and breeding, as well as a few depicting suspect heritage. Then Ruth yelled, "I fix ya, ya bums."

He turned around and batted righty for the first time in his career. Legend dictates that Ruth homered righty. Well, almost. He stepped in righty and watched the defense shift around. After taking a strike righty, he turned back around and hit lefty and watched the defense shift around again. Then he destroyed the strategy by hitting a homer, his 25th of the season. The Indians hung on to win 5-3.

Ruth did get in an entire righty at bat four days later.

On August 5, playing the St. Louis Browns, Ruth began lefty, as usual, and blasted two homers, numbers 26 and 27 off starter Ray Kolp. When relief pitcher Elam Vangilder, a righty, was called on to pitch to Ruth in the 11th inning, with two men on, Babe turned around to hit right-handed. Ruth reasoned that if he hit lefty, he'd be intentionally walked and if he hit righty, they'd pitch to him. To Vangilder, Ruth was just as intimidating righty as lefty, and he walked him intentionally in the 11th and again in the 13th, when Ruth again hit righty with two men on base. The Yanks won the game anyway, 9-8, when Bob Meusel followed Ruth's walk in the 13th with a single to drive in the winning run.

It is noteworthy to observe that it was Tris Speaker who commented on Ruth's move from being a full-time pitcher to a full-time hitter in 1920, saying, "Ruth made a grave mistake when he gave up pitching. Working once a week, he might have lasted a long time and become a great star."

THE DAY MIKE PAGLIARULO HIT RIGHT-HANDED

Following in Yankee tradition, New York slugger Mike Pagliarulo switched sides of the plate one day. On September 18, 1985, in the sixth inning of a game versus Detroit, Tiger lefty Mickey Mahler was on the mound. Since Pags had struck out his two previous at bats, Yankee skipper Billy Martin instructed him to bat from the right side. Pagliarulo was called out on strikes. It doesn't always work.

BASEBALL PAYBACK

Baseball etiquette teaches that paybacks have to happen, no matter how long it takes or what the circumstances are when the payback is administered.

In spring training 1991, Los Angeles Dodger pitcher John Candelaria intentionally hit teammate Juan Samuel in an intrasquad game and it cost him a dinner. Candelaria explained that six years earlier, Samuel had gotten the better of him in a game—when he was with Pittsburgh and Samuel was with the Phillies—and he had waited a long time to pay him back. He told Samuel in advance that he'd be plunked . . . and he was. For being a good sport, Candy took Samuel out to dinner. "We're even now," Candelaria explained.

ZAY AND BUDD

Two of baseball's shortest names are "Zay" and "Budd."

Zay was a pitcher-outfielder for Baltimore of the American Association who was picked out of a crowd to fill out the team (and start the game on the mound) one hot summer day in 1886. He never gave his first name (if he had one) and finished the contest going 0-for-1 and made one putout and one error. He was the losing pitcher, tossing two innings and allowing two runs on four hits for an ERA of 9.00. He walked four and struck out two and called it a career, retiring with baseball's shortest name.

"Budd" was plucked out of the stands during similar circumstances. On September 10, 1890, Patsy Tebeau, manager of Cleveland in the Players' League, was faced with forfeiting the game for lack of sufficient players. He spotted a muscular, athletic-looking man in the stands and yelled, "Hey, Budd, ya wanna play ball?" The man, who might have been a player for another team, nodded, took the field, and Tebeau announced that his new outfielder was "Budd." He reasoned that the man never corrected him when he called out the name. Budd went 0-for-4 and handled two outfield chances flawlessly.

ONE-DAY DEBACLES

Dickie Lowe was a catcher who played one game for Detroit in the National League in 1884. Why only one game? Manager Jack Chapman apparently didn't like what he saw during that single-game tryout with his last-place ball club. During the game, Lowe went 1-for-3, a respectable .333 batting average. But that was higher than his fielding percentage, as the catcher made seven errors in eight chances, for a horrible .125 fielding rate. Short career.

Dave Rowe had a longer career, but played one game that will go down in infamy. Rowe was a decent outfielder who lasted from 1877 to 1888 with a half dozen teams in an assortment of leagues. He pitched occasionally, starting a game a year in four different years.

But in 1882, for the infamous Cleveland Spiders of the National League, Rowe's manager Fred Dunlap, who was also the team's second baseman, punished Rowe for a difference of opinion and inserted him as the starting pitcher, and he forced him to remain in the game despite the travesty going on in the field. Rowe pitched a complete game. That's the good news. The bad news was he walked seven, struck out none, gave up 29 hits and 35 runs — 12 of them earned. Thirty-five runs allowed in a complete game. That record will stand.

But the worst pitching performance wasn't punishment, it was ego. In a Texas League game of June 15, 1902, at Ennis, Texas, the powerhouse Corsicana Oilers met the weak, last-place Texarkana squad. Texarkana owner-general manager and manager was C.B. DeWitt, who was also the team's pitcher. He declared he'd pitch the entire game come hell or high water, and both came that hot June day.

DeWitt pitched all nine innings and gave up 51 runs on 53 hits.

(He also walked three.) He gave up 21 home runs to eight players—only the opposing pitcher, Wright, failed to hit one. Oilers catcher J.J. Clark blasted a record eight homers and drove in 16 runs.

Only 26 of the runs were earned, but you'd think the pitcher would have given himself the hook. He didn't.

Note: Corsicana won the game 51-3 and when telegraph operators saw the score, they thought it was a misprint or missend. They reported the score to the papers as 5-3.

SEPTEMBER 15 WAS A WEIRD DAY

Three weird occurrences have happened on the same day, with twenty-five years separating the first from last event. The day is September 15.

On September 15, 1938, brothers Lloyd and Paul Waner hit back-to-back homers for the Pirates off New York Giants hurler Cliff Melton. It is the only time in Major League history that brothers have hit back-to-back homers.

On September 15, 1946, a game between the Brooklyn Dodgers and Chicago Cubs was called after five innings with the Dodgers winning 2-0. The game was called on account of gnats. There were so many insects in the air and on the field that players couldn't see, umpires couldn't see any better than they normally do, and fans couldn't make out the field or eat gnat-free hot dogs.

On September 15, 1963, in another brotherly love item, the Alou brothers—Felipe, Matty and Jesus—played in the outfield at the same time for the San Francisco Giants in a 13-5 route over the Pirates.

MORE GNATS

On August 27, 1990, The SkyDome in Toronto experienced a 35-minute gnat delay after Milwaukee pitcher Ted Higuera issued a buggy walk to Junior Felix in the fifth inning beause he "couldn't see the plate through the gnats." Umpires ordered the dome closed to keep more gnats from interrupting the game.

Five days later (September 1), Milwaukee again saw a swarm as their home park of County Stadium was inundated with thousands of flying invaders during the sixth inning of a game against the Baltimore Orioles.

The Brewers won 4-3, and Orioles manager Frank Robinson

went buggy saying a game should not have been played under those conditions.

AND A MOTH STORY

Houston Astros rookie first baseman-outfielder Mike Simms was a victim of a 1990 moth attack that left him dazed and confused.

Simms was standing in the on-deck circle in Atlanta and felt a moth flutter by his cheek. He swung at it, swiped at it and flicked at it, but it eluded his attack and nested on the earhole of his batting helmet. He tried to flick at it with his finger and ended up pushing it into his ear. The team trainer was called out to extricate the invader, but the cotton swab approach only pushed the moth farther into Simms's ear.

Finally resorting to tweezers, the trainer grabbed the insect by the leg and as he pulled the bug out, it flew away, to the cheers of Simms's teammates. Welcome to the Big Leagues, kid.

A ONE-TIME EXCUSE

Chicago White Sox shortstop Ozzie Guillen likes playing volleyball even more than he likes baseball. At age 17, he was playing in a baseball instructional league in San Diego and wanted to bolt the team to return home to Venezuela to try out for his national volleyball team.

He told the Padres that his mother had been killed and he had to go home. The Padres gave him a leave of absence and paid for his trip on the first plane home.

He didn't make the team and came back to San Diego with one less excuse in his arsenal.

THE PLAYER WHO NEVER WAS

In 1912, in a game between the Cleveland Indians and St. Louis Browns, "Proctor" was named as a pinch runner in the official Western-Union telegraphed account of the contest.

Proctor remained as an official player for 65 years until it was revealed that Lou Proctor was the telegraph operator who sent the box score out over the wire in Cleveland. He inserted his name as a runner for the Indians and remained in the official records from then on.

ONE THOUSANDTH STRIKEOUT

On August 29, 1992, Braves pitcher Charlie Leibrandt recorded his one thousandth strikeout and got an error on the play.

Playing against the Phillies, with Ricky Jordan at first and one out in the second inning, Leibrandt fanned Darren Daulton for the milestone. Atlanta catcher Greg Olson threw the ball to Leibrandt, who rolled it into the dugout for safekeeping. One thing, though, the pitcher forgot to call time-out. Realizing his mistake, Leibrandt ran after the ball, but got to it too late . . . it had already rolled into the dugout. Jordan was awarded second base and Leibrandt was awarded an error.

THE PACIOREK BROTHERS

The three baseball-playing Paciorek brothers—Jim, Tom and John—are never spoken of in the same terms as are the playing brothers from the DiMaggio, Alou, Boyer, Waner or even Canseco families. But they have made an impact on the sport nonetheless, in rather obscure fashion.

In 1984, Tom, a left fielder for the Chicago White Sox, played in the longest game (timewise) in Major League history, an eight-hour six-minute, 25-inning game won by the ChiSox over Milwaukee, 8-7. Tom went 5-for-9 with three RBIs.

In 1990, Jim Paciorek, playing in Japan, singled home the winning run in the 15th inning of the longest game in Japan League history, a five-hour, 51-minute battle won by the Yokohama Taiyo Whales, 6-5, over the Chunichi Dragons.

In 1963, eldest brother Jim set a Major League record that has never been duplicated. He played one game, the only game of his career, for the Houston Astros and went 3-for-3 with three RBIs to give him a career batting average of 1.000.

LONG SINGLE OR SHORT HOMER

On June 11, 1993, California Angels catcher Greg Myers punched a single into left field and never figured he would attain baseball lore immortality because of it.

In a game in which the Angels beat Seattle 8-2, there was nothing special happening when Myers stepped in against Mariners pitcher Erik Hanson with the Angels down 2-0. Hanson had loaded the bases on a hit batsman and two walks. Up came Myers, a slow-footed catcher, just trying to make contact. He hit the pitch into left and headed for first as outfielder Henry Cotto's throw sailed high over home plate.

Myers rounded first and sprinted for second. Hanson, backing up catcher Bill Hasselman, retrieved the ball and fired to third to keep Myers, who was now jogging, from taking the extra base. Hanson's throw was even higher than Cotto's and third baseman Mike Blowers wasn't within 10 feet of the toss as the ball skittered down the left-field line.

Myers then turned it on and made it home for a bases-loaded, bases-clearing single and two errors.

Myers, hitting .208, doubled to right field in the eighth inning and Jay Buhner bobbled the ball and allowed Myers to go to third. Seattle committed three errors that night, all on Myers's hits.

CEMETERIES

In 1919, the Cincinnati Reds held their spring training workouts in a Texas cemetery.

In an unrelated incident, catcher, speaker of 12 languages, future OSS spy, and rocket scientist-kidnapper for the American war effort Moe Berg was strolling through a Baltimore cemetery one night after a game in Baltimore, and to startled, amused and slightly scared teammates, he stood on the grave of Edgar Allan Poe and recited "The Raven" in its entirety.

UNPLAYABLE BALL FIELDS

In July 1994, several 15-pound ceiling tiles fell into the empty stands in Seattle's Kingdome prior to the game. This game was canceled as was the next homestand, as thousands of the tiles had to be removed to restore safety.

In September 1991, a 50-ton concrete beam fell on the promenade outside Montreal's Olympic Stadium. The incident forced the Expos to play all of their final 26 games on the road.

On October 17, 1989, at Candlestick Park in San Francisco, the third game of the World Series was called off after an earthquake measuring 7.1 hit the area. The Series resumed 10 days later, and Oakland won two straight to complete a four-game sweep.

On August 29, 1986, at Olympic Stadium in Montreal, explosions and fire on the site of the still-being-constructed stadium tower forced the postponement of an Expos-Padres game. An overheated acetylene tank set off the blast that set fire to wooden scaffolding.

On July 12, 1979, at Chicago's old Comiskey Park, the promotion that went terribly wrong occurred. Disco Demolition Night went out of control as 8,000 antidisco fans swarmed onto the field, cut it up, burned it and otherwise destroyed the place, forcing a forfeit of the second game of the doubleheader between the White Sox and Tigers.

In April, 1946, at Fenway Park, the crosstown Boston Braves played at the Red Sox's home park while paint dried at Braves Field.

On April 14 and 15, 1911, at the Polo Grounds in New York, a fire destroyed the park completely and forced the Giants to move to Hilltop Park for six weeks.

On August 6, 1903, at Baker Bowl in Philadelphia, fans rushing to the back of the left-field bleachers to watch a fistfight caused the stands to collapse onto 15th Street. The second game of the scheduled Phillies-Braves doubleheader was canceled.

In 1893, at West Side Park in Chicago, the White Stockings were forced to move to West Side Grounds to make room for the visiting Columbian Exposition.

ODD CHOICES FOR BATTING COACH

Now just because a guy can't hit doesn't mean he can't teach others how to hit. Borrowing from the old line: "Those who can, do; those who can't, teach."

But in a game in which "success begets success" and "leading by example" are maxims and credos by which players and teams live their lives, it is curious to see the lifetime batting averages of those men chosen to give tips, encouragement and instruction to slumping hitters. If these guys are so smart, how come they couldn't hit themselves?

And some of these guys never even made it as starters.

Some nonhitters who have become batting coaches and instructors in recent years, with their career stats, include:

Milt May, Pirates — .263 average in 1,192 games.

Walt Hriniak, White Sox — .253 in 47 games.

Denis Menke, Phillies — .250 in 1,598 games.

Terry Crowley, Twins — .250 in 865 games.

Clarence Jones, Braves — .248 in 58 games.

Tom McCraw, Mets — .246 in 1,468 games.

Tom Robson, Rangers — .208 in 23 games.

Charlie Manuel, Indians — .198 in 242 games.

Adrian Garrett, Royals — .185 in 163 games.

Jay Ward, Expos — .163 in 27 games.

Rick Down, Yankees — Never made it to the Majors. Hit .257 in seven years in the Minors.

Ben Hines, Astros — Never made it to the Majors. Hit .202 in three seasons in the Minors.

Greg Biagini, Orioles — Never made it to the Majors. Hit .289 in ten years in the Minors.

Rudy Jaramillo, Astros — Never played in the Majors. Hit .257 in four years in the Minors.

Special citation: The California Angels' roving Minor League instructor is Mario Mendoza, for whom the "Mendoza Line" was named. Ballplayers felt that if they hit lower than Mendoza they were in deep trouble, and soon The Mendoza Line came to mean "an average of .200." His career average: .215 in 686 games, with five seasons out of nine under .200.

WEIRD TRADES

Submitted for your approval . . . nine trades conceived and carried out in The Twilight Zone. And we're not even dredging up the Boston Red Sox's 1920 sale of Babe Ruth to the Yankees for $100,000 in cash and a $300,000 loan (mortgage on Fenway Park), which Boston owner Harry Frazee used to produce the Broadway play *No No, Nanette*. Books have been written on this, "The Curse of the Bambino," which has seen Boston go without a World Championship since the 1918 team led by Ruth. Since then, the dreaded rival Yankees who had zero titles before the deal (to the BoSox's five), have added 22 World Championships.

Even Up Trade

Harry Chiti, a catcher who played 502 games for the Cubs, A's, Tigers and Mets from 1950 to 1962, was traded April 26, 1962, by the Cleveland Indians, who had acquired him in the off-season, to the New York Mets for a player to be named later. That player turned out to be . . . Harry Chiti.

I Can't Believe We Made That Trade

In a pitcher-for-pitcher swap and reswap, the St. Louis Browns dealt righty hurler Dick Coffman to the Washington Senators for lefty pitcher Carl Fischer June 9, 1932. Unhappy with the deal, the clubs retraded the pitchers for each other December 13. Coffman was 1-6 for the Senators then came back to the Brownies to go 3-7 in 1933. Fischer went 3-7 for St. Louis in 24 games and was traded to Detroit with righty pitcher Firpo Marberry for lefty thrower Earl Whitehill before the 1933 season. Whitehill fashioned a 22-8 mark with the Browns while Fischer was 11-15 and Marberry 16-11 for the Tigers.

Managing a Swap

All-time Brooklyn Dodger great first baseman Gil Hodges was traded twice . . . as a manager. In 1963, the Mets dealt him to Washington for Jimmy Piersall and Hodges became the Senators' skipper. Four years later, the Nats sent him back to the Mets for Bill Denehy and $100,000, and Hodges became field boss in New York.

Managing a Swap 2

In 1976, Charlie O. Finley was the slickest trader of them all. When the Pittsburgh Pirates came hunting for a skipper, Finley agreed to part with Chuck Tanner who has just led the A's to an 87-74 second-place finish. Finley was quick to let Tanner fly, in exchange for top catcher Manny Sanguillen and $100,000. Tanner lasted nine years in the Steel City (one pennant). Sanguillen played one year in Oakland and then was peddled back to the Pirates for three more players (Miguel Dilone, Elias Sosa and Mike Edwards).

Managing a Swap 3

In August 1960, the Detroit Tigers were languishing in sixth place with a 44-52 mark under skipper Jimmy Dykes. Realizing it was time for a change, they searched for a winning manager and focused on the Cleveland Indians, who were in fourth place at 49-

46 under manager Joe Gordon. The Tribe felt a change could make them a contender. The two clubs swapped field generals, and in a trade that *really* made a difference, Gordon led the Bengals from sixth to sixth with a 26-31 mark, and Dykes managed the Tribe to a 26-32 fourth-place finish. Gordon was fired in mid-1961, and Dykes was booted out at the end of the 1961 season.

I Want You . . . Again and Again and Again

Catcher Ron Hassey was traded by the New York Yankees to the Chicago White Sox three times in less than one year. After the ChiSox dealt Hassey to the Bronx Bombers in 1984 in a six-player swap, Hassey returned to the Windy City from the Big Apple in a 1985 five-player deal. The Sox returned Hassey to the Yanks when Britt Burns was deemed damaged goods, then re-reacquired him in a four-player move two months later. After cutting him loose to let him re-reunite with the Yanks, the Sox brought him back again in a seven-player transaction in midseason.

Give Me Your Pitcher for Two Bats
and a Glove to Be Named Later

Lefty hurler Tim Fortugno, known in history as the pitcher who gave up George Brett's 3,000th hit and for striking out 24 men in a 16-inning game for El Paso, was toiling in the Minors for the independent Reno Silver Sox, who had an abundance of pitching, but a shortage of equipment. The Sox traded Fortugno to the Milwaukee Brewers on May 5, 1989, for $2,500 and 12 dozen baseballs. One thing though, the balls were American League issue and not considered official for Minor League games.

I'll Go, But I'll Take All of You With Me

World Series (1956) perfect game hurler Don "Gooney Bird" Larsen was traded six times in his 14-year, eight-team career in transactions involving a total of 42 players, including an 18-player Yankee-A's deal in 1954. He was involved in the swaps that sent Bob Turley to the Yankees, Roger Maris to the Yankees, and Billy Pierce to the White Sox.

When All Else Fails . . . Swap Wives

Lefty pitcher Fritz Peterson was one of the few bright spots in the Yankee dynasty's downfall of the mid-1960s to mid-1970s and went 20-11 in 1970. In 1972, Peterson and his fellow Yankee lefty hurler Mike Kekich became best buddies, and their families became best buddies, and their dogs became best buddies. So it seemed natural to them to make a trade—wife for wife, kids for kids, dogs for dogs. The Yankees, embarrassed by the affair, decided Cleveland was a better place for such activities. The Yanks sent Kekich to the Indians a few weeks later and dealt Peterson to the Tribe in early 1974—after Kekich was no longer in town. No wives were involved in the multiplayer deal for Peterson, but the Bronx Bombers got Chris Chambliss in return, and the classy first baseman led the Yanks to three American League titles. Fritzy was gone from the game in two years and Kekich pitched sporadically until 1977. Kekich lost the wife deal when Peterson's ex reneged and wanted out while Kekich's ex liked her new hubby and new surroundings. Eventually, that arrangement, too, went south. But Kekich didn't get his new wife, he didn't get his old wife back, and his kids disappeared on him. He didn't even get his dog back. Bad deal.

WEIRD LANGUAGE

Baseball has its own jargon, its own language and its own way of describing events, plays and people. Among the more colorful phrases adopted by the boys of summers are

Mullion—Old-time lingo for an ugly ballplayer. An inordinant number of catchers have been called mullions. "Andy Etchebarren, that mullion, could really catch."

Pine brother—A guy who sits on the bench and rarely plays. "With Lou Gehrig playing every game for 14 years, all other Yankee first basemen were pine brothers."

Lumber—Bat. After breaking his bat, one that didn't get him any hits, a hitter might go over to the bat rack and say, "I gotta get some new lumber" or "I had a bad piece of lumber."

Tater, dinger, roundtripper, homer, blast, smash, grand salami—Home run. "Mattingly's dinger with the bases loaded was his sixth grand salami of the season."

Back through the box—A ball hit by the batter directly at and past the pitcher. "Aaron hit one back through the box in the first inning, and the way Gibson glared at Henry, there's sure to be a payback this time up."

Payoff pitch — The next offering by a pitcher on a 3-2 count. "Clemons wheels, deals and here's the payoff pitch to Griffey."

Twin killing — A double play. "Torre banged into four twin killings yesterday."

Around the horn — A double play completed from third to second to first. "With runners at first and second and one out, Stargell hit a hard smash to third, but Schmidt turned it into an around-the-horn twin killing."

Keystone combo — The second baseman and shortstop. "With Kubek and Richardson as their keystone combo, the Yankees are steady in the infield."

Hot corner — Third base. "Nettles has turned the hot corner into his own playpen in this Series."

Death Valley — Any outfield region in a ballpark that plays deep and swallows up would-be home runs, particularly in old Yankee Stadium. "DiMaggio would have scored more homers in his career if Death Valley hadn't claimed his smashes."

Mendoza Line — A .200 batting average, named after Mario Mendoza, a shortstop for the Pirates in the 1970s who hit under .200 in four of five seasons, though he finished his career at .215 in nine years. "Bob Uecker hit the Mendoza Line on the button with a career mark of .200."

Double-dip, twin bill — Doubleheader. "In a current day rarity, the Mets and Phils will play a double-dip today at Shea."

Getting out the broom — Sweeping a series against another team, i.e. winning all three or four games. "The Rockies are looking to get out the broom tonight against the Expos."

Punched him out — A pitcher striking out a hitter or an umpire making the out sign (thumb extended) to a batter or runner. "Ryan punched out Henderson in the fifth."

Caught him looking — A batter who took a called third strike. "Johnson caught Brett looking in the third."

Caught him leaning — A runner who was moving toward the next base when either a pitcher or catcher picked him off base or a line drive hit by the batter caused him to be trapped off base. "Ford caught Aparicio leaning to end the inning."

Brush back, chin music, knock down, stick it in his ear — A pitcher taking control of the plate by throwing at or near a hitter. "Drysdale gave McCovey a little chin music in the top of the third, and after Marichal brushed Big D back in the bottom of the inning, you'll probably see Don stick it in Juan's ear in the fourth."

Career year — The best year of a player's life. "In 1987, the year of the rabbit ball, a lot of hitters with dubious power had career years in home runs." Many players were having "career months" in April and May of 1994 with excuses ranging from juiced balls to inferior pitching staffs to decrease of the ozone layer to better wood for bats.

Potential — A player who has all the tools and looks like he should produce, but so far, hasn't. "The Minors are filled with players full of potential, but who never became kinetic." And how long can a player have potential before he hasn't lived up to it?

Off year — A player who is expected to perform well but whose stats aren't up to par. "How many off years is a player entitled to before they all become normal production?"

So, too, does baseball have its own way of complimenting players. And there is a distinct difference between complimenting young players on their way up compared with old players on their way down.

And the main difference between old players and young players may not be the experience, the on-the-field performance or the age, but the way in which each is described. The older a player gets, the more oblique the compliment. And old players are miscomplimented. When referring to an aging player's performance in which he has reached back to the glory days for one last grab at the brass ring, it is said "he played like the *old*" player in question. In reality, he played like the *young* player in question and had been playing *old* until this blast from the past.

What follows, in baseball lingo, is the difference (OK, 30 differences) between young players and old players.

OLD PLAYERS VS. YOUNG PLAYERS

To a young player they say, "nice play" . . . to an old player they say, "nice try."

A young player is "a good base runner" . . . an old player is "a smart base runner."

A young player is "a good hitter" . . . an old player "finds a way to get on."

A young player is "a power pitcher" . . . an old player "mixes up his pitches and outsmarts the hitter."

A young player has "a strong arm" . . . an old player has "an accurate arm."

A young player "has all the tools" . . . an old player "knows how to get the most out of his ability."

A young player "has good range" . . . an old player "knows how to play the hitters."

A young player "has excellent wheels" . . . an old player "always hustles."

Speaking of a young player, a manager says he'd "like to have an entire team made up of guys like him" . . . speaking of an old player, the same manager says he'd "like to have a guy like him on the team."

A young player "can hit the breaking ball" . . . an old player "doesn't get fooled by the hitting tee."

A young player "will grow into his uniform" . . . an old player "has his unform shrunk by the clubhouse guy."

A young player "reminds us of a young Ozzie Smith" . . . an old player "reminds us of an old Ozzie Nelson."

A young player "hits better than Reggie Jackson at that age" . . . an old player "hits like LaToya Jackson."

A young infield "reminds us of Tinker-to-Evers-to-Chance" . . . an old infield "reminds us of Moe-to-Larry-to-Curly."

A young player "performs like a well-oiled machine" . . . an old player "sounds like Rice Krispies when he perfoms."

A young player is "good and dependable" . . . an old player is "experienced."

A young player is "a poised rookie" . . . an old player is "a crafty veteran."

A young player coming off a bad year "hasn't yet lived up to his potential or come into his own" . . . an old player coming off a bad year "has his best years behind him."

A young player is "versatile" ... an old player is "a utility ballplayer."

A young player "is coachable" ... an old player "can help coach our younger players."

A young player is a guy "we can build our team around" ... an old player "is good to have on the bench."

A young player is "a fiery competitor" ... an old player "provides quiet leadership."

A young player "picks up things quickly" ... an old player "drops tips for the younger guys."

A young player "can do the job" ... an old player "always gives 100 percent."

A young player "comes right at you" ... an old player "is deceptive."

A young player is "a take-charge guy on the field" ... an old player is "respected in the clubhouse."

A young player "can't miss" ... an old player "missed."

A young player is "big and strong" ... an old player "is in remarkable shape for a guy his age."

A young player is "on the way up" ... an old player is "on the way down."

A young player "sees fireworks on his highlight reel" ... an old player "sees the Energizer Bunny running out of power on his." And the music changes from "We Are the Champions," when you're young to either "The Way We Were" or "Send in the Clowns" when you're old.

WEIRD NUGGETS

"Broadway" Bill Schuster, an infielder who spent decades in the Minors and managed to play in The Show for five seasons from 1937 to 1945, had a series of eccentric acts he liked to perform. When he was hitting into a "sure" last out of a game, he'd often run to third base rather than first. And once, he hit a ground ball back to the mound, and instead of running hard to first, or third, he raced up the middle and slid in between the pitcher's legs. The pitcher, "Skinhead" Hunter, was not amused. He grabbed the ball and tagged Schuster on the head ... hard ... and knocked Schuster out. Both teams left him there.

Terry Mulholland, lefty pitcher for the Philadelphia Phillies, was on the hill facing the Mets' Keith Hernandez when the New

York first baseman drilled a hot one-hopper back to the mound. Mulholland fielded the hard smash, but found the ball had stuck in the webbing of his glove. Unable to extricate the ball, Mulholland tossed his glove, ball still attached, to first base to record the out.

Billy Bates, speedy second baseman for the Milwaukee Brewers and Cincinnati Reds in 1989 to 1990, may have earned a couple of footnotes in baseball history when he outran a cheetah in a Minor League promotional stunt, and then went on, in 1990, to become the first World Series player to go hitless during the regular season for a pennant-winning club—he hit .088 on the season, but went 3-for-29 for the Milwaukee Brewers in 14 games and 0-for-5 in eight games for Cincy—then bat 1.000 for that club in the World Series—he went 1-for-1. He then dashed home to score the winning run in game two of the Fall Classic that year and got a World Championship ring besides. Strangely, few will remember Bates's exploits or his high infield chopper against Dennis Eckersley that he beat out for a hit. For some reason, all most people talk about that game is teammate Billy Hatcher running his World Series streak to seven consecutive hits and nine consecutive times on base.

Minor League pitcher John Burgos, throwing for Scranton in 1991, came on with runners at first and third and one out and retired the side without throwing a pitch. He took the mound and immediately picked off the runner at first, forcing a rundown. After the putout was made at second, a throw home nailed the runner at third who was trying to score.

Oakland A's slugger Jose Canseco, who was married, divorced, seen in the company of Madonna, and reunited then reseparated from his wife, married former Miss Miami Esther Haddad following the 1988 World Series in order to win a $10,000 bet from teammate Dave Stewart. Ten thousand dollars isn't close to the community property the ex-Mrs. Canseco now enjoys.

When New York Yankee pitcher Andy Hawkins gave up five earned runs in one-third inning versus the Boston Red Sox at Fenway Park on September 1, 1990, in a 15-1 BoSox rout, the performance actually *lowered* his ERA. Prior to the outing, he had given up 13 earned runs in two-thirds inning for an ERA of 174.63. This cool stint on the mound lowered Hawkins's ERA to a low 162.00.

When pitcher Lew Burdette retired from baseball in 1967 following an 18-year career with Milwaukee, the Angels and five other teams, he drove to Anaheim Stadium, got a hammer and a nail out of the trunk of his car, and walked into the Angels clubhouse.

He announced to all in attendance, "I'm hanging up my glove."

He pounded a nail into the wall and hung his glove on it, retired, and walked out of the clubhouse. He never came back.

CHAPTER ELEVEN

Ludicrous Lists

In a kind of America's Least Wanted, what follows is a potpourri of all you always wanted (or never wanted) to see lumped together about baseball, but were afraid (or more intelligent than) to ask for.

Since baseball is a statistical game, its fans, stat freaks and students devoted to the "Top Ten" this, the "Worst Ten" that, the "Mediocre Ten" these, or the "Who Cares? Ten" those, this chapter is devoted to all readers who care, don't care, already knew or never wanted to know about strange groupings of ballplayers.

It's a quick read and may be useful in winning bar bets or when you're standing in line for tickets and need an opening line to talk to the attractive opposite-sex type standing next to you. It can be used as in "Hey, did you know who the worst hitters of all time were?" Or "Can you name the best players ever to wear uniform numbers from 1 to 99?" Or "I know the 'All-Weather' team, do you?"

These lists need no further explanation. They're only lists, not Shakespeare, for crying out loud.

SOME OF BILLY MARTIN'S FIGHTS

1. Clint Courtney, Browns catcher.................................... 1952
2. Jimmy Piersall, Red Sox outfielder 1952
3. Jimmy Piersall 2, Red Sox outfielder........................... 1952
   (under the stands at Fenway Park)
4. Clint Courtney 2, Browns catcher............................... 1952
5. Half-a-dozen Chicago White sox players 1957
   (a single brawl)
6. Jim Brewer, Cubs pitcher 1960
7. Dave Boswell, Twins Pitcher (Billy's own pitcher) 1969
8. Ray Hagar, *Nevada State Journal* reporter (tough questions) 1978

9. Joseph Cooper, marshmallow salesman 1979
10. Ed Whitson, Yankees pitcher (Billy's own pitcher) 1985
11. A bunch of guys at various bars around the country 1950s-1980s
12. A bunch of players in stadiums around the country 1940s-1960s

PLAYERS WHO HIT 60 OR MORE HOMERS IN A PRO BALL SEASON

1. Tony Lazerri, Salt Lake City, Pacific Coast League .... 60 ... 1925
2. John "Moose" Clabaugh, Tyler, East Texas League .... 62 ... 1926
3. Babe Ruth, New York Yankees, American League .... 60 ... 1927
4. Joe Hauser, Baltimore, International League .... 63 ... 1930
5. Joe Hauser, Minneapolis, American Association.............. 69 ... 1933
6. Bobby Crues, Amarillo, West Texas-New Mexico League....... 69 ... 1948
7. Joe Bauman, Roswell, Longhorn League .... 72 ... 1954
8. Bob Lennon, Nashville, Southern Association .... 64 ... 1954
9. Dick Stuart, Lincoln, Western League .... 66 ... 1956
10. Ken Guettler, Shreveport, Texas League .... 62 ... 1956
11. Forrest "Frosty" Kennedy, Plainview, Southwestern League .... 60 ... 1956
12. Roger Maris, New York Yankees, American League .... 61 ... 1961

SOME BASEBALL RULES OF THE PAST

1. Nine balls for a walk.
2. Five balls for a walk.
3. Five strikes for an out.
4. Fouls were not strikes.
5. Walks were counted as hits.
6. Batter could ask for a high or low pitch.
7. Ball had to be delivered by pitcher underhand.
8. Ball bouncing into the stands in fair territory was a home run.
9. Pitchers could spit on the baseball.
10. Pitchers had to bat in the American League.
11. The strike zone went from the batter's armpits to the bottom of his knees and was the width of home plate.

THE MAJOR LEAGUE OUTFIELDERS WHO WERE TEAMMATES THE LONGEST

1. Bob Skinner, left field
2. Bill Virdon, center field
3. Roberto Clemente, right field
   Pittsburgh Pirates from 1956 to 1963, eight years

BROTHERS WHO PLAYED SECOND
AND SHORT ON THE SAME TEAM

1. Granny and Wes Hamner, Philadelphia Phillies.................... 1945
2. Eddie and Johnny O'Brien, Pittsburgh Pirates 1953, 1955-1956
3. Milt and Frank Bolling, Detroit Tigers 1958
4. Cal and Billy Ripken, Baltimore Orioles 1987-1992

THE WORLD'S TOP SEVEN MAJOR
LEAGUE BASE STEALERS THROUGH 1993

1. Sophie Kurys, Racine Belles, All-American
   Girls League .... 1,114.... 1943-1952
2. Rickey Henderson, A's, Yankees, Blue Jays .... 1,095........ 1979-
3. Yutaka Fukumoto, Hankyu Braves Japan League ...... 1,065.... 1970-1988
4. Lou Brock, Cubs, Cardinals .... 938.... 1961-1979
5. "Sliding Billy" Hamilton, Kansas City (AA)
   Phillies, Braves................................. 915.... 1888-1901
6. Ty Cobb, Tigers, A's.............................. 892.... 1905-1928
7. Tim Raines, Expos, White Sox...................... 751........ 1979-

Note: If you consider Major League and Minor League stats, the top seven are:

1. Rickey Henderson 1,095 Majors, 250 Minors total 1,345
2. Billy Hamilton 915 Majors, 379 Minors total.......................1,294
3. Sophie Kurys 1,114 All-American Girls League total 1,114
4. Yutaka Fukumoto 1,065 Japan League total 1,065
5. George Hogriever 48 Majors, 948 Minors total 996
6. Lou Brock 938 Majors, 38 Minors total 976
7. Tim Raines 751 Majors, 224 Minors total 975
   This shoves Ty Cobb out of the magnificent seven.
   Cobb had *only* 892 Majors, 44 Minors total 936

MAJOR LEAGUE BASEBALL'S TOP HOME RUN
HITTERS, PER COUNTRY BORN

Austria-Hungary.........	Amos Cross...............	1	1885-1887
Australia...............	Craig Shipley..............	5	1986-1993
Belize..................	Chito Martinez.............	18	1991-1993
Canal Zone.............	Rod Carew................	92	1967-1985
Czechoslovakia	Elmer Valo...............	58	1940-1961
Cuba...................	Tony Perez...............	379	1964-1986
Curacao	Hensley Meulens...........	12	1989-1993
Denmark...............	Olaf Henriksen	1	1911-1917
England	Tom Brown................	64	1882-1898

France . . . . .Bruce Bochy 26 1978-1987
Germany. . . . . .Glenn Hubbard 70 1978-1989
Honduras . . . . .Gerald Young. 3 1987-1993
Ireland . . . . .John Doyle. 25 1889-1905
Italy. . . . . .Reno Bertoia 27 1953-1962
Nicaragua. . . . . .David Green. 31 1981-1987
Norway. . . . . .John Anderson. 48 1894-1908
Poland . . . . .Moe Drabowsky. 3 1956-1972
Puerto Rico . . . . .Orlando Cepeda. 379 1958-1974
Scotland. . . . . .Bobby Thomson. 264 1946-1960
Spain . . . . .Al Pardo. 1 1985-1989
Sweden . . . . .Eric Erickson 1 1914-1922
Switzerland . . . . .Otto Hess. 5 1902-1915
United States. . . . . .Henry Aaron. 755 1954-1976
Wales. . . . . .Jimmy Austin. 13 1909-1929
Note: Hector Espino of Mexico hit 484 homers in the Minor Leagues, and Sadaharu
Oh of Japan, hit 868 homers in Japan Leagues.

ALL-NATIONS TEAM BASED ON LAST NAMES

Frank Brazill . . . . .infielder . . . .A's. 1921-1922
Gus Brittain . . . . .catcher. . . . .Reds 1937
Woody English. . . . . .infielder . . .Cubs 1927-1938
Larry French. . . . . .pitcher . . . . .Pirates. 1929-1942
Les German . . . . .pitcher . . . . .Giants 1890-1897
Al Holland . . . . .pitcher . . . . .Phillies 1977-1987
Tim Ireland. . . . . .infielder . . . .Royals. 1981-1982
Ricky Jordan. .infielder . . . .Phillies 1988-
Hugh Poland .catcher. . . . .Braves. 1943-1948
Mark Portugal. . . . . .pitcher . . . . .Astros 1985-
Special citation: Germany Schaefer . . . . .infielder . . . .Senators 1901-1918

DIFFERENCES BETWEEN AMERICAN
AND JAPANESE BASEBALL

1. Ties are allowed and games can end after ten innings.
2. Managers order bunts in the first inning.
3. Even the top players can be benched for mistakes, real or imagined, or even a strikeout, as early as the first inning.
4. Catchers don't block the plate.
5. Players attempting to breakup double plays at second may only slide right on the bag.

6. American players are often walked, regardless of the situation, if they are closing in on a Japanese record.
7. American batters receive called strikes on virtually any pitch, regardless of location.
8. Tobacco chewing is not allowed.
9. Pitchers are asked to pitch every day and bow after hitting a batter.
10. Teams go through rigorous workouts every day . . . even on game days.
11. Postponed games are made up at the end of the season.
12. Team locker rooms are set up with different classes of players in different rooms (e.g., stars in one room, starting pitchers in another, relief pitchers in another, good players in another, and rookies and marginal players in another).
13. Schedule is 130 games.
14. Ballparks and the baseballs are smaller than in America.
15. Only two Americans (or foreigners — *gai jins* — of any nationality) are allowed on any team.
16. Team takes the name of the owning or parent corporation (e.g. the Tokyo-based Giants owned by Yomiuri Shinbun are not the Tokyo Giants, but the Yomiuri Giants).
17. Media can conduct interviews with players during the games.
18. Fans come to the park in suits and ties.
19. Fans seldom boo players, and then cheer for opponents having good games.
20. Players seldom argue with umpires.
21. Players wouldn't dream of striking.
22. The better team doesn't always win, as certain teams are expected to win and are helped along by umpires to put them in a position to win.

BEST PLAYERS PER UNIFORM NUMBER
(This one is worth an argument. You can't pick *everyone's* favorite.)

0 Al Oliver	8 Carl Yastrezmski	17 Dizzy Dean
1 Billy Martin	Yogi Berra	18 Mel Harder
Ozzie Smith	Bill Dickey	19 Bob Feller
2 Charlie Gehringer	09 Benito Santiago	20 Frank Robinson
3 Babe Ruth	9 Ted Williams	21 Roberto Clemente
4 Lou Gehrig	10 Phil Rizzuto	Warren Spahn
5 Jo DiMaggio	11 Carl Hubbell	Roger Clemens
6 Stan Musial	12 Mark Langston	22 Jim Palmer
Al Kaline	13 Ralph Branca	Will Clark
7 Mickey Mantle	14 Ernie Banks	23 Ryne Sandberg
	15 Dick Allen	Don Mattingly
	16 Whitey Ford	24 Willie Mays

25	Barry Bonds	39	Roy Campanella	51	Willie McGee
	Tommy John	40	Ken Harrelson	52	Jay Howell
26	Satchel	41	Tom Seaver	53	Don Drysdale
27	Juan Marichal		Ed Matthews	54	Goose Gossage
28	Vada Pinson	42	Jackie Robinson	55	Orel Hershiser
29	Rod Carew	43	Dennis Eckersley	56	Jim Bouton
30	Tim Raines	44	Hak Aaron	66	Jeff Ballard
31	Dave Winfield	45	Bob Gibson	72	Carlton Fisk
32	Sandy Koufax	46	Terry Mulholland	77	Jack Armstrong
33	Honus Wagner	47	Jack Morris	88	Rene Gonzalez
34	Nolan Ryan		Lee Smith	96	Bill Voiselle
35	Phil Niekro	48	Rick Reuschel	98	Jim McAnany
36	Robin Roberts	49	Ron Guidry	99	Willie Crawford
37	Casey Stengel	50	Sid Fernandez		Mitch Williams
38	Rick Aguilera				

Note: Eddie Gaedel wore number ⅛ and Minor League player John Neves, whose named spelled backward is "seven," wore a backward 7 on his uniform.

PLAYERS WHO HAD FIVE EXTRA-BASE HITS IN A GAME

George Strief . . . . Philadelphia (AA) . . .June 25, 1885 . . . .1 double, 4 triples
George Gore . . . . .Chicago (NL) . . .July 9, 1885 . . . . . .3 doubles, 2 triples
Larry Twitchell . . . . Cleveland (NL) . . .August 15, 1889 . . .1 double, 3 triples,
1 homer
Lou Boudreau . . . . Cleveland (AL) . . .July 14, 1946 . . . . .4 doubles, 1 homer
Joe Adcock . . . . .Milwaukee (NL) . . .July 31, 1954 . . . . .1 double, 4 homers
Willie Stargell . . . . Pittsburgh (NL) . . .August 1, 1970 . . . .3 doubles, 2 homers
Steve Garvey . . . . Los Angeles (NL) . . .August 28, 1977 . . .3 doubles, 2 homers

HITLESS WONDERS OVER AN ENTIRE SEASON

1. Bob Buhl, Braves, 1962 . . . . .0-for-70
2. Bill Wight, White Sox, 1950 . . . . .0-for-61
3. Ron Herbel, Giants, 1964 . . . . .0-for-47
4. Karl Drews, Browns, 1949 . . . . .0-for-46
5. Ernie Koob, Browns, 1916 . . . . .0-for-41
6. Randy Tate, Mets, 1975 . . . . .0-for-41
7. Ed Rakow, Tigers, 1964 . . . . .0-for-39

BOTTOM TEN: THE LOWEST
CAREER BATTING AVERAGES
Based on a minimum of 200 at bats

1. Ron Herbel 029 1963-1971
2. Don Carman 057 1983-1992
3. Dean Chance 066 1961-1971
4. Clem Labine 075 1950-1962
5. Dick Drago 077 1969-1981
6. Bill Hands 078 1965-1975
7. Terry Mulholland 079 1986-1993
8. Mike Bielecki 079 1984-1993
9. Lee Stange 079 1961-1970
10. Bruce Ruffin 080 1986-1993

Special citation: Bob Buhl, who hit .089 in 15 years from 1953 to 1967 and went 0-for-70 in 1962, compiled a 12-for-204 .059 average from 1961 through 1963.

MOST HOME RUNS HIT IN A SINGLE
PROFESSIONAL GAME IN AMERICA

Jay J. "Nig" Clarke . . .Corsicana, Texas League . . . . .June 15, 1902 . . .8 HRs
Lipman Pike . . . . .Philadelphia, Independent . . . . . . .July 16, 1866 . . . .6 HRs
Peter J. Schneider . . . .Vernon, Pacific Coast League . . . . .May 11, 1923 . . . .5 HRs
Louis Frierson . . . . . . .Paris, West Dixie League . . . . . . .May 30, 1934 . . . .5 HRs
Cecil Dunn . . . . .Alexandria, Evangeline League . . . .April 29, 1936 . . .5 HRs
Dick Lane . . . . .Muskegon, Central League . . . . . .July 3, 1948 . . . . .5 HRs

Note: Four homers have been hit in a Major League or Minor League game by a single player 80 times.

TOP HOME RUN HITTERS IN THEIR TEENS

1. Tony Conigliaro, Red Sox 24
2. Mel Ott, Giants 19
3. Ken Griffey, Jr., Mariners 16
4. Phil Cavaretta, Cubs 14
5. Mickey Mantle, Yankees 13

TOP HOME RUN HITTERS IN THEIR TWENTIES

1. Jimmy Foxx, A's 376
2. Eddie Mathews, Braves 370
3. Mickey Mantle, Yankees 361
4. Hank Aaron, Braves 342
5. Mel Ott, Giants 323

TOP HOME RUN HITTERS IN THEIR THIRTIES

1. Babe Ruth, Yankees 434
2. Hank Aaron, Braves 371
3. Willie Mays, Giants 348
4. Mike Schmidt, Phillies 314
5. Willie Stargell, Pirates 296

TOP HOME RUN HITTERS IN THEIR FORTIES

1. Darrell Evans, Tigers, Braves 60
2. Dave Winfield, Yankees, Blue Jays, Twins .... 57 through July 1994
3. Carl Yastrzemski, Red Sox 49
4. Stan Musial, Cardinals 46
5. Ted Williams, Red Sox 44

TOP HOME RUN HITTERS BY DECADES

1880s .... Harry Stovey .... Philadelphia (AA) 91
1890s .... Hugh Duffy .... Braves 85
1900s .... Harry Davis .... A's 67
1910s .... Gavvy Cravath .... Phillies 116
1920s .... Babe Ruth .... Yankees 467
1930s .... Jimmy Foxx .... A's 415
1940s .... Ted Williams .... Red Sox 234
1950s .... Duke Snider .... Dodgers 326
1960s .... Harmon Killebrew .... Twins 393
1970s .... Willie Stargell .... Pirates 296
1980s .... Mike Schmidt .... Phillies 313
1990-1993 .... Cecil Fielder .... Tigers 160

TOP HOME RUN-HITTING TEAMMATES
WHO HIT HOMERS IN THE SAME GAME

1. Hank Aaron and Eddie Mathews, Braves .... 75 games
2. Babe Ruth and Lou Gehrig, Yankees 73
3. Willie Mays and Willie McCovey, Giants 68
4. Duke Snider and Gil Hodges, Dodgers 67
5. Billy Williams and Ron Santo, Cubs 64
6. Harmon Killebrew and Bob Allison, Twins 61
7. Mickey Mantle and Yogi Berra, Yankees 56
7. Eddie Mathews and Joe Adcock, Braves 56
7. Jim Rice and Dwight Evans, Red Sox 56
10. Willie Mays and Orlando Cepeda, Giants 50

11. Babe Ruth and Bob Meusel, Yankees 47
12. Ernie Banks and Ron Santo, Cubs.......................43
13. Ernie Banks and Billy Williams, Cubs 42
13. Mickey Mantle and Roger Maris, Yankees 42
13. Harmon Killebrew and Tony Oliva, Twins 42
16. Tony Perez and Johnny Bench, Reds 41
17. Duke Snider and Roy Campanella, Dodgers..............39
17. Duke Snider and Carl Furillo, Dodgers 39
17. Mike Schmidt and Greg Luzinski, Phillies 39

THE OLDEST PLAYERS TO . . .

Steal a Base.........Arlie Latham .... New York Giants ... 1909.....age 49
Get a Base Hit ....Jim O'Rourke........ New York Giants ... 1904.....age 54
Hit a Double.........Jack Quinn......... Brooklyn Dodgers ... 1932.....age 49
Hit a Triple ....Nick Altrock..... Washington Senators ... 1924.....age 48
Hit a Home Run .....Jack Quinn...... Philadelphia Athletics ... 1930.....age 47
Throw a No-Hitter ....Nolan Ryan ....Texas Rangers ... 1991.....age 44
Pitch in a Game......Satchel Paige ... Kansas City Athletics ... 1965.....age 59
Pinch Hit ....Minnie Minoso .... Chicago White Sox ... 1980.....age 57
Designated Hit ....Minnie Minoso .... White Sox ... 1976.....age 54

FIRST BLACKS TO PLAY ORGANIZED BASEBALL

1. On a White Players Team .... Bud Fowler, Newcastle, Pennsylvania ... 1872
2. In Major League Game ..... Moses Fleetwood Walker, Toledo (AA) ... 1884
3. In the Minor Leagues After 1900 ....Jackie Robinson, Montreal ... 1945
4. In the Major Leagues After 1900 ....Jackie Robinson, Brooklyn ... 1945
5. In the American League .... Larry Doby, Cleveland ... 1947

THE FIRST NATIVE CANADIANS TO PLAY WITH THE TORONTO BLUE JAYS

1. Dave McKay.....infielder..... Vancouver, British Columbia.... 1977-1979
2. Paul Hodgson ...outfielder....Frederickton, New Brunswick......... 1980
3. Denis Boucher ...pitcher.................Lachine, Quebec......... 1991
4. Rob Ducey ......outfielder............Cambridge, Ontario.... 1987-1992
5. Vince Horsman ..pitcher......... Dartmouth, Nova Scotia......... 1991
6. Rob Butler ......outfielder.............. Toronto, Ontario........ 1993

MOST ERRORS IN AN INNING BY A PITCHER

3   J. Bentley Seymour, New York Giants ....May 21, 1898
     Tommy John, New York Yankees....................July 27, 1988
Note: John's were all on one play.

MOST SEASONS BY PLAYERS WHO SPENT THEIR ENTIRE CAREERS WITH ONE TEAM . . . BY POSITION

1B	Ed Kranepool, Mets	18
2B	Charlie Gehringer, Tigers	19
3B	Brooks Robinson, Orioles	23
SS	Luke Appling, White Sox	20
OF	Carl Yastrzemski, Red Sox	23
OF	Al Kaline, Tigers	22
OF	Mel Ott, Giants	22
C	Bill Dickey, Yankees	17
C	Johnny Bench, Reds	17
P	Walter Johnson, Senators	21
P	Ted Lyons, White Sox	21

THE ONLY TIMES THREE BROTHERS PLAYED IN THE MAJORS AT THE SAME TIME

1. The Sewell brothers — Joe, Luke and Tommy 1927
2. The DiMaggio brothers — Joe, Dom and Vince 1940-1942
3. The Sadowski brothers — Bob, Ted and Eddie 1963
4. The Alou brothers — Felipe, Jesus and Matty 1963-1974
5. The Allen brothers — Dick, Hank and Ron 1972
6. The Cruz brothers — Jose, Hector and Tommy .... 1973 and 1977

Note: In 1963, all three Alou brothers appeared in the same outfield in the same game at the same time for the San Francisco Giants.

MOST HOMERUNS IN A GAME BY A TEAM

10 Toronto Blue Jays, September 14, 1987, versus Baltimore — Ernie Whitt (3); Rance Mulliniks, George Bell (2); Lloyd Moseby, Fred McGriff, Rob Ducey (1)

MEMBERS OF BASEBALL'S 30-30 CLUB

(30 Homers and 30 Steals in the Same Season)

1922	Ken Williams, Cardinals	39 homers, 37 steals
1956	Willie Mays, Giants	36 homers, 40 steals
1957	Willie Mays, Giants	35 homers, 38 steals
1963	Hank Aaron, Brewers	44 homers, 31 steals
1969	Bobby Bonds, Giants	32 homers, 45 steals
1970	Tommy Harper, Brewers	31 homers, 38 steals
1973	Bobby Bonds, Giants	39 homers, 43 steals
1975	Bobby Bonds, Yankees	32 homers, 30 steals

1977 . . . .Bobby Bonds, Angels . . . . 37 homers, 41 steals
1978 . . . .Bobby Bonds, White Sox, Rangers . . . . 31 homers, 43 steals
1983 . . . .Dale Murphy, Braves . . . . 36 homers, 30 steals
1987 . . . .Eric Davis, Reds. . . . . 37 homers, 50 steals
          Darryl Strawberry, Mets . . . . 39 homers, 36 steals
          Howard Johnson, Mets . . . . 36 homers, 32 steals
          Joe Carter, Indians. . . . . 32 homers, 31 steals
1988 . . . .Jose Canseco, A's . . . . 42 homers, 40 steals
1989 . . . .Howard Johnson, Mets . . . . 36 homers, 41 steals
1990 . . . .Barry Bonds, Pirates . . . . 33 homers, 52 steals
          Ron Gant, Braves . . . . 32 homers, 33 steals
1991 . . . .Howard Johnson, Mets . . . . 38 homers, 30 steals
          Ron Gant, Braves . . . . 32 homers, 34 steals
1992 . . . .Barry Bonds, Pirates . . . . 34 homers, 39 steals
1993 . . . .Sammy Sosa, Cubs . . . . 33 homers, 36 steals
Note: Jose Canseco's 1988 season is the only 40-40 season in MLB history.

MOST CONSECUTIVE 30-STOLEN-BASE SEASONS
Rickey Henderson. . . . . .15 consecutive seasons 1979-1993
Lou Brock . . . . .14 consecutive seasons 1964-1977
Ty Cobb. . . . . .12 consecutive seasons 1907-1918
Honus Wagner . . . . .11 consecutive seasons 1899-1909
Willie Wilson. . . . . .11 consecutive seasons 1978-1988
Bert Campaneris . . . . .10 consecutive seasons 1965-1974

THE PLAYERS TO HIT HOMERS AS A TEENAGER
AND PAST THEIR FORTIETH BIRTHDAY
Ty Cobb. . . . . .1905 (1), 1927 and 1928 (6)
Rusty Staub . . . . .1963 (6), 1984 and 1985 (2)

FATHER AND SON . . . MOST . . .
Years . . . . 33 . . . . Gus Bell (15) and Buddy Bell (18)
Games . . . . . .4,146 . . . . .Gus Bell (1,741) and Buddy Bell (2,405)
Hits . . . . .4,337 . . . . .Gus Bell (1,823) and Buddy Bell (2,514)
Homers . . . . . . 554 . . . . Bobby Bonds (332) and Barry Bonds (222 through 1993)
Stolen Bases. . 782 . . . . Maury Wills (586) and Bump Wills (196)
Note: Through 1993, the Bonds family had 741 stolen bases—Bobby Bonds (461)
and Barry Bonds (280)

MOST STOLEN BASES BY PLAYERS
IN THEIR FORTIES

Cap Anson	1892-1897	90
Honus Wagner	1914-1917	61
Sam Rice	1930-1934	31
Willie Mays	1971-1973	28
Luke Appling	1947-1950	27
Ty Cobb	1927-1928	27
Davey Lopes	1986-1987	27

MOST 100-RBI MEN ON THE SAME TEAM

1936 Yankees—Five: Lou Gehrig (152), Joe DiMaggio (125), Tony Lazerri (109), George Selkirk (107) and Bill Dickey (107)

Teams with four 100-RBI men in the lineup include

Browns	1922
Pirates	1925
Yankees	1927, 1931, 1932 and 1939
Cubs	1929
Phillies	1929
Tigers	1934 and 1936
Red Sox	1940 and 1977
Brewers	1982

DONE BY JULY—WORST TEAM FINISHES

1.	Boston Braves	1906	66½ games behind
2.	Boston Braves	1909	65½ games behind
3.	St. Louis Browns	1939	64½ games behind
4.	Boston Red Sox	1932	64 games behind
5.	St. Louis Cardinals	1906	63 games behind
6.	Philadelphia Phillies	1942	62½ games behind
7.	Boston Braves	1935	61½ games behind
8.	New York Mets	1962	60½ games behind

WILLIE'S 31 SHORTSTOPS:
Double-Play Partners Willie Randolph Had During
His Thirteen Years With the Yankees (1976-1988)

Sandy Alomar	Luis Aguayo	Dale Berra
Paul Blair	Ivan DeJesus	Bucky Dent

Brian Doyle	Barry Evans	Mike Fischlin
Tim Foli	Damaso Garcia	Rex Hudler
Mickey Klutts	Jim Mason	Bobby Meacham
Larry Milbourne	Graig Nettles	Mike Pagliarulo
Domingo Ramos	Andre Robertson	Rafael Santana
Rodney Scott	Dennis Sherrill	Roy Smalley
Keith Smith	Fred Stanley	Wayne Tolleson
Randy Velarde	Dennis Werth	George Zeber
Paul Zuvella		

THIRTY ALL-TIME RECORDS THAT FIGURE TO STAND FOR AWHILE

Most Career Wins . . . . 511 . . . . .Cy Young
Most Career Losses. 316 . . . . .Cy Young
Most Career Shutouts . . . . 110 . . . . .Walter Johnson
Most Career Strikeouts by a Pitcher . . . . . . .5,714 . . . . Nolan Ryan
Most Career Walks by a Pitcher . . . . .2,795 . . . . Nolan Ryan
Most Career Innings Pitched . . . . .7,356 . . . . .Cy Young
Highest Career Batting Average . . . . .367 .Ty Cobb
Games Played Career . . . . .3,562 . . . . Pete Rose
Total Bases Career. . . . . .6,856 . . . . Hank Aaron
At Bats Career . . . . .14,053 . . . . Pete Rose
Hits Career. . . . . .4,256 . . . . Pete Rose
Doubles Career . . . . 793 . . . . Tris Speaker
Triples Career . . . . 312 . . . . Sam Crawford
Home Runs Career . . . . 755 . . . . Hank Aaron
RBIs Career . . . . .2,297 . . . . Hank Aaron
Runs Scored Career . . . . .2,245 . . . . .Ty Cobb
Batting Average in a Season. . . . . .438 . . . . Hugh Duffy (1894)
    Post-1900 Era . . . . .424 . . . . Rogers Hornsby (1924)
Total Bases in a Season . . . . 457 . . . . .Babe Ruth (1921)
RBIs in a Season . . . . 190 . . . . Hack Wilson (1930)
Runs Scored in a Season . . . . 196 . . . . .Billy Hamilton (1894)
    Post-1900 Era . . . . 177 . . . . .Babe Ruth (1921)
Triples in a Season . . . . 36 . . . . Owen Wilson (1912)
Wins in a Season . . . . 41 . . . . Jack Chesbro (1904)
Games Started by a Pitcher in a Season . . . . . 52 . . . . Amos Rusie (1893)
    Post-1900 Era . . . . 51 . . . . Jack Chesbro (1904)
Complete Games. . . . . 50 . . . . Amos Rusie (1893)
    Post-1900 Era . . . . 48 . . . . Jack Chesbro (1904)

Shutouts in a Season . . . . 16 . . . . . . Grover Alexander (1916)
Losses by a Pitcher in a Season . . . . 33 . . . . Red Donahue (1897)
    Post-1900 Era . . . . 29 . . . . Vic Willis (1905)
Innings Pitched in a Season . . . . 482 . . . . Amos Rusie (1893)
    Post-1900 Era . . . . 464 . . . . .Ed Walsh (1908)
Assists by an Outfielder in a Season . . . . 50 . . . . . . Orator Shaffer (1879)
    Post-1900 Era . . . . 44 . . . . Chuck Klein (1930)
Longest Consecutive Hitting Streak . . . . 56 . . . . .Joe DiMaggio (1941)
Most Consecutive Games Played . . . . .2,130 . . . . Lou Gehrig
(Note: Should Cal Ripken, Jr., break Lou Gehrig's record sometime in 1995, *that* record will be a mark that should stand as unmatchable.)

THE ALL-MONEY TEAM

Don Money . . . . Brewers
Bobby Bonds . . . . Giants
Ernie Banks . . . . Cubs
Randy Sterling . . . . .Mets
Charles "Silver" King . . . St. Louis (AA)
Elmer Pence . . . . White Sox

Norm Cash . . . . Tigers
Bob "Buck" Rodgers . . . . Angels
Kid Nichols . . . . Braves
Bill Pounds . . . . .Dodgers
Fred "Penny" Bailey . . . . Braves
Bill "Billy Bucks" Buckner . . . .Dodgers

THE ALL-FOOD TEAM

Johnny Oates . . . . .Orioles
Zack Wheat . . . . .Dodgers
Billy Bean . . . . Tigers
Jim Rice . . . . .Red Sox
Ty Cobb . . . . Tigers
Harold "Pie" Traynor . . . . Pirates
Francis "Salty" Parker . . . . Tigers
Coco Laboy . . . . .Expos
Darryl Strawberry . . . . .Mets
Bobby Wine . . . . Phillies
Bob Veale . . . . Pirates
Dusty Baker . . . . .Dodgers
Special citation: Tim Belcher, Dodgers

Ken Berry . . . . White Sox
Duke Carmel . . . . Cardinals
Ray Lamb . . . . .Indians
Candy Maldonado . . . . .Blue Jays
Wes Stock . . . . Orioles
Solly Salisbury (Steak) . . . . . . .A's (AA)
Laurin Pepper . . . . Pirates
Tony Curry . . . . Phillies
Jack Daniels . . . . Braves
Octavio "Cookie" Rojas . . . . . . Phillies
Dennis Cook . . . . Giants
Mark Carreon . . . . Giants

THE ALL-CRAYOLA TEAM

Vida Blue . . . . .A's
Bill White . . . . .Cardinals
Pete Rose . . . . Reds
Elijah "Pumpsie" Green . . . . . .Red Sox

Robert "Red" Rolfe . . . . .Yankees
Hal "Skinny" Brown . . . . .Orioles
Joe Black . . . . .Dodgers
Pete Gray . . . . .Browns

Rusty "Le Grande Orange" Staub Expos   Mark Clear.................Red Sox
Emerson "Pink" Hawley.......Pirates   Jim Golden .... Astros

THE ALL-WEATHER TEAM

J.T. Snow........... Yankees, Angels   Tim Raines......... Expos, White Sox
Sammy Hale ....A's   Rich Gale................. Royals
Curt Flood ....Cardinals   Storm Davis.................Orioles
Charles "Sonny" Siebert ......Indians   John "Champ" Summers....... Reds
Jesse "Nip" Winters ....Philadelphia Hilldales

THE ALL-CZECHOSLOVAKIAN TEAM
Elmer Valo (Only Czech-born player in the Majors.)

THE ALL-FOWL TEAM

Craig Swan ....Mets   Ed "Krane" Kranepool ....Mets
Joe "Ducky" Medwick ......Cardinals   Fred "Chicken" Stanley ......Yankees
Doug Bird .... Royals   Mark "The Bird" Fidrych ...... Tigers
George "Birdie" Tebbetts...... Tigers   Robin Roberts .... Phillies
Phil "The Vulture" Regan.....Dodgers   George Crowe .... Reds
Leon "Goose" Goslin .... Senators   Nelson "Chicken" Hawks ..... Phillies
Norman "Turkey" Stearnes........................Chicago American Giants

THE ALL-GAME TEAM

Ed "The Wild Elk of the Wasatch" Heusser ....Cardinals
Walter "Buck" Leonard .... Homestead Grays
Jimmy Foxx.....................A's   Walter "Rabbit" Maranville .... Braves
Bob Moose .... Pirates   Rob Deer .... Brewers
Ted Lyons .... White Sox   Roy "Squirrel" Sievers...... Senators
George "Possum" Whitted.... Phillies

THE ALL-BODY-PARTS TEAM

Ed Head...................Dodgers   Mike Palm.................Red Sox
Rollie Fingers .... Padres   Rich Hand .... Rangers
Bill Hands .... Cubs   Mike "Pinky" Higgins............A's
"Heinie" Manush .... Tigers   Wayne "Footsie" Belardi .....Dodgers
Len "Nails" Dykstra .... Phillies   Jim Ray Hart .... Giants
Dave Brain................Cardinals   George Bone ....Orioles
ElRoy Face................. Pirates   Peter LaCock.............. Royals
Bris "The Human Eyeball" Lord ...A's   Harry Cheek................ Phillies
Tom "Pee Wee" Butts........................Baltimore Elite Giants

Clarence "Spoony" Palm ....New York Black Yankees
Special citation: Walt "No-Neck" Williams .... White Sox

THE ALL-SEALIFE TEAM

Tim Salmon.................	Angels	Kevin Bass.................	Astros
Paul "Dizzy" Trout	Tigers	Jim "Catfish" Hunter	A's
Lipman Pike.........	Troy Haymakers	Ernie Koy.................	Dodgers
Jim "Mudcat" Grant..........	Twins	Sherman "Snapper" Kennedy ...	Cubs
Johnny Gill	Senators	Bob Kipper	Pirates
Dick Pole.................	Red Sox	Alex Hooks.................	Phillies
Arlie Pond.................	Orioles	Freddie Marsh...........	White Sox
Jim Walewander	Tigers	Newt Allen.....	Kansas City Monarchs

ALL THE PRESIDENTS MEN

Claudell Washington..........	Braves	Sparky Adams................	Cubs
Stanley Jefferson.............	Padres	Scotti Madison	Reds
Zach Monroe...............	Yankees	Glenn Adams.................	Twins
Reggie Jackson.............	Yankees	Roric Harrison	Braves
Lefty Tyler	Braves	Tony Taylor	Phillies
Billy Pierce	White Sox	Jim "Buck" Buchanan	Browns
Ezra Lincoln........	Cleveland Spiders	Walter Johnson	Senators
Jim "Mudcat" Grant..........	Twins	Charlie Hayes	Rockies
Reggie Cleveland	Cardinals	Hack Wilson	Cubs
Slim Harding...............	Tigers	Joe Hoover	Tigers
John Kennedy	Red Sox	Howard Johnson	Mets
Otis Nixon	Braves	Whitey Ford...............	Yankees
Gary Carter	Expos	Phil Regan...Tigers (OK, it's a stretch)
"Bullet Joe" Bush..........	Yankees	Lu Clinton	Red Sox

Dwight D. Eisenhower played for Abilene in The Minors under the name "Wilson" around 1911.

THE ALL-MUSIC TEAM

Frank Viola...................	Mets	Sam Horn	Red Sox
Buddy Bell................	Rangers	Steve Sax.................	Dodgers
Jody Reed	Red Sox	Tommy Harper	Reds
Frank "Piano Keys" Smith ..	White Sox	Dan Fife....................	Twins
Keith Drumright...............	A's	"Piccolo Pete" Elko	Cubs

Kevin Bass ....Astros (OK, it's mispronounced, but the spelling is the same)

SOME REALLY SHORT BASEBALL PLAYERS' NAMES

Budd . . . . Cleveland (Players' League), 1890
Fast . . . . Indianapolis (National League), 1887
Wall . . . . . . Washington Nationals (National Association), 1873
Wood . . . . Lord Baltimores (National Association), 1874
Zay . . . . .Baltimore (American Association), 1886

Note: These players had no official first names. Several players had three-letter last names to go with long first names (e.g., Bill Day, Ed Ott, Gus Gil, Chad See, etc.).

SOME REALLY LONG BASEBALL PLAYERS' NAMES

Calvin Coolidge Julius Caesar Tuskahoma "Cal" McLish . . . . Indians, 1944-64
Alan Mitchell Edward George Patrick Henry "Dirty Al" Gallagher . . Giants, 1970-73
John Phillips Jenkins "Count" Sensenderfer . . . . . Philadelphia A's (NA), 1871-74
Saturnino Orestes Armas Arrieta "Minnie" Minoso . . . . White Sox, 1949-80

THE LONGEST LAST NAMES IN BASEBALL HISTORY

Based strictly on family names, these monikers would have to be continued on another back, if adorning baseball uniforms. There have been a number of 12-letter last names, but to date, only thirteen 13-letter last names.

Ossee Schreckengost . . . . .catcher . . . . .A's 1897-1908
Lou Schiappacasse . . . . .outfielder . . . . . .Tigers 1902
Gene DeMontreville . . . . .infielder . . . . . . .Senators 1894-1904
Lee DeMontreville . . . . .infielder . . . . . . .Cards 1903
Ken Raffensberger . . . . .pitcher . . . . .Reds 1939-1954
Kirk Dressendorfer . . . . .pitcher . . . . .A's 1992
Austin Knickerbocker . . . . .outfielder . . . . . .A's 1947
Bill Knickerbocker . . . . .shortstop . . . . . .Indians 1933-1942
Al Hollingsworth . . . . .pitcher . . . . .Cards 1935-1946
Bonnie Hollingsworth . . . . .pitcher . . . . .Senators 1922-1928
Bill VanLandingham . . . . .pitcher . . . . .Giants 1994
Philomena T. Gianfrancisco . . . . .All-American Girls League 1945-1949
Fern Shollenberger . . . . .All-American Girls League 1946-1954

TWENTY CELEBRITIES IN OTHER FIELDS
WHO PLAYED PROFESSIONAL BASEBALL

"Gentleman Jim" Corbett . . .boxer . . . . .Minor League, 1895-1900
Zane Grey . . . . .author . . . . Minor League, 1890s
Sammy Baugh . . . . .football player . . . . .Minor League, 1938
Don Hutson . . . . .football player . . . . Minor League, 1930s
"Sweetwater" Clifton . . . . . . .basketball player . . . . .Minor League, 1949-1950

Tom Brookshier..........football player..............Minor League, 1954
Dick Shawn..............actor-comedian............Minor League, 1950s
Johnny Berardino.........actor.....Minor and Major League, 1930s to 1950s
Doug Harvey.............hockey player..............Minor League, 1940s
Bill Sharman.............basketball player...........Minor League, 1950s
Chuck Connors...........actor.......Minor and Major League, 1940s-1950s
Charlie Pride.............singer.............Negro Leagues, 1940s-1950s
Mario Cuomo.............governor of New York........Minor League, 1950s
Ron Shelton.............screenwriter................Minor League, 1980s
Randy Poffo..............Randy Savage-pro wrestler....Minor League, 1970s
Kurt Russell.............actor....................Minor League, 1970s
Drake Hogesteyn..........actor....................Minor League, 1970s
John Elway.............football player..............Minor League, 1982
Joe E. Brown*..........actor....................Major League tryout
Buster Keaton*..........actor....................Major League tryout
*Could have played in the Minors if he had so chosen

TWELVE MINOR LEAGUE RECORDS
THAT WILL STAND FOREVER

Games Played Career.................3,282.............George Whiteman
Runs Scored Career..................2,287..............Spencer Harris
RBIs Career.......................1,857.................Nick Cullop
Home Runs Career..................484.................Hector Espino
Most Career Wins....................383..................Bill Thomas
Most Career Strikeouts by a Pitcher......3,300 + (incomplete records) George Brunet
Hits in a Season.....................325.............Paul Strands (1923)
RBIs in a Season....................254.............Bobby Crues (1948)
Runs Scored in a Season..............202.............Tony Lazerri (1925)
Doubles in a Season.................100.............Lyman Lamb (1924)
Wins in a Season....................41............Stony McGlynn (1906)
Strikeouts by a Pitcher in a Season......456.............Bill Kennedy (1946)

TEN THINGS YOU'LL NEVER SEE AGAIN
ON A MAJOR LEAGUE BASEBALL FIELD

1. Checkered uniforms, as the Dodgers unveiled in 1916.
2. Baseball uniforms consisting of shorts and collared shirts as the Chicago White Sox tried in 1976.
3. A runner stealing first base ... when he was already on second as Germany Schaefer did in 1908.
4. A single player hitting more home runs than every other *team* in the league

... as Babe Ruth did when he hit 60 in 1927.

5. One city with three Hall of Fame center fielders for three teams, as New York had in the 1950s with Willie, Mickey and The Duke.

6. Disco Demolition Night at Comiskey Park.

7. A center fielder chasing a ball in and through and around the monuments at Yankee Stadium.

8. Major League fences in pristine fashion, without any advertising on them.

9. "Death Valley" ballparks that go 461 feet to dead center and 457 feet to the power alley. And pennant porches that measure 296 feet or 257 feet down the right-field line.

10. Kids in the stands opening packs of cards, looking to find their favorite player, and chewing a sugary-sweet stick of gum that comes with the collectibles, giving every card that unforgettable aroma of gum and cardboard.

BIBLIOGRAPHY

In researching this book, the following sources were used to corroborate, fact check, and add background biographical material and/or statistical accuracy to many of the stories included in this book.

Baseball America's Almanac. Durham, North Carolina: Baseball America, 1990-1994.

Blake, Mike. *Baseball Chronicles: An Oral History of Baseball Through the Decades*. Cincinnati: Betterway Books, 1994.

————. *The Incomplete Book of Baseball Superstitions, Rituals and Oddities*. Tarrytown, New York: Wynwood Press, 1991.

————. *The Minor Leagues: A Celebration of the Little Show*. Tarrytown, New York: Wynwood Press, 1991.

Cincinnati Enquirer, July 24, 1905.

Crasnick, Jerry. *Cincinnati Post*, August 22, 1990.

Cunningham, Dave. *Long Beach Press-Telegram*, April 12, 1993.

Harris, Otis. *Shreveport Journal*, June 18, 1930.

Johnson, Lloyd, and Miles Wolff. *The Encyclopedia of Minor League Baseball*. Durham, North Carolina: Baseball America, Inc., 1993.

Los Angeles Times, 1900, 1957, 1990-1994.

Santa Ana Orange County Register, 1990-1994.

Philadelphia Daily News, 1991-1993.

Ripp, Bart. "Big Time Superstition," *Tacoma Morning News Tribune*, June 18, 1989.

Ruggles, William B. *The History of the Texas League of Professional Baseball Clubs, 1888-1951*. Dallas: The Texas League, 1951.

SABR — The Society for American Baseball Research. *The Baseball Research Journal*. Vol. 19-22. Birmingham: EBSCO Media, 1990-1993.

————. *Minor League Baseball Stars*. Vol. II. Manhattan, Kansas: Ag Press, 1985.

————. *Minor League Baseball Stars*. Vol. III. Birmingham: EBSCO Media, 1992.

————. *The National Pastime: A Review of Baseball History*. Vol. 10-13. Birmingham: EBSCO Media, 1990-1993.

Shatzkin, Mike, ed. *The Ballplayers*. New York: Arbor House/Willim Morrow and Co., 1990.

Shreveport Times, May 31 and June 7, 1928; December 22, 1929; January 12, 1930.

Skipper, James K., Jr. *Baseball Nicknames, A Dictionary of Origins and Meanings*. Jefferson, North Carolina: McFarland & Co. Inc., 1992.

Treese, Bill. "Art (The Great) Shires, What a Man." Research paper. Shreveport, Lousiana, 1990.

Wolff, Rick, Editorial Director. *The Baseball Encyclopedia*. 9th Ed. New York: Macmillan Publishing Co., 1993.

Conversational tapes supplied by the following:
Bracciano, Jim. Sunflower Cablevision-6. Lawrence, Kansas.
McDonnell, Joe. KMPC Radio-710, Los Angeles.
Rowe, Bob. KMPC Radio-710, Los Angeles.
Topp, Richard. SABR, Chicago.

The Media Guides (1993 and 1994) and team magazines (covering many years) supplied by the following organizations:

Major League Baseball: *Major League Baseball Media Information Guide*. New York: The Commissioner's Office, 1993, 1994.

American League: American League Red Book, Media Guides and score books from Baltimore Orioles, Boston Red Sox, California Angels, Chicago White Sox, Cleveland Indians, Detroit Tigers, Kansas City Royals, Milwaukee Brewers, Minnesota Twins, New York Yankees, Oakland A's, Seattle Mariners, Texas Rangers, Toronto Blue Jays.

National League: National League Green Book, Media Guides

and score books from Atlanta Braves, Chicago Cubs, Cincinnati
Reds, Colorado Rockies, Florida Marlins, Houston Astros, Los
Angeles Dodgers, Montreal Expos, New York Mets, Philadelphia
Phillies, Pittsburgh Pirates, St. Louis Cardinals, San Diego Pa-
dres, San Francisco Giants.

INDEX

More Books of Interest

Baseball's All-Time Dream Team — Would your dream team have Ozzie at short and Johnny behind the plate? Key statistics and informed opinions will help you make the ultimate roster. *#70232/$12.95/240 pages/60 b&w photos/paperback*

Baseball Chronicles: An Oral History of Baseball Through the Decades — From Ty Cobb to Dave Winfield, 80 years of stories will take you on a journey through America's favorite pastime. *#70241/$16.95/336 pages/30 b&w illus./paperback*

Baseball Fathers, Baseball Sons — Win your next trivia bet! This guide brings you all the father and son combos to play pro ball — including chronology and stats. *#70008/$13.95/192 pages/paperback*

The Art of Doubles: Winning Tennis Strategies — Court diagrams, on-court drills, and at-a-glance checklists will bring you key strategies for improving your team game. *#70233/$14.95/144 pages/43 b&w illus./paperback*

Never Too Old to Play Tennis . . . And Never Too Old to Start — Don't watch from the grandstands — discover the joy of tennis! This guide has winning strategies for beginners age 55 and up. *#70188/$12.95/176 pages/paperback*

Intelligent Doubles: A Sensible Approach to Better Doubles Play — "Whether you're a social doubles player or serious competitor, this book is a must." — *Tennis Magazine* *#70059/$9.95/160 pages/paperback*

Intelligent Tennis — These on-the-court exercises are proven to focus your self-control, help you practice with purpose and prepare your game. *#70060/$11.99/160 pages/paperback*

The Junior Tennis Handbook — Parents, coaches, and players — get a complete rundown on the history of tennis and lessons on rules, strokes and strategies. *#70065/$12.95/176 pages/paperback/Ages 10 and up*

Spinning: A Guide to the World of Cycling — Get the most out of biking! You'll learn how to select the right bike and safety equipment, bike maintenance and much more! *#70187/$14.95/192 pages/paperback*

The Downhill Skiing Handbook — Witness the thrill of skiing through more than 180 photos as you learn beginner, intermediate and advanced skills. *#70145/$17.95/192 pages/paperback*

Underwater Adventures — From Cozumel to Aruba to Galapagos — You'll see 50 of the most exotic dive locations and names you can contact for information. *#70115/$19.95/160 pages/paperback*

Write to the address below for a FREE catalog of all Betterway Books. To order books directly from the publisher, include $3.50 postage and handling for one book, $1.00 for each additional book. Ohio residents add 5½% sales tax. Allow 30 days for delivery.

Betterway Books
1507 Dana Avenue
Cincinnati, Ohio 45207
VISA/MasterCard orders call TOLL-FREE
1-800-289-0963

Prices subject to change without notice.   Stock may be limited on some books.

Write to this address for a catalog of Betterway Books, plus information on *Writer's Digest* magazine, *Story* magazine, Writer's Digest Book Club, Writer's Digest School, and Writer's Digest Criticism Service.   3131